GCSE OCR
Computer Science

No doubt about it — OCR's Grade 9-1 GCSE Computer Science exams can be tricky to crack. But this CGP book is the perfect user guide...

It's full of detailed notes, clear diagrams and useful examples, not to mention plenty of practice questions — including new practical programming skills.

There's also a full practice exam, with answers and a complete mark scheme, so there'll be no compatibility errors when you finally face the real thing.

How to access your free Online Edition

This book includes a free Online Edition to read on your PC, Mac or tablet. You'll just need to go to **cgpbooks.co.uk/extras** and enter this code:

2997 2468 0668 7683

By the way, this code only works for one person. If somebody else has used this book before you, they might have already claimed the Online Edition.

Complete
Revision & Practice
<u>Everything</u> you need to pass the exams!

Contents

Component 01 — Computer Systems

Contents

Component 02 — Computational Thinking, Algorithms and Programming

Published by CGP

Editors: Liam Dyer, Sammy El-Bahrawy, Rob Harrison, Michael Weynberg.

Contributor: Colin Harber-Stuart.

With thanks to Shaun Harrogate and Simon Little for the proofreading.

With thanks to Lottie Edwards for the copyright research.

ISBN: 978 1 78908 558 7

Printed by Elanders Ltd, Newcastle upon Tyne.
Clipart from Corel®

Computer Systems

As it's the first page I'll start simple. Computer Science is all about computers. What, you already knew that?

A **Computer** is a **Machine** that Processes **Data**

1) The purpose of a computer is to take <u>data</u>, <u>process</u> it, then <u>output</u> it.
Computers were created to help process data and complete tasks <u>more efficiently</u> than humans.

2) A <u>computer system</u> consists of <u>hardware</u> and <u>software</u> that work together to process data/complete tasks.

- Hardware is the <u>physical</u> stuff that makes up your computer system, like the CPU, motherboard, monitor and printer.
- Software is the <u>programs</u> or <u>applications</u> that a computer system runs e.g. an operating system, a word processor or video game.

External pieces of hardware like the keyboard, mouse and printer are called peripherals.

3) There are <u>many types</u> of computer system. These range from small devices like calculators and watches, up to large <u>supercomputers</u> used by banks or for scientific applications. Computers may be <u>general purpose</u> (designed to perform <u>many tasks</u>, e.g. PCs and tablets) or <u>dedicated systems</u> (designed for <u>one particular</u> function, e.g. controlling traffic lights or an aeroplane).

Embedded Systems are Computers inside a **Larger System**

1) <u>Embedded systems</u> are computers <u>built into other devices</u>, like dishwashers, microwaves and TVs. They are usually dedicated systems.

2) Embedded systems are often used as <u>control systems</u> — they <u>monitor</u> and <u>control</u> machinery in order to achieve a desired result. E.g. In a <u>dishwasher</u> the embedded system could control the water pumps and water release mechanisms, manage the various dishwasher cycles and control the thermostat to keep the water at an appropriate temperature.

3) As they're <u>dedicated</u> to a single task, embedded systems are usually easier to <u>design</u>, cheaper to <u>produce</u>, and more <u>efficient</u> at doing their task than a general purpose computer.

Computers contain **Components** which **Work Together**

This section is all about the main hardware components of a computer.
As a warm-up, let's take a look inside a <u>typical desktop PC</u>.

Power supply — supplies power to motherboard, optical and hard drives, and other hardware.

Case cooling fan — extracts hot air from the computer case.

CPU heat sink and cooling fan — keeps the CPU at a steady temperature (CPUs generate a lot of heat).

CPU (hidden under the heat sink) — the most important component. Does all the processing (see p.2-3).

The <u>graphics card</u> slots in here (see p.7).

Optical drive — for read/writing of optical discs (see p.9).

RAM sticks (computer memory) slot in here (see p.6-7).

Motherboard — The main circuit board in the computer, where the hardware is connected.

Hard Disk Drive — Internal secondary storage (see p.8).

If you know your computer, you need not fear defeat...

There's a lot to take in on this first page. You should make sure you're comfortable with the components on this page before going any further, as they'll crop up a lot throughout this section.

The CPU

The CPU is very important — it's the main component of a computer, so here are two whole pages about it.

The **CPU** is the **Central Processing Unit**

1) The <u>CPU</u> is the <u>brain</u> of the computer system.

2) It processes all of the <u>data</u> and <u>instructions</u> that make the system work.

3) The processing power of a CPU depends on different characteristics, like its <u>clock speed</u>, <u>number of cores</u> and <u>cache size</u> — there's lots about this on p.7.

4) The CPU <u>architecture</u> describes the <u>main components</u> of the CPU, how they <u>interact</u> with each other, and with <u>other parts</u> of the computer system. <u>Von Neumann</u> and <u>Harvard</u> are the two main types of architecture. You will need to know about Von Neumann — see next page.

CPUs contain 1000s of gold pins — some of these transmit data, others supply power to the CPU.

The CPU has **Three Main Parts**

The Control Unit (CU)

- The control unit is in <u>overall control</u> of the CPU. Its main job is to manage the <u>fetching</u>, <u>decoding</u> and <u>execution</u> of <u>program instructions</u> by following the <u>fetch-execute cycle</u> (see next page).

- It controls the flow of data <u>inside</u> the CPU (to registers, ALU, cache — see below) and <u>outside</u> the CPU (to main memory and input/output devices).

The Arithmetic Logic Unit (ALU)

- The ALU basically does all the <u>calculations</u>.

- It completes simple <u>addition</u> and <u>subtraction</u>, <u>compares</u> the size of numbers and can do <u>multiplications</u> and <u>divisions</u> using repeated addition and subtraction.

- It performs logic operations such as <u>AND</u>, <u>OR</u> and <u>NOT</u> (see p.88) and <u>binary shifts</u> (see p.22) — remember, computers process <u>binary data</u>.

- It contains the <u>accumulator</u> register — see next page.

The Cache

- The cache is <u>very fast</u> memory in the CPU. It's <u>slower</u> than the <u>registers</u> (see below), but <u>faster</u> than <u>RAM</u> (see p.6).

- It stores <u>regularly used data</u> so that the CPU can access it <u>quickly</u> the next time it's needed. When the CPU requests data, it checks the <u>cache</u> first to see if the data is there. If not, it will fetch it from <u>RAM</u>.

- Caches have a very <u>low capacity</u> and are <u>expensive</u> compared to RAM and secondary storage.

- There are different <u>levels</u> of cache memory — L1, L2 and L3. <u>L1</u> is <u>quickest</u> but has the <u>lowest capacity</u>. L2 is <u>slower</u> than L1 but can <u>hold more</u>. L3 is <u>slower</u> than L2 but can <u>hold more</u>.

The CPU contains various <u>registers</u> which temporarily hold tiny bits of data needed by the CPU. They are <u>super-quick</u> to read/write to, much quicker than any other form of memory. You need to know about the <u>program counter</u>, <u>memory address register (MAR)</u>, <u>memory data register (MDR)</u> and the <u>accumulator</u> (see next page).

REVISION TASK

That's a lot to remember, for something so small...

It's important that you know all about the CU, ALU and cache. Try learning everything you can about each one, then cover up the page and write down as many notes as you can remember.

The CPU

Now let's look at the Von Neumann architecture and what the registers do in a bit more detail.
Von Neumann came up with his design in 1945 and it still describes how most computers work today.

Von Neumann's Design **Revolutionised** Computing

The Von Neumann architecture describes a system where the CPU runs <u>programs</u> stored in <u>memory</u>.
Programs consist of <u>instructions</u> and <u>data</u> which are stored in memory <u>addresses</u>.

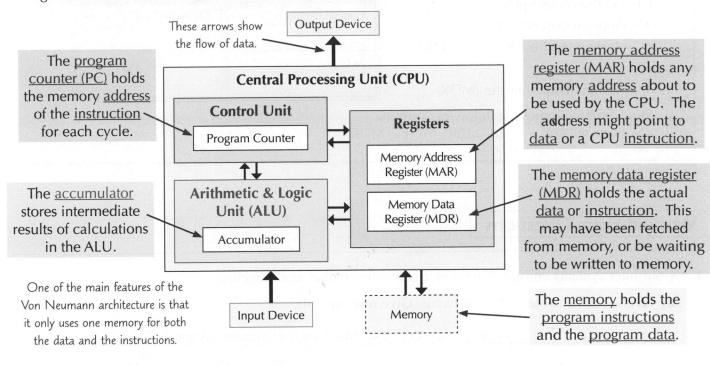

The <u>program counter (PC)</u> holds the memory <u>address</u> of the <u>instruction</u> for each cycle.

The <u>accumulator</u> stores intermediate results of calculations in the ALU.

These arrows show the flow of data.

One of the main features of the Von Neumann architecture is that it only uses one memory for both the data and the instructions.

The <u>memory address register (MAR)</u> holds any memory <u>address</u> about to be used by the CPU. The address might point to <u>data</u> or a CPU <u>instruction</u>.

The <u>memory data register (MDR)</u> holds the actual <u>data</u> or <u>instruction</u>. This may have been fetched from memory, or be waiting to be written to memory.

The <u>memory</u> holds the <u>program instructions</u> and the <u>program data</u>.

CPUs follow the **Fetch-Execute Cycle**

Essentially, <u>all a CPU does</u> is carry out instructions, one after another, billions of times a second.
The <u>Fetch-Execute</u> cycle (also called the <u>Fetch-Decode-Execute</u> cycle) describes how it does it.

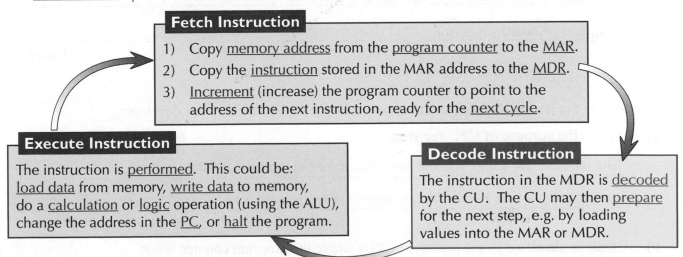

Fetch Instruction

1) Copy <u>memory address</u> from the <u>program counter</u> to the <u>MAR</u>.
2) Copy the <u>instruction</u> stored in the MAR address to the <u>MDR</u>.
3) <u>Increment</u> (increase) the program counter to point to the address of the next instruction, ready for the <u>next cycle</u>.

Decode Instruction

The instruction in the MDR is <u>decoded</u> by the CU. The CU may then <u>prepare</u> for the next step, e.g. by loading values into the MAR or MDR.

Execute Instruction

The instruction is <u>performed</u>. This could be: <u>load data</u> from memory, <u>write data</u> to memory, do a <u>calculation</u> or <u>logic</u> operation (using the ALU), change the address in the <u>PC</u>, or <u>halt</u> the program.

Learn this with the Revise-Assess-Review cycle...

To remember what each register does, look at its name to see if it stores an address or data. If you're confused about the difference between the PC and MAR, remember: the program counter just starts off the cycle by pointing to the instruction. The MAR is far busier — all addresses (data or instruction) being used must go into the MAR, meaning its value might change several times each cycle.

Warm-Up and Worked Exam Questions

There's a lot to learn on those first few pages — once you're happy with them, have a go at these questions.

Warm-Up Questions

1) Name five hardware components of a typical desktop computer.

2) Write the names of the parts of the CPU in the correct places:
   - Program Counter (PC)
   - Memory Address Register (MAR)
   - Accumulator
   - Memory Data Register (MDR)

   Central Processing Unit

Control Unit	Other Registers
ALU	

3) State the function of the following registers:
   a) Accumulator   b) MAR   c) MDR

Worked Exam Questions

1 Computer systems consist of hardware and software that work together.

   a) Define what is meant by hardware. Give **one** example.

      Definition: ...The physical components that make up a computer system.............

      Example: ...A mouse...

      There are loads of possible examples for each of these — far too many to list.

      [2 marks]

   b) Define what is meant by software. Give **one** example.

      Definition: ...The programs or applications that a computer can run...........

      Example: ...A word processor......................................

      [2 marks]

2 A tech firm are testing the registers in some prototype CPUs that they are developing.

   a) Explain the purpose of CPU registers.

      The registers are super fast memory that store tiny amounts of data

      or instructions that the CPU can access extremely quickly.

      [2 marks]

   b) A fault is identified in the prototype CPUs where the program counter is not incrementing with each cycle. Explain what will happen in the CPU in this case.

      The memory address of the next instruction will always be the same,

      so the CPU will carry out the same instruction repeatedly.

      [2 marks]

Exam Questions

3 A microwave contains an embedded system which controls its cooking modes.

a) What is an embedded system?

....

[1 mark]

b) Give **two** other examples of devices that may contain an embedded system.

1. ....

2. ....

[2 marks]

c) Explain **two** benefits of using an embedded system, rather than a general purpose computer, in a microwave.

1. ....

....

....

2. ....

....

....

[4 marks]

4 The control unit, arithmetic logic unit and cache memory are all parts of the CPU.

a) State **two** functions of the Control Unit.

1. ....

2. ....

[2 marks]

b) Describe the function of the Arithmetic Logic Unit (ALU).

....

....

[2 marks]

c) Explain how cache memory is used by the CPU.

....

....

....

[3 marks]

Memory

As you'll have gathered from earlier, memory is a pretty fundamental part of a computer. It contains all the instructions that the CPU follows. Without memory, a computer wouldn't know what to do with itself.

RAM is High Speed, Volatile memory

1) <u>RAM</u> (or Random Access Memory) is used as the <u>main memory</u> in a computer. It can be <u>read</u> and <u>written</u> to. RAM is <u>volatile</u>.

> • <u>Volatile</u> memory is <u>temporary</u> memory. It requires <u>power</u> to retain its data.
> • <u>Non-volatile</u> is <u>permanent</u> memory — it <u>keeps</u> its contents even when it has <u>no power</u>.

2) The main memory is where all <u>data</u>, <u>files</u> and <u>programs</u> are stored while they're <u>being used</u>.

3) When a computer boots up, the <u>operating system</u> is <u>copied</u> from <u>secondary storage</u> to <u>RAM</u>.

4) When <u>software applications</u>, <u>documents</u> and <u>files</u> are <u>opened</u>, they are <u>copied</u> from secondary storage to RAM. They stay in RAM until the files or applications are <u>closed</u>.

Secondary storage is covered on p.8-9.

5) RAM is <u>slower</u> than the CPU cache, but <u>much faster</u> than secondary storage.

Virtual Memory is Secondary Storage used as extra RAM

1) Computers have a limited amount of RAM. As applications are opened, RAM <u>fills</u> with <u>data</u>.

2) When RAM is full, the computer needs <u>somewhere else</u> to put application data. It <u>moves</u> data that hasn't been used recently to a location on <u>secondary storage</u> (p.8) known as <u>virtual memory</u>.

3) Virtual memory may be needed if there are <u>too many applications</u> open at once, or if a particularly <u>memory-intensive</u> application is being used (or both).

4) If the CPU needs to <u>read data</u> stored in virtual memory, it must move the data back to RAM. This is slow as data transfer rates are <u>much slower</u> on secondary storage than RAM.

5) Using virtual memory can make a computer <u>slow to respond</u> when <u>switching</u> between applications (while data for one application in virtual memory is swapped with the other) or when using a <u>memory-intensive</u> application (due to data <u>constantly moving</u> between virtual memory and RAM just to keep the program running).

ROM tells the CPU how to Boot Up

1) <u>ROM</u> ('Read Only Memory') is <u>non-volatile</u> memory. As it says on the tin, it can <u>only be read</u>, not written to.

2) ROM comes on a small, factory-made <u>chip</u> built into the <u>motherboard</u>.

3) It contains all the <u>instructions</u> a computer needs to properly <u>boot up</u>. These instructions are called the <u>BIOS (Basic Input Output System)</u>.

The BIOS is a type of firmware — hardware-specific software built in to a device. Embedded systems (p.1) are controlled by firmware.

4) As soon as the computer is powered on, the CPU <u>reads</u> the instructions from ROM. This tells the CPU to perform <u>self checks</u> and <u>set up</u> the computer, e.g. test the memory is working OK, see what hardware is present and copy the operating system into RAM.

5) Although the CPU can only read ROM, it <u>is</u> possible to update ('flash') the BIOS on a ROM chip.

Get all this information stored on your brain's non-volatile memory...

RAM is where the computer puts everything it's working on. Don't confuse memory with secondary storage — if a computer has a 2 TB (see p.19) hard drive, that doesn't mean it has 2 TB of memory.

CPU and System Performance

All sorts of things affect the speed of a computer system, but the biggest factors are usually to do with the hardware. Choice of CPU, RAM and GPU (see below) can all have big effects on performance.

CPU Performance depends on Clock Speed, Cores and Cache

Clock speed

- This is the <u>number of instructions</u> a single processor core can carry out per <u>second</u> (Hz). For most desktop computers, this will be somewhere around 3.5 GHz (3.5 billion instructions per second).
- The <u>higher</u> the clock speed, the <u>greater</u> the number of instructions that can be carried out per second.
- Some CPUs can be <u>overclocked</u> to make them run at a higher clock speed than the factory-set rate. But it's risky if not done properly — it can make CPUs <u>overheat</u>, causing <u>crashes</u> or permanent <u>damage</u> to the system. High performance <u>cooling systems</u> (e.g. water cooling) are usually needed.

Number of Cores

- Each <u>core</u> in a CPU can process data <u>independently</u> of the rest.
- The <u>more cores</u> a CPU has, the <u>more instructions</u> it can carry out at once, so the faster it can process a batch of data.
- Most PCs and smartphones have 4 or more cores these days.

It's <u>not</u> quite as simple as 'doubling the number of cores doubles performance'. Software needs to be <u>designed</u> to use multicore processing. And not all processing tasks can be split evenly between cores — some steps will <u>depend</u> on others, meaning one core may end up waiting for another core to catch up.

Cache Size

- The cache (p.2) is data storage inside the CPU that's much <u>faster than RAM</u>.
- A <u>larger</u> CPU cache gives the CPU faster access to <u>more data</u> it needs to process.

Generally speaking, CPUs with <u>higher clock speeds</u>, <u>more cores</u> or <u>larger caches</u> will have better performance, but will also be more expensive.

More RAM can mean a Faster or Smoother System

1) If a computer has <u>too little</u> RAM it may run slowly due to the use of <u>virtual memory</u> (see previous page).
2) The <u>more RAM</u>, the <u>more applications</u> or more <u>memory-intensive</u> applications it can smoothly run, making it faster overall.
3) It's easy to <u>upgrade</u> RAM on a PC or laptop — it's just a matter of replacing the RAM sticks with higher <u>capacity</u> (or higher speed) ones.
4) If the computer <u>already</u> has plenty of RAM to run everything the user wants, increasing RAM may make <u>no</u> difference to performance.

RAM comes on sticks which plug into slots on the motherboard.

GPUs help CPUs process Images

1) <u>GPUs</u> (graphics processing units) are specialised circuits for handling <u>graphics</u> and <u>image</u> processing. They relieve the <u>processing load</u> on the CPU, freeing it to do other things.
2) Computers have <u>basic</u> GPUs integrated onto the <u>motherboard</u> or the <u>CPU</u>. For better graphics performance, a <u>dedicated</u> GPU (graphics card) is often used.
3) Using high-end graphics cards can greatly improve performance in graphics-intensive applications, e.g. PC <u>gaming</u> and design software.

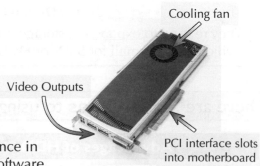

Cooling fan

Video Outputs

PCI interface slots into motherboard

High-end hardware tends to be very expensive...

There are other factors that affect CPU performance, but you don't need to worry about them at GCSE. Using SSDs rather than traditional hard drives is another way to speed up a computer — more info on p.8.

Secondary Storage

When you think of memory, you might think of USB sticks, CDs, hard drives, etc. — these are all types of 'secondary storage'. All that RAM and ROM stuff from p.6 was actually what we call 'primary storage'.

There are **Two Main Tiers** of **Storage**

1) Primary storage refers to the memory areas that the CPU can access very quickly, like CPU registers, cache, ROM and RAM. Primary storage has the fastest read/write speeds and is mostly volatile (p.6).

2) Secondary storage is non-volatile — it's where all data (operating systems, applications and user files) are stored when not in use. It includes magnetic hard disk drives, solid state drives, CDs and SD cards. Read/write speeds are much slower compared to primary storage.

> There's also tertiary storage, which is used for long term data storage (it's mainly used for archives and back-ups of massive amounts of data).

Hard Disks are **High-Capacity**, **Reliable Storage**

1) Hard disk drives (HDDs) are the traditional internal storage in PCs and laptops — they are often just called hard drives.

2) A hard disk drive is made up of a stack of magnetised metal disks that spin thousands of times a second.

3) Data is stored magnetically in small areas on the disk's circular tracks.

4) A moving arm can access these areas and read or write data.

5) Portable HDDs are popular for backing up and transporting large amounts of data.

6) Despite their moving parts, HDDs are generally very long lasting and reliable, although they could be damaged by large impacts like being dropped.

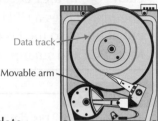
Data track
Movable arm

Solid State Drives are **Fast** and **Reliable Secondary Storage**

1) Solid State Drives (SSDs) are storage devices with no moving parts. SSDs are used for the same purpose as HDDs — for internal / external storage.

2) Most SSDs use a type of flash memory (a common type of non-volatile memory).

3) SSDs have significantly faster read/write times than HDDs. Using a SSD rather than traditional HDD can give much quicker times for booting up and opening programs and files.

4) Hybrid drives exist which use solid state storage for the OS and programs, and a hard disk for data.

5) Like HDDs, portable SSDs can be used to back up and transport data.

> ### Other types of flash storage
>
> USB pen drives and memory cards (e.g. SD cards) are also flash-based, solid-state storage.
>
> They're much slower than SSDs and have a much shorter read/write life.
>
> They're used to expand the storage capacity of small devices like cameras, smartphones and tablets (which are too small for SSDs or HDDs). Their capacity is very high relative to their tiny size.

There are **Advantages** to using **HDDs** and **SSDs**

Advantages of HDDs	Advantages of SSDs
• HDDs are cheaper.	• SSDs are faster.
• Both are high capacity, but HDDs are higher.	• SSDs don't need defragmenting (see p.15).
• HDDs have a longer read/write life than SSDs — SSDs can only be written a certain number of times before they begin to deteriorate.	• SSDs are more shock-proof than HDDs.
	• HDDs make some noise, SSDs are silent.

Secondary Storage

Optical Discs are Cheap and Robust Secondary Storage

1) Optical discs are things like <u>CDs</u>, <u>DVDs</u> and <u>Blu-ray</u>™ discs.

2) CDs can hold around 700 MB of data, DVDs can hold around 4.7 GB and Blu-rays can hold around 25 GB.

3) Optical discs come in three forms:

> – <u>read-only</u> (e.g. CD-ROM / DVD-ROM / BD-ROM)
> – <u>write-once</u> (e.g. CD-R / DVD-R / BD-R)
> – <u>rewritable</u> (e.g. CD-RW / DVD-RW / BD-RW)

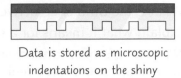

Data is stored as microscopic indentations on the shiny surface of the disc.

4) Nowadays, their use is <u>declining</u>:

- As Internet speeds have increased, <u>streaming</u> and <u>download</u> services like Netflix, Spotify® and Steam® have removed the need for optical discs.
- Modern devices like <u>phones</u> and <u>tablets</u> don't have optical drives.
- DVD-Rs and DVD-RWs used to be popular for backing up data, but they have <u>low capacity</u> per disc, very <u>slow</u> read/write speeds and poor <u>reliability</u> compared to flash storage devices.

5) They do have some <u>advantages</u> — they're very cheap (per GB), portable, and won't be damaged by <u>water</u> or <u>shocks</u> (although they are easily <u>scratched</u>).

Magnetic Tapes are used for Archiving

1) <u>Magnetic tape</u> has much <u>greater storage capacity</u> than HDDs. It also has an extremely <u>low cost</u> per GB.

2) Magnetic tapes are often used by <u>large organisations</u> in archive libraries to store <u>huge amounts</u> of data.

3) It comes in plastic <u>cassettes</u> (containing reels of tape). Cassettes require a special tape-drive for read/writing.

4) Tape is read/written <u>sequentially</u>, meaning it is read/written from the <u>beginning</u> to the <u>end</u>, or until it is stopped by the computer. This means tape is very <u>slow</u> when <u>finding</u> specific data stored on it, but has a <u>fast</u> read/write speed once it is in the correct place to begin reading/writing.

Magnetic tapes are most suitable for businesses who do large, frequent back-ups.

A quick Summary...

Here's a summary of the relative <u>speeds</u>, <u>costs</u> and <u>capacities</u> of all these different types of storage.

Optical disc	Memory Card		Magnetic Tape	HDD		SSD
Slowest			**Average read/write speed**			*Fastest*

Magnetic Tape		Optical disc	HDD		Memory Card	SSD
Cheapest			**Average cost (per GB)**			*Priciest*

Optical disc	Memory Card		SSD	HDD		Magnetic Tape
Lowest			**Average capacity**			*Highest*

Be sure to learn the pros and cons of all these types of storage...

Be careful with your terminology. Storage <u>media</u> refers to the actual thing that holds the data, e.g. an optical disc. Storage <u>devices</u> read/write data to media, e.g. optical drives, or HDDs.

Warm-Up and Worked Exam Questions

Once you've got all the different memory and storage terms learnt, it's time to have a go at some questions. If you're confident with the warm-up questions, then test yourself against the exam questions.

Warm-Up Questions

1) What is the difference between RAM and ROM?
2) Explain what it means for a single-core processor to have "a clock speed of 3 GHz".
3) Name a type of secondary storage that:
   a) usually comes on a reel in a cassette   b) uses flash storage
   c) stores data on a stack of magnetic disks
4) Give one advantage of storing data on a USB pen drive over an optical disc.

Worked Exam Questions

1   Sabina runs a piece of software to analyse the performance of her computer.
     It recommends that she should install more RAM in her computer.

     a)   State the purpose of RAM in a computer system.

          RAM holds any data that is currently in use.
                                                                              [1 mark]

     b)   Give **two** reasons why Sabina may need to install more RAM in her computer.

          1. Her computer may be running slowly.

          2. She may want to run more programs at once.
                                                                              [2 marks]

2   Shaun is going on a two week skiing trip. Each night, he will
     copy photos and videos to his laptop's secondary storage.

     a)   Give **three** characteristics to consider when choosing a suitable type
          of secondary storage for a computer system.

          You could also mention how quickly they transfer data, or how portable they are.

          1. Capacity

          2. Cost

          3. Durability —— Durability is how much physical damage it can take without breaking.
                                                                              [3 marks]

     b)   Shaun will be using a helmet-mounted action camera while skiing.
          The camera records videos onto a solid state memory card.
          Give **two** reasons why this is a suitable storage type for an action camera.

          1. It's resistant to impacts, so it's unlikely to be damaged when the camera is in use.

          2. It can be very compact and lightweight.
                                                                              [2 marks]

Exam Questions

3 Diana has bought a new laptop. The laptop contains 3 GB RAM and 128 GB secondary storage.

  a) Explain why secondary storage is needed in addition to RAM.

    ....

    ....

    ....

[3 marks]

  b) Diana wants to back up the data on her laptop twice a week.
Give **two** advantages and **two** disadvantages of storing her backup data on optical discs.

    Advantages: 1. ....

                   2. ....

    Disadvantages: 1. ....

                      2. ....

[4 marks]

4 Jackson is considering upgrading his PC. Will offers to sell his old CPU to Jackson.
Will's CPU is the same type as Jackson's CPU but has a different specification.

Jackson's CPU	Will's CPU
8 cores	4 cores
6 MB cache	3 MB cache
1.6 GHz clock speed	2.8 GHz clock speed

  a) Explain why using a CPU with a large cache capacity may increase CPU performance.

    ....

    ....

[2 marks]

  b) Do you think Jackson should buy Will's CPU? Give reasons to justify your decision.

    ....

    ....

    ....

    ....

There's no wrong answer, as long as your answer is properly justified.   *[4 marks]*

  c) Jackson increases the RAM in his PC from 4 GB to 8 GB, but is disappointed to find no
noticeable increase in his computer's performance. Explain why this may be the case.

    ....

    ....

[2 marks]

Systems Software — The OS

Systems software is software designed to run and maintain a computer system. By far the most important one is the operating system (OS). There's also utility software (see p.15), but that's very much the runner up.

Operating Systems manage Hardware and run Software

An Operating System (OS) is a complex piece of software found on most computer systems.

Main Functions of an OS

- Communicate with <u>internal</u> and <u>external hardware</u> via the <u>device drivers</u> (see below).

- Provide a <u>user interface</u>, allowing a user to interact with the computer (see p.13).

- Provide a <u>platform</u> for different <u>applications</u> to run (see p.13).

- Allow the computer to <u>multi-task</u> by controlling <u>memory resources</u> and the <u>CPU</u> (see p.13).

- Deal with <u>file management</u> and <u>disk management</u> (see p.14).

- Manage the <u>security</u> of the system, e.g. through <u>user accounts</u> (see p.14).

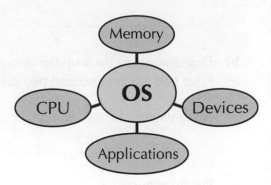

The words 'application' and 'program' can be used interchangeably to describe computer software.

Device Drivers let the OS and Hardware Talk to Each Other

Operating systems use device driver software to <u>communicate</u> with <u>internal hardware</u> or <u>peripherals</u> connected to the computer system:

- Every piece of hardware connected to the computer system requires a <u>device driver</u>. Drivers essentially act as a 'translator' for the <u>signals</u> between <u>OS</u> and <u>hardware</u>.

- When a computer is booted up, the OS will choose the correct device drivers for the hardware it <u>detects</u>. If new hardware is connected to the computer, the system will <u>install</u> the new, matching driver.

- Device manufacturers may release <u>updates</u> to device drivers in order to fix <u>bugs</u>, add <u>features</u> or improve the <u>performance</u> of their hardware. Updates may be installed <u>automatically</u> by the OS or <u>manually</u> by the user.

Some OSs will automatically find and install the drivers when you plug in a new device.

A driver lets a computer speak to a mouse? If you say so...

The OS is the boss of the computer system. It gives you a way to interact with your computer, controls hardware via drivers, and allows the computer to run applications and multi-task. There's loads more to learn about the OS, so make sure you've got your head around everything on this page before moving on.

Systems Software — The OS

One of the most recognisable functions of an OS is its user interface. It's one of the first things you imagine when you think about a particular system. But there's much more to an operating system than how it looks...

Operating Systems provide a **User Interface**

1) A <u>User Interface</u> allows the user to interact with a computer system.

2) <u>Graphical User Interfaces</u> (GUIs) are the most common type — they're designed to be easy for <u>everyday users</u> by making them visual, interactive and intuitive.

3) GUI systems are <u>optimised</u> for specific <u>input methods</u>. In the past, GUIs have been <u>WIMP</u>-based (using <u>windows</u>, <u>icons</u>, <u>menus</u> and <u>pointers</u>). <u>Android</u>™ and <u>iOS</u> were created for <u>touchscreen devices</u>, using <u>finger</u> gestures like pinching and swiping in place of a mouse.

4) A <u>command-line interface</u> is <u>text</u>-based. The user enters specific commands to complete tasks. Command-line interfaces are less <u>resource-heavy</u> than GUIs.

5) Command-line interfaces aren't suitable for everyday users. But for advanced users, they can be far more <u>efficient</u> and <u>powerful</u> than a GUI. They can be used to <u>automate</u> processes using <u>scripts</u> (simple programs).

You can swipe between screens or tap an icon to open it on Android™.

You type instructions into a command-line interface.

The OS allows **Multi-Tasking** by managing **Resources**

1) Operating Systems provide a <u>platform</u> to run applications (by configuring hardware so they can use it, and giving access to the CPU and memory).

2) Operating Systems that can run <u>multiple applications</u> at the same time are called <u>multi-tasking OSs</u>.

3) The OS helps the CPU carry out multi-tasking by efficiently <u>managing memory</u> and <u>CPU processing time</u>:

- When an application is <u>opened</u>, the OS moves the <u>necessary</u> parts of the application to <u>memory</u>, followed by <u>additional</u> parts when they are required. The OS will decide if applications or features have been used recently — if <u>not</u>, they may be <u>removed</u> from memory.

- To run <u>multiple</u> applications, the OS needs to make sure that the applications <u>don't overwrite</u> or <u>interfere</u> with each other. A memory manager allocates certain applications certain memory addresses, to make sure their processes are placed into separate locations.

- Only <u>one</u> application is processed by the CPU at a time, so the other processes must <u>wait</u>. The OS <u>divides CPU time</u> between open applications and may <u>prioritise</u> certain processes in order for instructions to be executed in the most <u>efficient</u> order.

Fortunately the CPU can switch between applications extremely quickly.

- When required, the OS organises the movement of data to and from <u>virtual memory</u>.

- The OS also helps manage the <u>flow of data</u> in the system by using <u>memory buffers</u>. Different types of computer components, devices and processes will <u>send</u>, <u>receive</u> and <u>process</u> data at different <u>speeds</u> — temporary memory buffers <u>store the data</u> until the component, device or process is <u>ready</u>.

Make sure you understand how multi-tasking works...

Take a look at a few different types of OS (e.g. desktop computer, smartphone, game console). What differences can you see between the GUIs? How have they been adapted to suit the device?

Systems Software — The OS

It's also the job of the OS to make sure that all your files are where they're meant to be.
So when you go looking for carKeys.txt or tvRemote.exe, they'll be right where you left them.

The OS handles **File** and **Disk Management**

1) Computers store data as <u>files</u>. Images, music, videos and spreadsheets are all just collections of data. <u>File extensions</u> (for example .jpg, .mp3, .mpeg) tell the computer which <u>type</u> of file it is.

2) The OS is responsible for <u>file management</u> — the organisation of data into a usable <u>hierarchical structure</u>. It also deals with the <u>naming</u>, <u>saving</u>, <u>movement</u>, <u>editing</u> and <u>deletion</u> of data.

3) The OS manages the <u>hard disk</u>. It splits the <u>physical disk</u> into storage <u>sectors</u>, decides which sectors to <u>write data</u> to, and keeps track of <u>free space</u> on the disk. Ideally, the data for a single file would be placed in <u>adjacent</u> sectors, but this isn't always possible (see p.15).

4) The OS may also include <u>utility software</u> to help it manage files and disks. <u>File compression</u> software can reduce the <u>size</u> of individual files and <u>encryption</u> software is used to <u>secure</u> the contents of files. <u>Defragmentation</u> software can help to <u>organise</u> and <u>maintain</u> the hard disk by collecting all the free space together.

Utility software can be used for loads of different things. For example, File Explorer in Windows® allows users to navigate and edit the file structure or access their files. See p.15 for more about utilities.

Operating Systems deal with **User Accounts**

1) Operating Systems can be <u>single-user</u> or <u>multi-user</u>.

- <u>Single-user</u> operating systems allow only <u>one user</u> to use the computer <u>at once</u>. Most common OSs, such as macOS, are single-user operating systems, even if the computer has multiple <u>user accounts</u>, or is connected to a <u>network</u> (see p.34).

- <u>Multi-user</u> OSs (e.g. UNIX® server) allow <u>several users</u> to use the computer at the <u>same time</u>. They're often used on <u>mainframes</u> (huge supercomputers) and give many users <u>simultaneous access</u>. For example, <u>ATMs</u> allow thousands of people access to a large bank's mainframe at the same time.

2) The OS is also responsible for <u>user account control</u>. User accounts allow different users to be granted <u>access</u> to specific data or resources on a computer system.

3) On most desktop operating systems each user has access to <u>their own</u> <u>personal data</u> and <u>desktop</u>, but cannot access other users' personal data.

4) Operating systems may have anti-theft measures to <u>prevent</u> other users from accessing locked devices or accounts to steal information. User accounts may be <u>password</u>, or <u>pin</u> protected. Some devices also require a user to draw a specific <u>pattern</u> on the screen, or have <u>fingerprint</u> or <u>retina</u> scanners.

Two people at one computer doesn't count as a multi-user OS...

Make sure you know the difference between multi-user and single-user OSs. A single user OS may have multiple user accounts, but only a single person can use the computer at any one time.

Systems Software — Utilities

Utility system software helps to maintain or configure a computer. Many useful utilities are installed with the operating system, but extra utility software can be installed to perform additional tasks.

Defragmentation Utilities put **broken up** files back together

1) Files are stored on a <u>hard disk</u> in <u>available spaces</u>. Ideally, <u>entire files</u> would be stored together.

2) However, as <u>files</u> are <u>moved</u>, <u>deleted</u> and <u>change size</u>, lots of <u>small gaps</u> begin to appear on the disk. When writing files to the disk, the OS <u>splits</u> files into smaller <u>blocks</u> to fill up the gaps.

3) Over time, the disk becomes more and more <u>fragmented</u>. This makes reading and writing files <u>slower</u> as the <u>read/write head</u> has to move back and forth across the disk.

4) <u>Defragmentation</u> software <u>reorganises</u> data on the hard drive to put fragmented files back together. It also moves files to collect all the <u>free space</u> together. This helps to <u>prevent</u> further <u>fragmentation</u>.

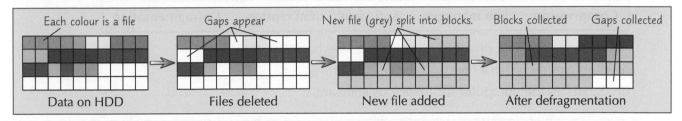

Each colour is a file — Gaps appear — New file (grey) split into blocks. — Blocks collected — Gaps collected

Data on HDD · Files deleted · New file added · After defragmentation

5) As <u>SSDs</u> use flash storage with no moving parts, fragmentation <u>doesn't</u> cause them any problems — they can access data just as quickly however it's arranged. In fact, as SSDs have a limited number of read/writes, defragmenting them can actually <u>shorten</u> their <u>lifespan</u>.

Compression Software makes files **Smaller**

1) Compression software reduces the <u>size</u> of files by <u>permanently</u> or <u>temporarily</u> removing data from them.

2) Compressed files take up <u>less disk space</u> and are <u>quicker to download</u>.

3) Standard file formats include <u>.zip</u> and <u>.rar</u>.

4) Compressed files need to be <u>extracted</u> before they can be used.

There is a <u>whole page</u> about compression on p.30.

Encryption Software can help **Protect** files

1) Encryption software <u>scrambles</u> (encrypts) data to stop <u>third-parties</u> from <u>accessing it</u>.

2) The main <u>benefit</u> of encryption is that <u>intercepted</u> or <u>stolen</u> data is still <u>secure</u>, as only the <u>intended readers</u> of the data can <u>unscramble</u> and <u>understand</u> the data.

There's more about encryption on p.46.

3) To <u>decrypt</u> the data, a special '<u>key</u>' is needed. A <u>computer</u> uses the key and a <u>set of instructions</u> to turn the data back into its <u>original form</u>.

4) The <u>strong</u> forms of encryption that are used today are <u>very difficult</u> to <u>crack</u> (break). Hackers can't use <u>brute force attacks</u> (see p.44) to guess the key.

There are many more examples of utility software...

Remember, utilities are bits of software that help maintain your system. You need to know the three above, but it's worth knowing some others for the exam, e.g. disk/registry cleaners, system restore, file managers, anti-virus / anti-spyware / firewalls, automatic updating, system diagnosis tools.

Warm-Up and Worked Exam Questions

You've made it to the end of Section One, and I think that calls for a bit of a celebration. But not before having a go at these questions — better get them out of the way while it's all fresh in your mind...

Warm-Up Questions

1) Tick the correct box in each row of the table below.

	System Software	Not System Software
Operating System		
Word Processor		
Disk defragmenter		

2) Choose the utility software from the box that best matches each description below:

Compression	File manager	Anti-virus	Encryption	Defragmentation

   a) Reorganises data on a hard drive to put files back together.

   b) Reduces the size of files and folders.

   c) Searches the computer for malicious software.

Worked Exam Question

1   Selina has customised the graphical user interface (GUI) on her computer's operating system.

   a)   Describe the purpose of a graphical user interface.

   A graphical user interface allows the user to interact with the computer in
   a visual and intuitive way (e.g. through windows, menus and pointers).

   [2 marks]

   b)   Selina's operating system also has an optional command line interface.
   i)   Define what is meant by a command line interface.

   A command line interface allows the user to interact with a computer
   only by typing in commands from a set list.

   [1 mark]

   ii)   Identify **two** benefits of using a command line interface instead of a GUI.

   1.   Command line interfaces give greater control than GUIs.

   2.   They are less resource-heavy than GUIs.
        You could also mention scripts as a possible benefit.

   [2 marks]

   c)   The operating system includes an encryption utility that can be used to encrypt folders and files. Explain **one** reason why Selina may use the encryption utility.

   To keep her data private in the event of a third party, like a hacker,
   gaining access to her files.   It may also protect her data from malware.

   [2 marks]

Exam Questions

2   Darpan has just installed a new operating system on his computer.

   a)   State **three** functions of an operating system.

   1. ....

   2. ....

   3. ....

   [3 marks]

   After the new OS was installed, it automatically downloaded and installed the device drivers.

   b)   Describe what is meant by device drivers.

   ....

   ....

   [2 marks]

3   Keri's operating system includes an encryption utility that helps to keep her personal data secure.

   a)   Describe the process of data encryption and decryption.

   ....

   ....

   ....

   [2 marks]

   b)   Identify **two** other features or utilities the operating system
          may provide to help protect Keri's personal data.

   1. ....

   2. ....

   [2 marks]

4   Josephine's computer has a multi-tasking operating system. Explain how the
       operating system manages memory and CPU time to allow the computer to multi-task.

   ....

   ....

   ....

   ....

   ....

   ....

   ....

   [6 marks]

Revision Questions for Section One

Sometimes the first section is the easy one — but not this time. There's lots to learn here, so:
- Try these questions and <u>tick off each one</u> when you <u>get it right</u>.
- When you've done <u>all the questions</u> for a topic and are <u>completely happy</u> with it, tick off the topic.

Computer Systems and the CPU (p.1-3) ☑

1) What is a computer?
2) Define hardware and software.
3) What is an embedded system?
4) Explain the role of the control unit in the CPU.
5) Write down the names of three registers in the CPU.
6) What does ALU stand for and what does it do?
7) What is cache memory and what is it used for?
8) Sketch a Von Neumann computer.
9) Describe what happens at each stage of the CPU fetch-execute cycle.

Memory and Computer Performance (p.6-7) ☑

10) What is the difference between volatile and non-volatile memory?
11) What does RAM stand for? Describe how RAM is used in a computer system.
12) Could changing the amount of RAM affect the performance of the computer?
    Give reasons for your answer.
13) Explain when and how virtual memory is used.
14) Explain why ROM is required by a computer system.
15) Name three characteristics of a processor that may affect its performance.
16) State three components that could be upgraded to speed up a computer system.

Secondary Storage (p.8-9) ☑

17) Define primary and secondary storage. Give an example of each.
18) List three types of flash storage device or media.
19) List the advantages and disadvantages of HDDs and SSDs.
20) Why might someone choose magnetic tape as a form of storage?
21) What are the pros and cons of optical discs?
22) Draw a diagram to summarise cost, speed and capacity for different types of secondary storage.

Types of Software (p.12-15) ☑

23) List six functions of an operating system.
24) Explain how device drivers are used in a computer system.
25) Briefly describe a GUI and a Command-line interface.
26) Describe how the OS manages resources to allow multi-tasking.
27) What is a memory buffer?
28) What is a multi-user OS? Give an example of where one might be used.
29) List three types of utility software.
30) Explain how defragmentation software works.
31) Why does using encryption software make data more secure?

Units

Just like you have units like centimetres, metres and kilometres for measuring distance, computers need units for measuring digital information. You'll need to learn all of the unit names on this page and their sizes.

Bits are the Smallest Measure of Data

1) Computers use 1s and 0s to represent the flow of electricity.
   <u>1</u> is used to show that electricity <u>is</u> flowing, and <u>0</u> shows that it is <u>not</u> flowing.

2) All the data we want a computer to process must be converted into <u>binary code</u> (1s and 0s).

3) Each 1 or 0 in a binary code is a <u>bit</u> (binary digit). For example, 1010 is 4 bits.

4) The table below shows <u>the size</u> of other units of data:

A <u>byte</u> is big enough to store one <u>character</u> (like x, e, M or £). See p.27 for more info.

Most <u>files</u> (like <u>songs</u>, <u>pictures</u> and <u>documents</u>) are measured in <u>kB</u> or <u>MB</u>.

High definition <u>videos</u> and complex <u>applications</u> are often measured in <u>gigabytes</u>.

<u>Secondary storage</u> capacity is measured in <u>gigabytes</u> or <u>terabytes</u>.

Name	Size
Bit (b)	A single binary digit (1 or 0)
Nibble	4 bits
Byte (B)	8 bits
Kilobyte (kB)	1000 bytes
Megabyte (MB)	1000 kilobytes
Gigabyte (GB)	1000 megabytes
Terabyte (TB)	1000 gigabytes
Petabyte (PB)	1000 terabytes

You might see each unit defined to be 1024 (not 1000) times bigger than the previous unit. The main reason is that 1024 is a power of 2 which is helpful when dealing with binary data.

5) Each <u>bit</u> can take one of <u>two different values</u> (either 1 or 0). This means that a <u>nibble</u> (4 bits) can take 2^4 = <u>16 different values</u>, and a <u>byte</u> (8 bits) can take 2^8 = <u>256 different values</u>.

You can Convert between Different Units

<u>Converting</u> between units of data is usually pretty straightforward — Just watch out when you have to switch between <u>bits</u> and <u>bytes</u>.

EXAMPLE: **Ashley has downloaded some images to her computer. Each image is 300 kilobytes.**

a) How many bits are in each image?

1) First, convert to bytes by <u>multiplying by 1000</u>:   300 kB = 300 × 1000 = 300 000 Bytes

2) There are 8 bits in a byte, so <u>multiply by 8</u>:   300 000 Bytes = 300 000 × 8
                                                                              = 2 400 000 bits

b) She wants to copy 400 of these images onto her USB flash drive, which has 0.15 GB of free space left. Does she have enough space to store them all?

1) Work out the <u>total size</u> of all the images: 400 × 300 = 120 000 kB

2) Now convert this to GB — first, <u>divide by 1000</u> to get it in MB, then <u>again</u> to get it in GB: 120 000 kB = 120 000 ÷ 1000 = 120 MB
   120 MB = 120 ÷ 1000 = 0.12 GB

So yes, she has enough space.

This page has me in bits...

Keep working your way through that unit table until the size order is clear in your head — it might just show up on your exam. A bit is smaller than a nibble, and a nibble is less than a full byte. I know, hilarious.

Binary Numbers

As computers only understand 1s and 0s, all data must be converted into binary to be processed.
Binary can be used to represent all numbers in our standard number system.

Counting in Binary is a bit like Counting in Denary

1) In our standard number system we have ten different digits (0, 1, 2, 3, 4, 5, 6, 7, 8, 9). This is called <u>denary</u>, <u>decimal</u> or <u>base-10</u>.

2) <u>Binary</u> only uses <u>two</u> different digits (0 and 1) — we call this <u>base-2</u>.

3) Counting in binary is similar to counting in denary, but the place values from <u>right</u> to <u>left</u> increase by <u>powers of 2</u> (e.g. 8, 4, 2, 1), instead of powers of 10 (e.g. 1000, 100, 10, 1).

4) The following table shows the <u>binary equivalents</u> of the <u>denary numbers 0-15</u>:

0 = 0	4 = 100	8 = 1000	12 = 1100
1 = 1	5 = 101	9 = 1001	13 = 1101
2 = 10	6 = 110	10 = 1010	14 = 1110
3 = 11	7 = 111	11 = 1011	15 = 1111

5) Most binary numbers are given as <u>8-bit</u> numbers, e.g. 01101011, which can represent the denary numbers <u>0 to 255</u>. The bit with the <u>largest</u> value (the <u>left-most bit</u>) is called the <u>most significant bit</u>, and the bit with the <u>smallest</u> value (the <u>right-most bit</u>) is called the <u>least significant bit</u>

Binary Numbers are easier to Convert using Tables

Drawing a table with binary <u>place values</u> in the first row makes binary to denary conversion easier.

EXAMPLE: **Convert the 8-bit binary number 0011 0101 to a denary number.**

Each column is just a power of 2. i.e. 2^3, 2^2, 2^1, 2^0.

1) Draw up a table with binary place values in the top row. Start with 1 at the right, then move left, <u>doubling</u> each time.

2) Write the binary number 0011 0101 into your table.

128	64	32	16	8	4	2	1
0	0	1	1	0	1	0	1

3) <u>Add up</u> all the numbers with a 1 in their column:

32 + 16 + 4 + 1 = 66. So 0011 0101 is **66** in denary.

This works with all binary numbers — just draw as many columns as you need, doubling each time.

Convert Denary to Binary by Subtracting

When converting from <u>denary</u> to <u>binary</u>, it's easier to draw a <u>table</u> of binary place values, then <u>subtract them</u> from <u>largest</u> to <u>smallest</u>. Have a look at this example:

EXAMPLE: **Convert the denary number 79 into an 8-bit binary number.**

1) Draw an 8-bit table.

2) Move along the table, <u>only</u> subtracting the number in each column from your <u>running total</u> if it gives a <u>positive</u> answer.

3) Put a 1 in every column that gives a positive answer, and a 0 in the rest.

128	64	32	16	8	4	2	1
0	1	0	0	1	1	1	1

79 − 128 = −49   79 − 64 = 15   15 − 32 = −17   15 − 16 = −1   15 − 8 = 7   7 − 4 = 3   3 − 2 = 1   1 − 1 = 0

So 79 converted to an 8-bit binary number is **0100 1111**.

There are other methods to convert denary to binary, so just choose the one you are most comfortable with.

REVISION TASK

Use powers of 2 to convert between binary and denary...

There's a really easy way to test yourself on this stuff. Write down a denary number between 0 and 255 and convert it to binary. Then write down an 8-bit binary number and convert it to denary.

Binary Numbers

Add **Binary Numbers** using **Column Addition**

As binary only uses 1s and 0s we <u>can</u> comfortably do 0 + 0 = 0, 1 + 0 = 1 and 0 + 1 = 1.
Using binary we <u>can't</u> write 1 + 1 = 2. Instead, we have to write <u>1 + 1 = 1 0</u>.

EXAMPLES: **1.** **Add the following 8-bit binary numbers together: 1000 1101 and 0100 1000**

1) First, put the binary numbers into columns. —

2) Starting from the right, add the numbers in columns.

3) When doing 1 + 1 = 10, carry the 1 into the next column.

So 1000 1101 + 0100 1000 = 1101 0101

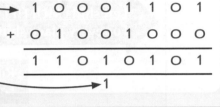

```
  1 0 0 0 1 1 0 1
+ 0 1 0 0 1 0 0 0
  1 1 0 1 0 1 0 1
                1
```

2. **Add the two 8-bit binary numbers below:**

```
   0 0 1 1 0 0 1 1
 + 0 1 1 1 1 0 0 1
   1 0 1 0 1 1 0 0
   1 1 1     1 1
```

1) Start at the right-hand side and add each column.

2) Sometimes you'll get something like 1 + 1 + 1 = 11, so you need to write 1, then carry 1 to the next column.

So 0011 0011 + 0111 1001 = 1010 1100

You can check your answer by converting the numbers and answer to denary, to make sure it still works.

Overflow Errors occur when a Number has Too Many bits

1) Sometimes, during binary arithmetic you will get a result that requires <u>more</u> bits than the CPU is expecting — this is called <u>overflow</u>.

2) For example, in binary the <u>8-bit</u> calculation 1111 1111 + 0000 0001 gives the <u>9-bit</u> answer <u>1 0000 0000</u>. Computers will see the 1 as an <u>overflow error</u> and just output 0000 0000, which is nonsense.

3) Computers usually deal with these extra bits by <u>storing</u> them elsewhere.

4) Overflow <u>flags</u> are used to show that an overflow error has occurred.

The most significant bit will be the first to overflow.

EXAMPLE: **a)** **Add the 8-bit binary numbers below, giving your answer as an 8-bit binary number.**

1) <u>Add</u> the binary numbers in the usual way.

2) The final calculation is 1 + 1 = 10, so <u>carry the 1</u>.

3) You are left with a <u>9-bit answer</u> — this is an <u>overflow error</u>.

4) <u>Ignore</u> the overflow to give your 8-bit answer. **0110 0101**

```
    1 1 0 1 0 0 0 1
 +  1 0 0 1 0 1 0 0
  1 0 1 1 0 0 1 0 1
  1         1
```

b) **Identify any problems that could be caused by giving your answer as an 8-bit number.**

There is an overflow error which can lead to a loss of data and a loss of accuracy in your answer. It could also cause software to crash if it doesn't have a way of dealing with the extra bit.

Binary, binary, quite contrary, how do you overflow...

Overflows occur when a calculation gives a result with more bits than are available to store it. This can be a real problem — programmers must make sure that they can't occur, or that they are dealt with.

Binary Numbers

Binary Shifts can be used to Multiply or Divide by 2

1) A <u>binary shift</u> (also known as a <u>logical shift</u>) moves every bit in a binary number left or right a certain number of places.

2) <u>Gaps</u> at the <u>beginning</u> or <u>end</u> of the number are filled in with <u>0s</u>.

3) The <u>direction</u> of the binary shift indicates whether it <u>multiplies</u> or <u>divides</u> the binary number:

> **Left shifts MULTIPLY a binary number.**
> **For every place shifted left, the number is <u>doubled</u>.**

> **Right shifts DIVIDE a binary number.**
> **For every place shifted right, the number is <u>halved</u>.**

4) If a number is shifted <u>3 places right</u>, it would be <u>halved three times</u> (i.e. divided by $2^3 = 8$). If a number were shifted <u>4 places left</u>, it would be <u>doubled four times</u> (i.e. multiplied by $2^4 = 16$).

5) Left shifts can cause <u>overflows</u> (if extra bits are needed), and right shifts cause bits to 'drop off' the end. Bits dropping off or overflowing can lead to a <u>loss of accuracy/data</u>.

Examples of Binary Shifts

EXAMPLE: **Perform a 3 place left shift on the 8-bit binary number 0010 1001.**
Explain the effect this will have on the number and problems that may occur.

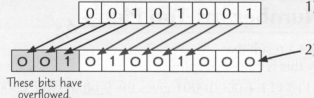

| 0 | 0 | 1 | 0 | 1 | 0 | 0 | 1 |

| 0 | 0 | 1 | 0 | 1 | 0 | 0 | 1 | 0 | 0 | 0 |

These bits have overflowed.

1) Write down the original binary number, then shift all digits 3 places to the left.

2) Fill in the gaps on the right with 0s.

The number has been doubled three times, so it has been multiplied by $2^3 = 8$.

If there are only 8 bits available to store the number then the 3 most significant bits will **overflow**. Some data/accuracy may be lost and an overflow flag will be displayed.

EXAMPLE: **Perform a 2 place right shift on the binary number 0011 1100.**
What effect will this have on the number?

1) Write down the original binary number, then shift all digits 2 places to the right.

| 0 | 0 | 1 | 1 | 1 | 1 | 0 | 0 |

2) Fill in the gaps on the left with 0s.

| 0 | 0 | 0 | 0 | 1 | 1 | 1 | 1 | X | X |

A 2 place right shift gives the binary number 0000 1111. As this is a 2 place shift, the original number will have been halved twice (so divided by $2^2 = 4$).

Dividing using a right binary shift has the same effect as using the <u>DIV</u> operator (p.77) — your answer would <u>not</u> take into account any <u>remainders</u>.

Shift left to multiply and shift right to divide...

Binary shifts are really good for doing fast multiplication and division by powers of 2. Watch out for bits overflowing or dropping off the end — if this happens then you'll lose accuracy in your answer.

Hexadecimal Numbers

Hexadecimal (hex) is another number system used regularly in programming.
Hex uses a combination of digits and letters in order to represent a number.

Hexadecimal numbers are Shorter than Binary

1) Hexadecimal (or base-16) uses sixteen different digits.

2) A single hex character can represent any denary number from 0-15. To represent 0-15 in binary would require 4 bits (a nibble), so each hex character equates to a nibble in binary.

3) The table shows the denary and binary value of each hex character.

4) Programmers often prefer hex when coding, because:

- It's simpler to remember large numbers in hex — they're far shorter than binary numbers.
- Due to hex numbers being shorter, there's less chance of input errors.
- It's easier to convert between binary and hex than binary and denary.

Computers themselves do not use hex — they still have to convert everything to binary to process it.

Denary	Hex	Binary	Denary	Hex	Binary
0	0	0000	8	8	1000
1	1	0001	9	9	1001
2	2	0010	10	A	1010
3	3	0011	11	B	1011
4	4	0100	12	C	1100
5	5	0101	13	D	1101
6	6	0110	14	E	1110
7	7	0111	15	F	1111

Convert Hex to Denary by Multiplying each Character

In hex, moving right to left, place values increase in powers of 16.

4096	256	16	1

To convert from hex to denary, draw up a table, fill in the boxes, then multiply — just like in this example:

EXAMPLES:

1. Convert the hexadecimal number 87 into denary.

Luckily in the exam you'll only have to convert two digit hex numbers like in these examples.

1) First, draw this table, then write in your hex number.

16	1
8	7

2) Multiply the numbers in each column.

$8 \times 16 = 128$ $7 \times 1 = 7$

3) Add up the results: → $128 + 7 = 135$ So the hex number 87 is 135 in denary.

To convert from denary to hex, draw the table but use division to fill it in.

2. Convert the denary number 106 into hexadecimal.   *Remember, hex goes from 0-9, then A to F.*

1) Start at the left. Divide 106 by 16, then hold onto the remainder.

$106 \div 16 = 6 \text{ r } 10$

16	1
6	A

2) Divide the remainder from the last calculation by 1.

$10 \div 1 = 10 = A$

So the denary number 106 is 6A in hexadecimal.

Hex can be a blessing and a curse...

REVISION TASK

Hex and denary can look fairly similar (as they both contain 0-9), so make sure you've got them the right way round when converting — 65 in hexadecimal is NOT the same as 65 in denary. Memorise the hex table and its advantages, then cover it up and write everything you remember.

Hexadecimal Numbers

Convert **Binary** to **Hex** by splitting it into **Nibbles**

1) Each hex character is equal to a <u>nibble</u> in binary, so it is possible to convert from binary to hex by splitting the binary code into <u>4-bit chunks</u>.

2) Binary to hex conversions can be much <u>easier</u> than converting from binary to denary, as you only have to deal with the nibbles <u>one at a time</u>.

EXAMPLE: **Convert the binary number 1011 1001 to hexadecimal.**

> Remember, hex only uses letters for denary values between 10-15.

1) Firstly, <u>split</u> the binary number into <u>nibbles</u>:   1011   1001

2) Draw a table with columns labelled 1, 2, 4, 8, then <u>repeat</u> the values for as many nibbles as you require.

3) Fill in the table with your binary number.

8	4	2	1	8	4	2	1
1	0	1	1	1	0	0	1

4) For <u>each nibble</u>, add up the numbers with a 1 in the column, then convert this value to hex.

$$8 + 2 + 1 = 11$$
$$= B$$

$$8 + 1 = 9$$

5) Finally put the hex values <u>together</u>.

The binary number 10111001 is B9 in hexadecimal.

If the binary number can't be split into nibbles, you'll have to stick some zeros on the front.

EXAMPLE: **Convert the binary number 11 1110 to hexadecimal.**

1) Add <u>zeros</u> to the <u>front</u> of the binary number, so that you can split it into nibbles.   0011   1110

2) Draw a repeating table of 1, 2, 4 and 8, as above.

3) Write your binary number in the table.

8	4	2	1	8	4	2	1
0	0	1	1	1	1	1	0

4) Add up <u>each nibble</u> and <u>convert</u> each value to <u>hex</u>.

$$2 + 1 = 3$$

$$8 + 4 + 2 = 14$$
$$= E$$

5) Put the hex values together.

The binary number 111110 is 3E in hexadecimal.

For **Hex** to **Binary**, use each **Character's Denary Value**

To convert the <u>opposite</u> way (from <u>hex</u> to <u>binary</u>) convert each hex character into binary, then just put the binary numbers together.

EXAMPLE: **Convert the hexadecimal number 8C to binary.**

1) First, find the denary value of each character: 8 = 8 in denary   C = 12 in denary

2) Find the binary value of each denary number:

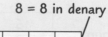

8	4	2	1
1	0	0	0

8	4	2	1
1	1	0	0

8 = 1000 in binary   12 = 1100 in binary

3) Put the nibbles together to get the equivalent binary number.   The hexadecimal number 8C is 10001100 in binary.

This page has so many nibbles it could spoil your lunch...

When converting binary to hex just remember to split the binary up into chunks of 4 bits, each with columns labelled 1, 2, 4 and 8. Then work out the individual hex values and put them together.

Warm-Up and Worked Exam Questions

Converting between binary, denary and hexadecimal tests your maths skills just as much as your computing knowledge. Have a go at these warm-up questions before diving into the exam questions on the next page.

Warm-Up Questions

1) How many bits are in a nibble?

2) Convert:
   a) 01011001 from binary to denary
   b) 69 from denary to binary

3) Add the following 8-bit binary numbers together: 01101000 and 10001010

4) Explain how overflow errors occur.

5) Perform a 3 place right shift on 10111000. Give your answer as an 8-bit number.

6) What is the effect of a 1 place left shift?

7) Convert:
   a) 48 from denary to hex
   b) C6 from hex to denary
   c) 10100010 from binary to hex
   d) 3D from hex to binary

Worked Exam Questions

1 Work out these conversions.

   a) Convert the 8-bit binary number 10010011 into a denary number.

   128 + 16 + 2 + 1 = 147

   ....147...........
   [1 mark]

   b) Convert the denary number 252 into an 8-bit binary number.

   Drawing an 8-bit table can help.

128	64	32	16	8	4	2	1
1	1	1	1	1	1	O	O

   252 − 128 = 124
   124 − 64 = 60
   60 − 32 = 28
   28 − 16 = 12
   12 − 8 = 4
   4 − 4 = O

   ....11111100...........
   [1 mark]

2 Daniel is a programmer. He makes the following two claims about hex numbers.

   Claim 1: "Hex is much easier to work with than binary."

   Claim 2: "Converting from denary to hex is easier than converting from binary to hex."

   Would other programmers agree with Daniel's claims? Explain your answers.

   Claim 1: They're likely to agree with claim 1. Hex numbers are shorter so are easier to identify, remember, edit and share than binary codes.

   Claim 2: They're likely to disagree with claim 2. Converting binary to hex is easier as binary numbers can be split into nibbles to quickly read off the hex values.

   [4 marks]

Exam Questions

3 Misha wants to save some music onto a solid state drive (SSD).

a) State which SSD has the largest capacity:
250 gigabyte (GB), 200 000 megabyte (MB) or 0.3 terabyte (TB).

....
[1 mark]

b) Calculate how many 5 MB music files Misha could save onto a 250 GB SSD.

....
[2 marks]

4 Binary shifts can be used to quickly multiply and divide binary numbers.

a) State an appropriate binary shift to divide a binary number by 4 and use it on 11010100.

....
[2 marks]

b) Yasha says "Adding a binary number to itself is the same as a 2 place left shift."
Is he correct? Explain your answer.

....

....
[2 marks]

5 A security program encrypts passwords using a hexadecimal conversion.
The binary code of each letter for the password 'CAT' is shown below.
01000011   01000001   01010100

a) Convert each binary number above to a hexadecimal number to encrypt the password 'CAT'.

....
[3 marks]

b) The password 'DOG' is encrypted as 44 4F 47.
  i) Convert the first encrypted letter to binary.

....
[1 mark]

  ii) What password would be encrypted as 43 4F 44 45?

Look back at previous question parts.

....
[2 marks]

Characters

Almost everything can be represented as binary code — words, images and sound can all be turned into bits and processed by a computer. Firstly let's look at words, which are made up of different characters.

Binary can be used to represent Characters

1) Alphanumeric characters are used to make words and strings (see p.80). They include uppercase and lowercase letters, the digits 0-9, and symbols like ? + and £.

2) Computers are unable to process these characters directly as they only process binary code. So they need a way of converting these characters to binary code and vice versa. They can do this using character sets.

> Character sets are collections of characters that a computer recognises from their binary representation.

Don't mistake a character set for a font. A character set is what determines the letter — the font you use just displays that letter in a certain way.

3) Character sets also contain special characters which do certain commands (e.g. enter and delete).

4) Pressing a button on your keyboard sends a binary signal to the computer telling it which key you pressed. The computer then uses the character set to translate the binary code into a particular character.

The number of Bits you'll need is based on the Character Set

Different character sets can have different amounts of characters. The number of characters in a character set determines how many bits you'll need. Here are some standard character sets you should know about:

ASCII

- ASCII is the most commonly-used character set in the English-speaking world. Each ASCII character is given a 7-bit binary code — this means it can represent a total of 128 different characters, including all the letters in the English alphabet, numbers, symbols and commands.

- An extra bit (0) is added to the start of the binary code for each ASCII character (see the table on the right). This means each ASCII character fits nicely into 1 byte.

- The codes for numbers, uppercase letters and lowercase letters are ordered (A comes before B comes before C....) with symbols and commands scattered around.

Character	Binary	Hex	Decimal
Backspace	0000 1000	8	8
0	0011 0000	30	48
1	0011 0001	31	49
=	0011 1101	3D	61
A	0100 0001	41	65
B	0100 0010	42	66
a	0110 0001	61	97
b	0110 0010	62	98

Some examples of ASCII characters.

Unicode®

- Unicode® comes in several different forms and tries to cover every possible character or symbol that might be written. Unlike ASCII, Unicode® uses multiple bytes for each character.

- The best thing about Unicode® is that it covers all major languages, even those that use a completely different alphabet like Greek, Russian and Chinese.

- The first 128 codes in Unicode® are the same as ASCII.

You can work out the size of a text file using this formula:

> **File size (in bits) = number of bits per character × number of characters**

E.g. a text file that uses 8 bits per character (like ASCII) and contains 200 characters will have a file size of 8 × 200 = 1600 bits.

Character sets are used to turn binary data into characters...

You don't need to remember the ASCII codes for any specific characters, but if you're given the ASCII code of one character (e.g. T) you should be able to work out the ASCII code for another character (e.g. W).

Storing Images

Images and sounds are pieces of data stored on computers — so, naturally, they're made of bits (p.19).

Images are stored as a series of Pixels

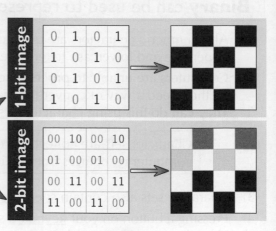

1) Most images you use are <u>bitmap</u> images — e.g. photos. They're made up of lots of tiny dots, called <u>pixels</u>.

2) The <u>colour</u> of each pixel is represented by a <u>binary</u> code. The number of colours available in an image is related to the number of <u>bits</u> the code has.

3) <u>Black-and-white</u> images only use two colours, so they need <u>1-bit</u> for each pixel — e.g. <u>0 for white</u> and <u>1 for black</u>.

4) <u>2-bit images</u> can be made up of four colours. Each pixel can be one of four binary values — <u>00</u>, <u>01</u>, <u>10</u> and <u>11</u>.

5) You can make a <u>greater range</u> of shades and colours by <u>increasing the number of bits</u> for each pixel.

Increasing Colour Depth and Resolution increases the File Size

1) The <u>colour depth</u> is the <u>number of bits</u> used for <u>each pixel</u>.

2) Given the colour depth you can work out <u>how many colours</u> can be made using this <u>formula</u>:

> **Total number of colours = 2^n (where n = number of bits per pixel, or bpp)**

> 1-bit image: $2^1 = 2$ colours   4-bit image: $2^4 = 16$ colours   24-bit image: $2^{24} = 16\ 777\ 216$ colours

3) Most devices use a <u>24-bit colour depth</u>, with 8 bits for the levels of <u>red</u>, <u>green</u> and <u>blue</u> in each pixel. This colour depth can produce more colours than the human eye can see (estimated to be 10 million).

4) The image <u>resolution</u> is the <u>number of pixels</u> in the image. It's sometimes given as <u>width × height</u>. The <u>higher the resolution</u>, the more pixels the image is made of, so the <u>better the quality</u> of the image.

5) To work out <u>how many bits</u> an image will take up, use the <u>formula</u>:

> **File size (in bits) = image resolution × colour depth = width × height × colour depth**

6) Using a <u>greater</u> image resolution or colour depth means that there are <u>more bits</u> in the image. This can give a <u>higher-quality image</u>, but also increases the <u>file size</u>.

EXAMPLE: **Calculate the file size, in MB, of an 8-bit image that is 2000 pixels wide and 1000 pixels high.**

1) First, use the <u>formula</u> to find the <u>size in bits</u>:   2000 × 1000 × 8 = 16 000 000 bits

2) <u>Divide by 8</u> to convert to <u>bytes</u>:   16 000 000 ÷ 8 = 2 000 000 bytes

3) Finally, <u>divide by 1000 twice</u> to convert to <u>MB</u>:   2 000 000 ÷ 1000 ÷ 1000 = 2 MB

Devices need Metadata to display the images

1) <u>Metadata</u> is the <u>information</u> stored in an image file which helps the computer recreate the image on screen from the binary data in each pixel. *It can also include information like the time and date that the image was created or last edited.*

2) Metadata usually includes the image's <u>file format</u>, <u>height</u>, <u>width</u>, <u>colour depth</u> and <u>resolution</u>.

3) Without metadata, devices would not be able to <u>display</u> the image on screen as intended.

Images are stored as long strings of bits...

Remember that these types of images are called bitmaps — they're the ones made out of pixels. There are also vector images — vectors are not made of pixels, and can resized without loss of quality.

Storing Sound

Sound is made up of bits and stored in files on a computer. Or rather, digital sound is — the other type of sound, analogue, doesn't get on well with computers very much, so we've got to turn it into digital first.

Sound is **Sampled** and stored **Digitally**

1) Sound is recorded by a microphone as an <u>analogue</u> signal.
   Analogue signals are pieces of <u>continually changing</u> data.

2) Analogue signals need to be converted into <u>digital</u> data so that computers can read and store sound files. This is done by <u>analogue to digital converters</u>, which are found in most modern recording devices.

3) The process of converting analogue to digital is called <u>sampling</u>:

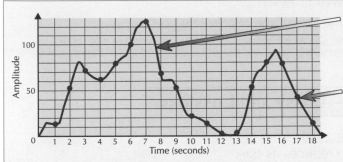

The blue line shows the analogue sound wave — it's one <u>continuous</u> piece of data which <u>keeps changing</u>.

To convert the analogue recording to digital data, we <u>sample</u> the <u>amplitude</u> of the wave at <u>regular intervals</u> (shown by the dots on the graph). The <u>amplitude</u> can only take certain values depending on the <u>bit depth</u> (see below).

Once the device has sampled the recording, it creates the curve <u>digitally</u> like this.

Each block of data matches where each sample was taken.

The digital data is about the same shape as the analogue wave, but it's <u>not continuous</u>. It's <u>lost</u> a lot of data — e.g. the last peak in the analogue wave is much flatter in the digital data.

The digital data can be improved by taking samples <u>more regularly</u> — most music isn't sampled every second but every couple of <u>milliseconds</u>.

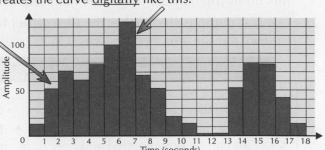

Several factors affect the **Size** and **Quality** of **Sound Files**

1) <u>Sample rate</u> (or <u>sampling frequency</u>) is how many samples you take in a second — it's usually measured in hertz (Hz) or kilohertz (kHz). E.g. a common sample rate is 44,100 samples per second (44 100 Hz or 44.1 kHz).

2) <u>Bit depth</u> is the number of bits available for each sample.

Sample rate × bit depth is often called the bit rate.

3) You can calculate the <u>size</u> of a sound file using this <u>formula</u>:

> **File size (in bits) = Sample rate (in Hz) × bit depth × duration (in seconds)**

4) For example, if you were to sample <u>30 seconds</u> of audio with a bit depth of <u>8 bits</u> and a sample rate of <u>500 Hz</u>, your file would be 500 × 8 × 30 = 120 000 bits.

5) <u>Increasing</u> the sample rate means the analogue recording is sampled more often. The sampled sound will be <u>better quality</u> and will more <u>closely match</u> the original recording.

6) <u>Increasing</u> the bit depth means the digital file picks up <u>quieter sounds</u>, even if they're happening at the same time as louder ones. This will also result in a sampled sound that is closer to the <u>quality</u> of the original recording.

7) However, increasing the sample rate or bit depth will <u>increase the file size</u>.

You can change the size and quality of sound files...

Bit depth is the sound equivalent of colour depth from the previous page — it's the number of bits used for each 'piece' of data in the file. The file size is the number of bits used for the entire file.

Compression

How can we possibly store all of these images and sound files? Well, the answer is down to data compression.

Sometimes we need to **Compress** files

1) <u>Data compression</u> is when we make <u>file sizes smaller</u>, while trying to make the compressed file as <u>true to the original</u> as possible.

2) Compressing data files has many <u>uses</u>:

- Smaller files take up <u>less storage space</u> on a device.
- <u>Streaming</u> and <u>downloading</u> files from the Internet is quicker as they take up less <u>bandwidth</u> (p.36).
- It allows <u>web pages</u> to <u>load more quickly</u> in web browsers.
- <u>Email</u> services normally have restrictions on the size of the attachment you can send — compressing the file allows you to send the same content with a much smaller file size.

There are **Two Types** of compression — **Lossy** and **Lossless**

1) <u>Lossy compression</u> works by permanently <u>removing data</u> from the file — this limits the number of bits the file needs and so reduces its size.

2) <u>Lossless compression</u> makes the file smaller by <u>temporarily</u> removing data to store the file and then restores it to its <u>original state</u> when it's opened.

	Pros	Cons	E.g. of File Types
Lossy	• Greatly <u>reduced file size</u>, meaning more files can be stored. • Lossy files take up <u>less bandwidth</u> so can be downloaded and streamed more quickly. • <u>Commonly used</u> — lots of software can read lossy files.	• Lossy compression <u>loses</u> data — the file can't be turned back into the original. • Lossy compression <u>can't be used</u> on text or software files as these files need to retain all the information of the original. • Lossy files are <u>worse quality</u> than the original. But, this loss in quality is normally <u>unnoticeable</u>.	• MP3 (audio) • AAC (audio) • JPEG (image)
Lossless	• Data is only removed temporarily so there is <u>no reduction in quality</u> — the compressed file should look or sound like the original. • Lossless files can be <u>decompressed</u> — turned back into the original. • Lossless compression can be used on <u>text</u> and software <u>files</u>.	• Only a <u>slight reduction</u> in file size, so lossless files still take up quite a bit of space on your device. E.g. a lossless song may have a file size of around 30 MB, while the same song with lossy compression may be 5 MB.	• FLAC (audio) • TIFF (image) • PNG (image)

 **EXAMPLE:** **Phil has just heard a new band on the radio. He wants to download fifty of their songs from the Internet and store them on his smartphone to take on holiday. State which type of compression would be most appropriate in this situation and explain why.**

<u>Lossy</u> compression would be the most appropriate. Lossy files are <u>smaller</u> so they would take up less bandwidth, meaning Phil could <u>download</u> the songs more quickly. Their smaller file size would also allow him to <u>store</u> them all on his smartphone without taking up too much storage space.

The best compression type? I'm afraid I'm at a loss...

Lossy files aren't as high quality as the originals, but the difference is normally unnoticeable to us unperceptive humans. This helps to explain why lossy file formats like JPEG (for photos) and MP3 (for music) are so popular — they save a lot of storage space and their inferior quality is hardly noticeable.

Warm-Up and Worked Exam Questions

That was a tricky bunch of pages to get your head around, so make sure it's all sunk in by trying these warm-up and exam questions. As always, make sure you look back over anything you're unsure about.

Warm-Up Questions

1) What is the difference between the character sets ASCII and Unicode®?
2) How many different colours are possible with a colour depth of 4?
3) What would be the effect on the file size of an image if:
   a) the colour depth was increased?
   b) the resolution was decreased?
4) What is the file size in bits of a 10 second audio file with a sample rate of 50 kHz and a bit depth of 4 bits?
5) What would be the effect on the file size and quality of an audio sample if:
   a) the bit depth was increased?
   b) the sample rate was decreased?
6) Name the two types of compression.

Worked Exam Questions

1 A singer uses a microphone that is connected to her computer to sample her voice. Describe the process of sound sampling.

Analogue sound is inputted and the recording device / computer software converts the analogue signal to digital. The converter reads the amplitude of the sound at specific intervals and stores these values as binary data. This creates a digital approximation of the real sound.

[3 marks]

The key thing to get across is that analogue waves are sampled to be turned into digital (or binary) data.

2 State and explain which type of compression would be most appropriate in these examples.

a) Uploading 100 holiday photographs to a social media account.

Make sure the explanation relates to the context of the question.

Type Of Compression: Lossy compression

Explanation: Lossy compression will greatly reduce the size of the files so uploading them will be quicker.

[2 marks]

b) Uploading a photograph of a model for a fashion magazine.

Type Of Compression: Lossless compression

Explanation: An image with all original detail may be preferred so they can edit it and print it at the best possible resolution.

[2 marks]

Exam Questions

3 Helena is writing a news article using a word processor.

a) Define the term 'character set'.

....

....

[1 mark]

b) Helena presses a key on her keyboard, and her monitor displays a character.
Describe how the computer recognises the character she enters.

....

....

....

[2 marks]

4 Fatima records herself reading two extracts from a novel to use in an audiobook.
The duration, sample rate and bit depth of each recording are shown below.

	Duration	Sample Rate	Bit Depth
Recording 1	102 seconds	20 000 Hz	4 bits
Recording 2	100 seconds	50 000 Hz	8 bits

a) Explain which recording you would expect to have better sound quality.

....

....

[2 marks]

b) Give **one** drawback of using recording 2 rather than recording 1 for the audiobook.

....

[1 mark]

5 An image has a colour depth of 32 bits and an image resolution of 200 × 100.

a) i) Define the term 'image resolution'.

....

[1 mark]

ii) Calculate the file size, in bits, of this image.

.... bits

[2 marks]

b) Explain the purpose of metadata in an image file.

....

....

[2 marks]

Revision Questions for Section Two

Section Two is done and dusted, so all you've got to do now is try these revision questions.
- Try these questions and <u>tick off each one</u> when you <u>get it right</u>.
- When you've done <u>all the questions</u> for a topic and are <u>completely happy</u> with it, tick off the topic.

Units (p.19) ☑
1) Why is binary used by computers?
2) How many bits are in a byte?
3) Put these units in order of size: Terabyte, Petabyte, Kilobyte, Gigabyte, Megabyte
4)* A hard drive has a storage capacity of 2000 gigabytes.
   a) How many terabytes is this?   b) How many megabytes is this?

Binary and Hexadecimal (p.20-24) ☑
5)* Convert the following denary numbers to: a) binary   b) hexadecimal
          (i) 17   (ii) 148   (iii) 240
6)* Convert the following binary numbers to: a) denary   b) hexadecimal
          (i) 0011 1000   (ii) 1001 1111   (iii) 10 1011
7)* Convert these hexadecimal numbers to: a) denary   b) binary
          (i) 4A   (ii) 75   (iii) D9
8)* What is the most significant bit in the binary number 1010?
9)* Add the binary numbers 0101 1101 and 0011 0010.
10) What is an overflow error?
11) What effect do left and right shifts have on binary numbers?
12) Give three reasons why programmers prefer hexadecimal over binary and denary.

Characters (p.27) ☑
13) What is the definition of a character set?
14) Give the four types of character that are included in a character set.
15) What are the two main character sets? Give a feature of each.
16)* What is the size of a text file (in bits) that uses 32 bits per character and contains 100 characters?

Images, Sound & Compression (p.28-30) ☑
17) Define the following terms:
   a) pixel   b) bitmap   c) colour depth   d) image resolution
18) Give two effects of choosing a greater image resolution or colour depth for an image.
19) What is metadata and what is it used for?
20) In no more than four bullet points, explain how audio sampling works.
21) Give a definition for each of the following and explain what happens when you increase each of them:
   a) sample rate   b) bit depth
22) Give four reasons why you might want to compress data.
23) What is the difference between lossy compression and lossless compression?
24) Give three reasons why you might want to use:
   a) lossy compression   b) lossless compression

Networks — LANs and WANs

When you connect a device to another one, you're creating a network — networks allow devices to share information and resources. Here we'll look at the two types of network you'll need to know for your exam.

A LAN is a Local Area Network

1) A LAN covers a <u>small geographical area</u> located on a <u>single site</u>.

2) All the hardware for a LAN is <u>owned</u> by the organisation that uses it.

3) LANs are either <u>wired</u> (e.g. with <u>Ethernet</u> cables) or <u>wireless</u> (e.g. using <u>Wi-Fi</u>®).

4) You'll often find LANs in <u>businesses</u>, <u>schools</u> and <u>universities</u>.

5) Lots of homes have a LAN to connect various devices, such as <u>PCs</u>, <u>tablets</u>, <u>smart TVs</u> and <u>printers</u>.

Why Use A LAN?

- <u>Sharing files</u> is easier — network users can access the same files, <u>work collaboratively</u> on them (at the same time) and <u>copy files</u> between machines.
- You can share the same <u>hardware</u> (like <u>printers</u>) on a LAN.
- The <u>Internet connection</u> can be shared between every device connected to the LAN.
- You can install and update <u>software</u> on all computers at once, rather than one-by-one.
- You can <u>communicate</u> with LAN users <u>cheaply</u> and <u>easily</u>, e.g. with <u>instant messaging</u>.
- <u>User accounts</u> can be stored centrally, so users can <u>log in</u> from <u>any device</u> on the network.

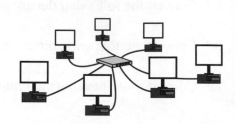

A WAN is a network that Connects LANs

1) WAN stands for <u>Wide Area Network</u>.

2) A WAN connects LANs that are in <u>different geographical locations</u>. For example, a business with offices in three different countries would need a WAN for all their devices to connect together.

3) Unlike a LAN, organisations <u>hire infrastructure</u> (e.g. communication lines) from telecommunications companies, who own and manage the WAN. This is because a WAN is much more <u>expensive</u> to set up than a LAN.

4) WANs may be connected using fibre or copper <u>telephone lines</u>, <u>satellite links</u> or <u>radio links</u>.

5) The <u>Internet</u> is actually one big WAN (see p.43).

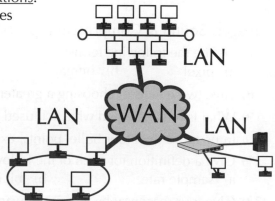

Don't LANguish at the bottom of the class — learn this page...

Make sure you're absolutely clear about the differences between LANs and WANs before moving on. Remember, companies use their own cables for LANs but for WANs they almost always hire lines.

Networks — Hardware

Connecting devices doesn't magically happen. To create a network, you need certain pieces of hardware...

NICs, Switches and Routers

1) A <u>Network Interface Controller</u> (NIC) is an internal piece of hardware that allows a device to connect to a network. These used to be on separate <u>cards</u>, but nowadays they're <u>built into</u> the motherboard. NICs exist for both <u>wired</u> and <u>wireless</u> connections.

2) Switches <u>connect devices</u> on a LAN. Switches receive data (in units called <u>frames</u>) from one device and <u>transmit</u> this data to the device on the network with the correct <u>MAC address</u> (see p.41).

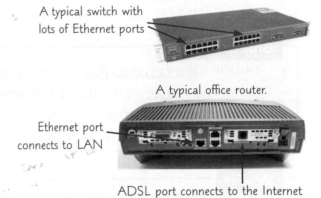

A typical switch with lots of Ethernet ports

A typical office router.

Ethernet port connects to LAN

3) <u>Routers</u> are responsible for transmitting data <u>between</u> networks — they're always connected to at least two different networks.

4) Routers have a crucial role on the Internet, directing data (in units called <u>packets</u>) to their destination.

ADSL port connects to the Internet

5) Routers are used in <u>homes and offices</u> to connect the LAN to the <u>Internet</u>.

> Most home 'routers' are in fact a router, switch and WAP (see p.36) <u>all-in-one</u>.

Wired Ethernet Connections are Fast and Reliable

1) <u>Ethernet (wired) networks</u> can use different types of <u>Ethernet cables</u> to connect devices on a LAN.

2) The most common Ethernet cables are <u>CAT 5e</u> and <u>CAT 6</u>. They are '<u>twisted pair</u>' cables, containing four pairs of <u>copper wires</u> which are twisted together to reduce internal <u>interference</u>.

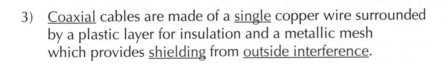

Twisted pair of copper wires

CAT 6 cable

3) <u>Coaxial</u> cables are made of a <u>single</u> copper wire surrounded by a plastic layer for insulation and a metallic mesh which provides <u>shielding</u> from <u>outside interference</u>.

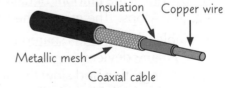

Insulation   Copper wire

Metallic mesh

Coaxial cable

4) <u>Fibre optic</u> cables transmit data as <u>light</u>. They are <u>high performance</u> (and therefore expensive) cables — they don't suffer <u>interference</u> and can transmit over <u>very large distances</u> without loss of signal quality.

Fibre optic cable

Hardware — nothing to do with concrete jackets...

Make sure you understand how switches and routers are different — it might take a while to click.

Wireless Networks

If you don't like the sound of all those cables, don't worry — you can throw them all away and use wireless networking instead. You'll still have to learn about both of them for the exam though, I'm afraid.

Wireless uses Radio Waves to transmit data

1) Like mobile phones and TVs, wireless networks use <u>radio waves</u> to transmit data.

2) Wireless networks are more <u>convenient</u> than wired networks as you can <u>move around</u> while still being <u>connected</u> — they are also <u>cheaper</u> as you need <u>fewer wires</u>.

3) Bluetooth® and Wi-Fi® are two common wireless technologies:

Bluetooth®

- Usually a <u>direct connection</u> between <u>two</u> devices so that data can be <u>shared</u>.
- Connection <u>range</u> varies, but mobile devices are typically <u>10 metres</u>.
- <u>Low bandwidth</u> (see below) compared to <u>Wi-Fi®</u>.
- Often used in <u>mobile/wearable devices</u> — smartphones/watches, headphones, etc.

Wi-Fi®

- Can be used by <u>multiple devices</u> to connect to a <u>LAN</u> at the <u>same time</u>.
- Connections have a <u>range</u> between <u>40</u> and <u>100 metres</u>.
- <u>High bandwidth</u> compared to <u>Bluetooth®</u>.
- Often used in the home — <u>routers</u>, <u>desktops</u>, <u>laptops</u>, <u>smartphones</u>, etc.

4) To set up a Wi-Fi® network, you need a <u>Wireless Access Point (WAP)</u> device. The WAP is basically a <u>switch</u> that allows devices to connect wirelessly.

5) To connect, devices need a <u>wireless NIC</u>. This is often built in, but if not you can use a <u>dongle</u>.

- <u>USB dongles</u> can be plugged into computers to allow them to connect wirelessly to the Internet.

- <u>HDMI dongles</u> can use wirelesss networks to stream high-quality video to a TV.

Many Factors can affect the Performance of Networks

1) <u>Bandwidth</u> is the <u>amount of data</u> that can be transferred in a <u>given time</u>, e.g. 500 Mbps. The greater the bandwidth, the better the network can perform.

2) Available <u>bandwidth</u> is <u>shared</u> between the devices on a network — <u>too many</u> devices or <u>heavy use</u> (e.g. streaming video) may cause congestion and slow the network. You can <u>limit</u> the bandwidth available to individual users to address this.

Mbps stands for megabits per second, a measure of bandwidth.

3) <u>Wired</u> connections are generally <u>faster</u> and <u>more reliable</u> than wireless. <u>Fibre optic cables</u> can give much better performance than <u>copper cables</u> (see p.35).

4) <u>Wireless</u> performance depends on <u>signal quality</u> so is affected by the <u>range</u> of the device, the amount of <u>interference</u> from other wireless networks and <u>physical obstructions</u> like thick walls in buildings.

5) Choice of <u>hardware</u> other than cables (see p.35) and network <u>topology</u> (see p.38) also have a big effect.

Remember, Wi-Fi® is a separate thing from the Internet...

Wi-Fi® allows a device to wirelessly connect to a network with a WAP — that network would then need to be connected to a router in order for the device to be able to access the Internet.

Client-server and Peer-to-Peer Networks

Don't think we're finished with networks yet — we've barely started. If you want to set up a network, you need to decide what form the network is going to take — and whether you're going to need a server or not.

Client-server networks are made up of a **Server** and **Clients**

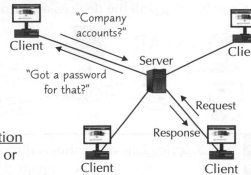

1) A client-server network is <u>managed</u> by a <u>server</u>. The devices connected to the server are <u>clients</u>.

2) Files and software are usually <u>stored centrally</u> on the server rather than on individual client devices.

3) Clients send <u>requests</u> to the server, e.g. asking for data. The server <u>processes</u> the request and <u>responds</u>. This is the <u>client-server relationship</u>.

4) The server stores <u>user profiles</u>, <u>passwords</u> and <u>access information</u> — it may <u>request a password</u> before fulfilling certain requests or <u>deny requests</u> to users without the right access level.

5) Most uses of the <u>Internet</u> work on a <u>client-server</u> relationship. E.g. <u>websites</u> are hosted on <u>web servers</u>. Web browsers are <u>client programs</u> which send requests to <u>web servers</u>. Web servers fulfil requests (e.g. by sending web pages) for thousands (or hundreds of thousands) of clients.

Pros
- Easier to <u>keep track of</u> files as they are stored centrally.
- Easier to perform <u>back-ups</u>.
- Easier to install and update <u>software</u>.
- Easier to manage <u>network security</u> (e.g. anti-malware software and user access levels).
- Servers are very <u>reliable</u> and are <u>always on</u>.

Cons
- <u>Expensive</u> to set up and needs <u>IT specialists</u> to <u>maintain</u> the network and server.
- <u>Server dependence</u> — if the server goes down <u>all clients</u> lose access to their work.
- The server may become <u>overloaded</u> if too many clients are accessing it at once.

Peer-to-Peer networks don't use servers

1) In Peer-to-Peer (P2P) networks all devices are <u>equal</u>, connecting <u>directly</u> to each other without a server.
2) You store files on <u>individual devices</u> and share them with <u>others</u>.
3) You may use a P2P network at <u>home</u> to <u>share files</u> between devices, or connect devices to a <u>printer</u>.

Pros
- <u>Easy</u> to <u>maintain</u> — you don't need any expertise or expensive hardware.
- <u>No dependence</u> on server — if one device fails the whole network isn't lost.

Cons
- <u>No centralised management</u> — devices need their updates and security installed individually. <u>Backups</u> are also more <u>complicated</u>.
- Copying files between devices creates <u>duplicate</u> files — it's easy to <u>lose track</u> of what's stored where and which files are <u>up-to-date</u>.
- Peer machines are <u>less reliable</u> and data may be <u>lost</u> if one <u>fails</u>.
- Machines are prone to <u>slow down</u> when other devices access them.

Although most Internet use is <u>client-server</u> based, there are some common P2P applications such as <u>video calling</u> (like Skype) and <u>file sharing</u> (sadly this is often used for illegal sharing of copyrighted material).

Luckily, these networks are exactly what their names suggest...

Look into whether the network at home or school is client-server or peer-to-peer. Draw a diagram showing the devices and how they're connected (you can simplify it if there are a lot of devices).

Network Topologies

A topology is essentially the layout of the network. Networks can be arranged in lots of different topologies, but star and mesh are the two important ones you'll need to know for the exam.

In a **Star Topology** all devices are connected to the centre

In a star topology, all the devices are connected to a central switch or server that controls the network.

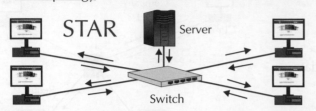

STAR

Server

Switch

The central switch allows many devices to access the server simultaneously.

Star networks may be wired or wireless.

Pros
- If a device fails or a cable is disconnected, the rest of the network is unaffected.
- It's simple to add more devices to the network.
- Better performance than other setups — data goes straight to the central device so all devices can transmit data at once (unlike ring network) and there are few data collisions (unlike bus network).

Cons
- In wired networks, every device needs a cable to connect to the central switch or server. This can be expensive, e.g. for an office building with 50 terminals.
- If there is a problem with the switch/ server, the whole network is affected.

It's worth taking a quick look at some traditional network setups for comparison with star networks:

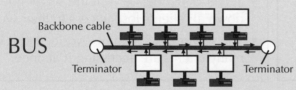

BUS

Backbone cable

Terminator   Terminator

In a bus topology, all devices are arranged in a line, connected to a single backbone cable. Devices send data in both directions. This causes data collisions, which slows the network.

RING

In a ring topology, data moves in one direction around the ring, preventing collisions. But only one device can send data at a time and data passes through many devices before reaching its destination.

In a **Mesh Topology** all devices are connected to each other

1) A mesh topology is a relatively new network layout. It is decentralised — networking devices are either directly or indirectly connected to every other one without the need for one central switch or server. Mesh networks work by sending data along the fastest route from one device to another.

2) The main advantage of a mesh topology is that there is no single point where the network can fail. If the central switch or server of a star network fails then the whole network fails — in a mesh network, if one device fails then the data is sent along a different route to get to its target.

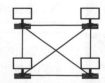

Full mesh topology

3) The traditional problem with mesh networks has been that they were very expensive — you needed a lot of wire to connect so many devices together. But now more people are using wireless technology, mesh networks are a more practical option.

4) A full mesh topology is where every device is connected to every other device. In a partial mesh topology, not all devices are fully-connected.

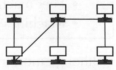

Partial mesh topology

I tried to set up a star network, but it all ended up a bit of a mesh...

Don't let all this stuff about different types of network confuse you — remember, these diagrams are about the layout of a network, while the client-server/P2P diagrams showed the roles of the devices on the network.

Warm-Up and Worked Exam Questions

Now that you know what networks are made of and what they look like, test yourself against these questions. If anything catches you out, just have another read over it until you're happy.

Warm-Up Questions

1) State one piece of hardware needed in order to set up a LAN.
2) Which type of wireless technology has higher bandwidth, Bluetooth® or Wi-Fi®?
3) Briefly explain the relationship between client and server in a client-server network.
4) Give one type of software that uses a P2P connection across the Internet.
5) Complete the table showing different network topologies by correctly filling in the white cells:

No. of devices	Star	Partial Mesh	Full Mesh
4			
5			
6			

Worked Exam Question

1 In an office there are six computers, a scanner and a router connected together in a Local Area Network (LAN).

a) Define the term Local Area Network (LAN).

A group of devices connected to share data over a small geographical area.

[1 mark]

b) State **three** advantages of connecting the computers together into a Local Area Network.

1. The business' six computers can share one Internet connection.

2. The computers can share the scanner and any other hardware.

3. It is easier to install and update software.

[3 marks]

They can also share files more easily, communicate with instant messaging and store user accounts centrally.

Exam Questions

2 Jane connects her laptop to her home LAN using a home router.
Jane's home router functions as a switch, router and Wireless Access Point (WAP) all in one.
Outline the function of each of these devices.

Switch: ....

....

Router: ....

....

WAP: ....

....

[6 marks]

3 Explain **one** advantage and **one** disadvantage of mesh topologies compared to star topologies.

Advantage: ....

....

Disadvantage: ....

....

[4 marks]

4 The staff at a graphic design company work together by sharing files between their computers, which are connected together in a Peer-to-Peer (P2P) network. An IT consultant suggests the company should adopt a Client-Server network setup.

a) Describe what is meant by Peer-to-Peer and Client-Server networks.

Peer-to-Peer: ....

....

Client-Server: ....

....

[4 marks]

b) Identify **two** benefits and **two** drawbacks of changing from a Peer-to-Peer (P2P) network to a Client-Server network.

Benefits: 1. ....

2. ....

Drawbacks: 1. ....

2. ....

[4 marks]

Network Protocols

Moving data on a network is like going on a car journey — you need a destination, something to tell you how to get there, and rules to stop you crashing into anyone else on the road. That's where protocols come in.

Networks need **Protocols** to set the rules

1) A network standard is a set of agreed requirements for hardware and software.

2) Standards are important as they allow manufacturers to create products and programs that will be compatible with products and programs from other manufacturers.

3) A network protocol is a set of rules for how devices communicate and how data is transmitted across a network.

4) Communication protocols specify how communication between two devices must start and end, how the data must be organised, and what the devices must do if data goes missing.

See p.42 for some standard protocols that are commonly used.

Communication on the same network uses **MAC Addresses**

1) Every device needs a unique identifier so it can be found on a network.

2) MAC addresses are assigned to all network-enabled devices by the manufacturer. They are unique to the device and cannot be changed.

3) MAC addresses are 48 or 64-bit binary numbers (i.e. a long string of 48 or 64 0s and 1s). To make them easier to use they're converted into hexadecimal.

```
10011000 10000001 01010101 11001101 11110010 00101111  ➔  98-81-55-CD-F2-2F
```

This binary MAC address is translated into six hexadecimal numbers.

See p.23-24 for more on binary to hex conversion.

4) MAC addresses are mainly used by the Ethernet protocol on LANs. LAN switches read the MAC addresses and use them to direct data to the right device.

Communication between different networks uses **IP Addresses**

1) IP addresses are used when sending data between TCP/IP networks, e.g. over the Internet.

2) IP addresses are assigned either manually or automatically before the device can access the network.

3) There are two versions of IP addresses — IPv4 (which uses 32 bits) and IPv6 (which uses 128 bits).

4) IPv6 was created due to the increasing number of devices that need unique IP addresses. IPv4 has 2^{32} (over 4 billion) IP addresses, whereas IPv6 has a whopping 2^{128} addresses.

5) IPv6 addresses are split into 16-bit chunks and each one is given as a hexadecimal number. IPv4 addresses are split into 8-bit chunks and each one is given as a denary number, for example:

See p.20 for a reminder on binary to denary conversion.

```
00100101.10011001.00111110.10001000  ➔  37.153.62.136
```

This 32-bit binary IP address is translated into four denary numbers.

IPv6 addresses separate groups of hex numbers with a colon : (instead of a decimal point like in IPv4)

I hope this useful tIP addresses any confusion you have...

You'll find out lots more about TCP/IP and its uses on page 42. But for now, just remember: MAC addresses are wired into devices' hardware and are used to communicate within networks. IP addresses are assigned to devices and are used for communication between networks.

Network Protocols

This is where we get to the protocols themselves, so it's no surprise that there's a lot of information here.

TCP/IP is the most important protocol

1) TCP/IP is the protocol which dictates how data is sent between networks. It's made up of <u>two protocols</u>.

2) <u>Transmission Control Protocol</u> (TCP) sets the rules for how devices <u>connect</u> on the network. It's in charge of splitting the data into <u>packets</u> and reassembling the packets back into the <u>original data</u> once they reach the receiving device. It's also responsible for checking the data is correctly <u>sent</u> and <u>delivered</u>.

3) <u>Internet Protocol</u> (IP) is responsible for <u>directing</u> packets to their destination across the network.

4) Several other protocols build upon TCP/IP to do specific Internet-based tasks:

Protocol	Stands for...	What is it used for?
HTTP	Hyper Text Transfer Protocol	Used by <u>web browsers</u> to access <u>websites</u> and communicate with <u>web servers</u>.
HTTPS	HTTP Secure	A more <u>secure</u> version of HTTP. <u>Encrypts</u> all information sent and received.
FTP	File Transfer Protocol	Used to access, edit and move <u>files</u> between devices on a network, e.g. to access files on a server from a client computer.
POP3	Post Office Protocol — version 3	Used to <u>retrieve emails</u> from a server. The server holds the email <u>until you download it</u>, at which point it is <u>deleted</u> from the server.
IMAP	Internet Message Access Protocol	Used to <u>retrieve emails</u> from a server. The server holds the email <u>until you delete it</u> — you only download a <u>copy</u>. Used by most web-based email clients.
SMTP	Simple Mail Transfer Protocol	Used to <u>send emails</u>. Also used to transfer emails between servers.

Network protocols are divided into Layers

1) A <u>layer</u> is a group of protocols which have <u>similar functions</u>.

2) Layers are <u>self-contained</u> — protocols in each layer don't need to know what's happening in other layers.

3) Each layer <u>serves</u> the layer above it — it does the hidden work needed for an action on the layer above. So in the example <u>4-layer model</u> below, when you send an email (on layer 4), this triggers actions in layer 3, which triggers actions in layer 2, <u>all the way down</u> to layer 1.

Layer	Protocols in this layer cover...	Protocol examples
4	Turning <u>data</u> into <u>websites</u> and other <u>applications</u> and vice versa.	HTTP, FTP, SMTP
3	Splitting data into <u>packets</u> and checking data is <u>sent</u> and <u>delivered</u>.	TCP
2	Making <u>connections</u> between networks and directing data.	IP
1	Passing data (as electrical signals) over the <u>physical network</u>.	Ethernet

4) Data can only be passed between <u>adjacent layers</u>. E.g. layer 2 can pass data to layers 1 and 3, but layer 1 can only pass data to layer 2.

Advantages of Using Layers

- It breaks network communication into <u>manageable pieces</u>. This helps developers concentrate on only <u>one area</u> of the network without having to worry about the others.

- As layers are <u>self-contained</u>, they can be <u>changed</u> without the other layers being affected.

- Having <u>standards</u> for each layer forces companies to make <u>compatible</u>, <u>universal</u> hardware and software, so different brands will work with <u>each other</u> and always work in basically the <u>same way</u>.

Lots of layers and plenty of protocols to ponder...

Make sure you know what the TCP/IP protocol is all about, as well as all the other protocols on this page.

Networks — The Internet

The Internet is so much a part of everyday life, it's easy to forget that it's actually just a really big network.

The **Internet** is a **Worldwide** collection of networks

1) The Internet is a <u>network of networks</u> — it's a <u>WAN</u> which connects devices and networks from all over the world. It's based around the protocol <u>TCP/IP</u>.

2) The <u>World Wide Web</u> (WWW) is a collection of <u>websites</u> that are <u>hosted</u> on <u>web servers</u> and accessed through the <u>http</u> protocol.

The world wide web is an example of a client-server network (see p.37).

3) <u>URLs</u> are <u>addresses</u> used to access web servers and resources on them.

> URL: https://www.cgpbooks.co.uk/secondary-books/gcse/computer-science
>
> HTTPS is the protocol used (see page 42). | The domain name of the website. This is linked to an IP address. | Path to the specific file or page. May also contain a query for the web server.

4) A <u>Domain Name Server</u> (DNS) translates a website's <u>domain name</u> into its IP address. The Internet has a network of Domain Name Servers, meaning you don't need to remember IP addresses to access websites — you can use domain names instead.

The **Cloud** uses the Internet to store files and applications

1) <u>Hosting</u> is when a business uses its servers to <u>store</u> files of another organisation.

2) The <u>traditional</u> use for this on the Internet is the hosting of <u>websites</u> on web servers.

3) <u>Businesses</u> also use their <u>servers</u> to offer a greater range of <u>services</u> — clients can access <u>data storage</u>, <u>software</u> and <u>processing power</u> remotely over the Internet.

4) This is known as <u>cloud computing</u>, or simply '<u>the cloud</u>'. It acts like an <u>extension</u> of a traditional <u>client-server</u> network where user files are stored centrally on a network server.

This is called a "freemium" model. Customers can try some parts of the service for free, then have the option to pay to upgrade to the full "premium" service.

5) There is often a <u>subscription fee</u> to access cloud services, but some providers offer a <u>limited service</u> for <u>free</u>.

6) <u>Cloud</u> applications can be run on the <u>remote server</u>, which means the user can access <u>large</u>, <u>powerful</u> applications with a computer that has <u>less expensive</u> hardware.

7) The cloud can also provide increased <u>computing power</u>. A user has access to <u>more</u> processing power, so they can perform more <u>memory-intensive tasks</u> than they could on a single computer.

Pros

- Users can access files and applications from <u>any connected device</u>.
- Easy to <u>increase</u> how much <u>storage</u> is available
- <u>No</u> need to buy <u>expensive hardware</u> to store data or run complex applications.
- <u>No</u> need to pay <u>IT staff</u> to manage the hardware.
- Cloud host provides <u>security</u> and <u>back ups</u> for you.
- Cloud software will be <u>updated automatically</u>.

Cons

- Need <u>connection to the Internet</u> to access files or applications.
- <u>Dependent on host</u> for security and back-ups.
- Data stored in the cloud can be <u>vulnerable</u> to hackers.
- Unclear who has <u>ownership</u> over cloud data.
- Subscription fees for using cloud <u>storage</u> and <u>software</u> may be expensive.

Learn the difference between the Internet and the WWW...

Don't make the mistake of thinking the WWW and the Internet are the same. The Internet is the network behind the WWW, but it also has many other uses, e.g. email, FTP and instant messaging.

Network Security Threats

Networks are great for lots of reasons, but they can also be very vulnerable to attacks by criminals.
Hackers can be very imaginative when it comes to attacking and stealing data stored on networks.

Network **Attacks** come in different forms

1) A passive attack is where someone monitors data travelling on a network and intercepts any sensitive information they find. They use network-monitoring hardware and software such as packet sniffers. Passive attacks are hard to detect as the hacker is quietly listening. The best defence against passive attacks is data encryption (see p.46).

> Government agencies sometimes use data interception for cyber-security purposes — this is called Lawful Interception.

2) An active attack is when someone attacks a network with malware (see below) or other planned attacks. They are more easily detected. The main defence against them is a firewall (see p.46).

3) In an insider attack someone within an organisation exploits their network access to steal information.

4) A brute force attack is a type of active attack used to gain information by cracking passwords through trial and error. Brute force attacks use automated software to produce hundreds of likely password combinations, e.g. combining real words with predictable number sequences. Hackers may try lots of passwords against one username or vice versa. Simple measures like locking accounts after a certain number of failed attempts and using strong passwords will reduce the risk of a brute force attack.

5) A denial-of-service attack (DoS) is where a hacker tries to stop users from accessing a part of a network or website. Most DoS attacks involve flooding the network with useless traffic, making the network extremely slow or completely inaccessible.

Malware is software that can harm devices

1) Malware (malicious software) is installed on someone's device without their knowledge or consent.

2) Typical actions of malware include:

> - Deleting or modifying files.
> - Scareware — e.g. it tells the user their computer is infected with loads of viruses to scare them into following malicious links or paying for problems to be fixed.
> - Locking files — ransomware encrypts all the files on a computer. The user receives a message demanding a large sum of money be paid in exchange for a decryption key.
> - Spyware — secretly monitors user actions, e.g. key presses, and sends info to the hacker.
> - Rootkits alter permissions, giving malware and hackers administrator-level access to devices.
> - Opening backdoors — holes in someone's security which can be used for future attacks.

3) Malware can access your device in different ways.

> - Viruses attach (by copying themselves) to certain files, e.g. .exe files and autorun scripts. Users spread them by copying infected files and activate them by opening infected files.
> - Worms are like viruses but they self-replicate without any user help, meaning they can spread very quickly. They exploit weaknesses in network security.
> - Trojans are malware disguised as legitimate software. Unlike viruses and worms, Trojans don't replicate themselves — users install them not realising they have a hidden purpose.

There is more than one way to attack a network...

You don't need to know every single type of malware out there, but learning all of the examples here will give you a great overview of how malware gets in to a system, and the damage it can do once it's there.

Network Security Threats

Often, security threats arise because organisations fail to secure their network properly — they might forget to encrypt their data or use bad code. Other instances are a result of hackers manipulating employees.

People are often the **Weak Point** in secure systems

1) <u>Social engineering</u> is a way of gaining sensitive information or illegal access to networks by <u>influencing people</u>, usually the employees of large companies.

2) A common form of social engineering takes place over the <u>telephone</u> — someone rings up an employee of a company and <u>pretends</u> to be a network administrator or somebody else within the organisation. The social engineer gains the employee's trust and persuades them to disclose <u>confidential information</u> — this might be personal (e.g. their login details) or sensitive company data.

3) Another type of social engineering is <u>phishing</u>. Phishing is when criminals send <u>emails</u> or texts to people claiming to be from a well-known business, e.g. a bank or online retailer. The emails often contain links to <u>spoof</u> versions of the company's <u>website</u>. They then request that the user <u>update</u> their <u>personal information</u> (e.g. password or bank account details). When the user inputs this data into the website they hand it all over to the criminals, who can then access their genuine account.

4) Phishing emails are often sent to <u>thousands</u> of people, in the hope that someone will read the email and believe its content is legitimate.

5) Many email programs, browsers and firewalls have <u>anti-phishing</u> features that will reduce the number of phishing emails received. There are often giveaways that you can spot, e.g. <u>poor grammar</u>. Emails asking users to follow links or update personal details should always be treated with caution.

SQL Injections give criminals easy access to insecure data

1) Networks which make use of <u>databases</u> are vulnerable to <u>SQL injection</u> attacks.

2) SQL stands for Structured Query Language — it's one of the main coding languages used to <u>access information</u> in <u>databases</u> — see p.98 for more about it.

3) SQL injections are pieces of SQL typed into a website's <u>input box</u> which then reveal sensitive information.

4) A website may allow you to view your account information, as long as you enter your password into an input box. If the website's SQL code does not have strong enough input <u>validation</u>, then someone may be able to enter a piece of <u>SQL code</u> which allows them to access other people's account information as well as their own.

- For example, to access an online retail account you may need to put in a PIN number. When you put in your PIN number, 12345, the website's <u>SQL code</u> may be executed like this:
- SELECT name, address, account number WHERE pin = 12345
- However, this SQL code does not have strong <u>validation</u> because it <u>doesn't specify</u> that the PIN value has to be numerical. This can be exploited by entering the code "12345 OR 1=1". This code is an <u>SQL injection</u>. Now the SQL query looks like this instead...
- SELECT name, address, account number WHERE pin = 12345 OR 1=1
- 1=1 is always <u>true</u> in SQL, so rather than just showing your details, the website instead shows the details of <u>everyone</u> on the website's database.

5) If a website's SQL code is <u>insecure</u>, this can be an easy way for hackers to get past a website's <u>firewall</u>.

No amount of security software can protect against human error...

The best way to prevent social engineering in the workplace is to make employees aware of the dangers. The bottom line is: don't give away any details unless you're sure of who you're giving them to.

Network Security Threats

Organisations want to prevent their network from having any vulnerabilities. They'll often follow a set of rules and procedures to ensure their network is protected against attacks and unauthorised access.

Organisations should...

- Regularly <u>test</u> the network to find and fix security weaknesses and <u>investigate</u> any problems.
- Use <u>passwords</u> to prevent unauthorised people from accessing the network.
- Enforce <u>user access levels</u> to limit the <u>number</u> of people with access to sensitive information.
- Install <u>anti-malware</u> and <u>firewall</u> software to prevent and destroy malicious software attacks.
- <u>Encrypt</u> sensitive data.

Penetration Testing

- <u>Penetration testing</u> (or pentesting) is when organisations employ specialists to <u>simulate</u> potential attacks on their network.
- Pentesting is used to <u>identify possible weaknesses</u> in a network's security by trying to exploit them. The results of the pentest are then <u>reported back</u>.

Physical Security

- <u>Physical security</u> protects the <u>physical parts</u> of a network from either <u>intentional</u> or <u>unintentional damage</u> (e.g. fire, flooding, theft, vandalism, etc).
- Physical security can involve <u>many different things</u>, for example:
  – <u>Locks</u> and <u>passcodes</u> to restrict <u>access</u> to certain areas, e.g. server rooms.
  – <u>Surveillance equipment</u>, e.g. <u>cameras</u> or <u>motion sensors</u> to deter intruders.

Passwords

- <u>Passwords</u> help prevent <u>unauthorised users</u> accessing the network.
- Passwords should be <u>strong</u> — they should be many characters long, use a <u>combination</u> of letters, numbers and symbols — and be <u>changed regularly</u>.

User Access Levels

- <u>User access levels</u> control which parts of the network different groups of users can access.
- E.g. business managers are likely to have a <u>higher access level</u> allowing them to access <u>more sensitive data</u>, like pay information. They may also have <u>write access</u> to files that others can only read and the ability to change employees' access levels.
- User access levels help <u>limit</u> the number of people with access to important data, so help prevent <u>insider attacks</u> on the network (see p.44).

Anti-Malware

- <u>Anti-malware software</u> is designed to find and stop <u>malware</u> from damaging a network and the devices on it. There are lots of different types of anti-malware software, including <u>antivirus</u> programs which isolate and destroy computer viruses.
- Companies use <u>firewalls</u> to <u>block unauthorised access</u>. Firewalls examine <u>all data</u> entering and leaving the network and block any potential threats.

Encryption

There's more information about encryption on page 15.

- <u>Encryption</u> is when data is translated into a code which only someone with the <u>correct key</u> can access, meaning unauthorised users cannot read it.
- Encrypted text is called <u>cipher text</u>, while non-encrypted data is called <u>plain text</u>.
- Encryption is essential for sending data over a network <u>securely</u>.

Learn these pages and your exam grade should be fairly secure...

Try to find a recent news article about a network attack. Identify the type of attack/malware used. See if you can find out how the attack was carried out and suggest some ways that it may have been prevented. Then try to get over the inevitable fear of ever using the Internet again...

Warm-Up and Worked Exam Questions

That's another section down. There are lots of little things to remember, like the different protocols and types of malware, so go over them until they're secure in your mind. Then have a go at some questions.

Warm-Up Questions

1) Complete the table showing the names and functions of various network protocols:

Protocol	Function
TCP	
	Responsible for directing data packets across a network.
HTTP	
	A more secure version of HTTP.
FTP	
SMTP	
	Used to retrieve emails from a server. The user downloads a copy of the email and the server holds the original email until the user deletes it.
	Used to retrieve emails from a server. The server holds the email until the user downloads it, at which point the server deletes it.

2) Name the type of malware that:
   a) disguises itself as legitimate software.
   b) alters permissions and access levels on the user's device.
   c) spreads by self-replicating without any user help.
   d) encrypts the data on the user's device, making them pay money to the hacker in exchange for the key to decrypt it.

Worked Exam Question

1 Hannah often receives fake emails claiming to be from well-known banks and other organisations.

   a) State the name given to the practice of sending fake or spoof emails.

   Phishing
   ....

   [1 mark]

   b) Explain the purpose of these fake emails.

   They are used to trick people into thinking they are from legitimate organisations
   ....

   so that they give away their personal information, e.g. account login details.
   ....

   [2 marks]

   c) Hannah also receives suspicious emails that contain attachments, sometimes from names in her own contacts list. Explain the dangers of opening untrusted email attachments.

   The email attachment could contain a virus. Opening the attachment would activate the
   ....

   virus and cause it to infect the device.
   ....

   [2 marks]

Exam Questions

2 The Internet offers access to a variety of services, including the World Wide Web.

a) Explain the difference between the Internet and the World Wide Web.

....

....

[2 marks]

b) State the function of a Domain Name Server (DNS).

....

[1 mark]

3 An online supermarket stores customer account information in a database.
The supermarket recently suffered a security breach where customer information was stolen.

a) A common way for databases to be breached is through SQL injection.
Explain how SQL injection works.

....

....

[2 marks]

b) The supermarket believe the data was stolen through social engineering.
Describe an example of how the thieves could have used social engineering to steal the data.

....

....

[2 marks]

4 Aysha is a network administrator at a secondary school. She has put measures in place
to prevent attacks on the school's network, including having different user access levels.

a) Explain why the school's network needs to have different user access levels.

....

....

....

[3 marks]

b) A hacker recently broke through the school's network security using a brute force attack.

i) Explain what is meant by a brute force attack.

....

....

[2 marks]

ii) Identify **two** steps the school can take to protect against a brute force attack.

1. ....

2. ....

[2 marks]

5 Sally works in an office. Her computer has a MAC address, which helps Sally to access files from the company's server.

a) Describe what is meant by a MAC address.

....

....

....

[2 marks]

b) The network managers at Sally's company work with layers of network protocols.
   i) Describe what is meant by a layer of network protocols.

....

....

....

[2 marks]

   ii) Identify **three** benefits of using layers when working with network protocols.

   1. ....

   2. ....

   3. ....

[3 marks]

6 A magazine publishing company based in rural Scotland connect their computers in a LAN using a Client-Server setup. Their writers live elsewhere in the UK and either email or post their articles to the company, where they are edited in time for the weekly deadline.

Discuss the advantages and disadvantages to the company of changing from their current system to one which uses the cloud.

[6 marks]

Make sure your answer includes both advantages and disadvantages, otherwise you won't be able to get full marks.

7 A law firm has 100 members of staff in an office building in London. The firm stores confidential data about its clients on a server.

Discuss the security methods that the law firm could use to protect the data against network threats.

Consider the threats posed to the firm's network and how they could be prevented.

[8 marks]

Revision Questions for Section Three

From passwords to packets to peer-to-peer to protocols — this section has been quite the mouthful...
- Try these questions and tick off each one when you get it right.
- When you've done all the questions for a topic and are completely happy with it, tick off the topic.

LANs, WANs and Hardware (p.34-36) ☑

1) What's the difference between a LAN and a WAN? ☑
2) Give one similarity and one difference between a switch and a router. ☑
3) Give one advantage of using wired network connections over wireless. ☑
4) What is the purpose of a Wireless Access Point (WAP)? ☑
5) Describe the features of these wireless technologies: a) Bluetooth®   b) Wi-Fi® ☑
6) Give three factors that can affect the performance of a network. ☑

Network Types and Topologies (p.37-38) ☑

7) Draw diagrams of a Client-Server network and a Peer-to-Peer (P2P) network. ☑
8) Compare the client-server relationship with the relationship of peers in a P2P network. ☑
9) Give two reasons why someone might choose to set up a peer-to-peer network. ☑
10) Give three advantages and two disadvantages of using a star network. ☑
11) Describe the key features of a mesh network. ☑

Protocols and The Internet (p.41-43) ☑

12) Why are standards helpful for manufacturers? ☑
13) What is the definition of a network protocol? ☑
14) What is the difference between a MAC address and an IP address? ☑
15) How many bits are used in an IPv6 address? ☑
16) What does each of the following stand for? Describe in a sentence what each one does:
      TCP, IP, FTP, HTTP, HTTPS, SMTP, POP3, IMAP ☑
17) Give three reasons why we divide protocols into layers. ☑
18) True or false? Data can only be passed between adjacent layers. ☑
19) Describe how a Domain Name Server (DNS) works. ☑
20) What is meant by the cloud? ☑
21) Give five advantages and five disadvantages of using the cloud. ☑

Network Security Threats (p.44-46) ☑

22) Describe, in a sentence each, five different types of network attack. ☑
23) List six actions that malicious software might carry out. ☑
24) Describe three ways that malware can access a device or network. ☑
25) What is social engineering? Give two examples of it. ☑
26) Explain how an SQL injection works. ☑
27) Give five security measures that will help protect a network against attacks. ☑
28) Give three precautions you should take with your passwords. ☑
29) What do organisations use firewalls for? ☑

Ethical and Cultural Issues

Despite what you might think, computer science doesn't just exist in a well-ventilated bubble — it affects all of our lives. Computers, new technology and the Internet all impact different people in different ways.

Use of Technology can raise all sorts of **Tricky Issues**

1) <u>Ethical</u> issues are about what would be considered <u>right</u> and <u>wrong</u> by society.

2) <u>Legal</u> issues are about what's actually <u>right</u> and <u>wrong</u> in the eyes of <u>the law</u>.

3) <u>Cultural</u> issues are about how <u>groups of people</u> with particular beliefs, practices or languages may be affected, e.g. ethnic groups, religions, countries.

4) <u>Environmental</u> issues are about how we impact the natural world.

These categories will often overlap — many environmental and cultural questions could also be considered questions of ethics.

If a company acted <u>legally</u> but ignored all questions of ethics, it could lose <u>public trust</u>. Many companies have a <u>code of conduct</u> (a set of rules that the company and its employees will follow) to show that they take these issues seriously. A company may invent <u>its own</u> code or agree to follow a <u>standard</u> one.

New technologies affect **Different Groups Of People**

1) As new <u>digital technology</u> becomes available, it can <u>directly</u> or <u>indirectly affect</u> many people.

2) E.g. the actions of a technology company can affect the <u>owners</u>, its <u>employees</u>, the <u>shop</u> that sells the company's product, <u>customers</u>, the company's hardware <u>suppliers</u> and the <u>local community</u>.

3) Each group of people that are affected have different <u>priorities</u> which may conflict with those of the others.

4) In the exam, you may be given a <u>scenario</u> and asked to discuss the ethical, legal, cultural or environmental issues it raises for <u>certain groups</u> of people.

You may see the term "stakeholder" — in computing this is anyone with an interest in, or who may be affected by a technology.

EXAMPLE:

Sally pays to download movies from a major on-demand streaming service. Her friend suggests that she should use a website where the movies are free but that probably isn't legal. Discuss the impact of using the website. You might consider the impact on Sally, the movie industry, the streaming service and the government, and any potential ethical or legal issues.

If Sally uses the website, she faces ethical and legal dilemmas. She would <u>save money</u>, but may be supporting <u>copyright theft</u> and, indirectly, other <u>criminal activities</u>. She may also be breaking the <u>law</u> herself and could face <u>prosecution</u>. By using a website of dubious nature, she will put herself at risk from computer <u>viruses</u> and other <u>malware</u>. She may argue that the website is <u>easily accessible</u>, the legality is a <u>grey area</u> and that the <u>government</u> or <u>film company</u> should shut down these websites if they don't want people to use them.

The movie <u>creators, publishers and employees</u> are affected as they may <u>lose money</u> as a result of people using these websites. This could affect their ability to employ staff and make films in the future. They could use copyright laws, e.g. the Copyright, Design and Patents Act to attempt to prosecute the website's <u>owners</u> or the website's <u>users</u>. However, if they targeted users, it could also create <u>bad press</u>.

<u>Owners</u> of the legitimate streaming service are also affected as they would <u>lose money</u>, which could affect their ability to <u>employ</u> staff or <u>stay in business</u>.

<u>Governments</u> could also be affected. The film company governments will want to <u>protect</u> their companies and will be <u>under pressure</u> to take action. However this may be very expensive and technically difficult. If the website is hosted in a <u>different country</u> with different copyright laws, tricky <u>political negotiations</u> may be required. The governments may also be concerned that money from these websites could be funding further illegal activities.

These are really common essay questions in the exam...

When you're answering questions on these issues, get in the habit of thinking about what groups are affected and what issues (legal/ethical/cultural/environmental) it raises.

Ethical and Cultural Issues

It's quite concerning to think how many people have access to your social media profile. However, some people in the world don't get to access social media at all — so maybe you're the lucky one...

It's hard to keep information **Private** on the Internet

1) Many websites (e.g. social media, banking and retail) require users to provide personal information in order to set up an account, e.g. date of birth and address.

2) Social media websites actively encourage you to post even more personal information, including photographs and details of your job and social life.

3) Cloud computing websites allow users to upload personal files to their servers.

4) Companies may make your personal information, photos, etc. available to other website users or the whole Internet. They may also sell your personal details, buying habits, likes / dislikes etc. to other organisations (who might use it to send you targeted adverts or spam emails). Companies can do lots with your information as long as they stay within the bounds of the privacy agreement.

5) Users will accept a privacy agreement before using many websites and software. The trouble is that very few people actually read these so are unaware of what they're agreeing to. Even if they do read the terms, users often have no choice but to agree if they want to use the website or software at all.

6) Users can take steps to make the information they share more private, e.g. change their privacy settings on social media sites. Websites often have fairly relaxed privacy settings by default. They also can have privacy settings that are hard to find and hard to understand.

7) Users have to trust companies to keep their data secure. But this doesn't always happen — there have been various high profile cases where customer data held by large companies has been leaked or stolen.

8) There are also issues around having so much personal information accessed via mobile devices, which might be stolen.

Censorship and Surveillance are controversial issues

Censorship

1) Internet censorship is when someone tries to control what other people can access on the Internet. Some countries' governments use censorship to restrict access to certain information.

2) One of the strictest countries for censorship is China, where they restrict access to websites which are critical of the government. China also censors many major foreign websites, including Facebook®, Twitter and YouTube™. In Cuba, citizens can only access the Internet from government-controlled access points.

3) Many governments use some form of censorship. Many countries (including the UK) restrict access to pornography, gambling and other inappropriate websites in order to protect children.

Surveillance

1) Computer surveillance is when someone monitors what other people are accessing on the Internet.

2) Many countries use some form of surveillance. Government intelligence agencies may use packet sniffers and other software to monitor internet traffic, looking out for certain key words or phrases that might alert them to illegal activities, terrorism, etc. In some countries Internet Service Providers (ISPs) keep records of all websites visited by all its customers for a certain amount of time.

Censorship and surveillance are controversial topics. Some people support them in some form, e.g. to protect children or to stop terrorism. Others are completely against them, including several non-profit organisations which campaign against what they call cyber censorship and mass surveillance.

You should have seen this page before it was censored...

The weird thing about this stuff is that everyone knows it's happening but no-one does anything about it — the Internet is such a big part of modern life that for many people their loss of privacy is a price worth paying. Other people aren't so keen about losing their privacy though, which is why these issues are so controversial.

Ethical and Cultural Issues

This page might talk about trolls, but there's nothing fantastical or whimsical about it.
In fact, this page gets into some serious issues which have damaged people's lives.

New technology can impact our **Social Well-being**

1) Companies release <u>new technology</u> regularly, and pay for <u>advertisements</u> to promote it. These techniques often try to <u>influence</u> and pressure people into buying or <u>upgrading</u> to the latest device.

2) Technology has also increased <u>peer pressure</u> — children feel pressure to own the latest device for fear of being <u>bullied</u> by their peers. Parents feel pressured into buying them.

3) <u>Smartphones</u> make it easier for people's <u>work</u> to intrude into other areas of life. Employees may be expected to carry a smartphone all the time, so that they can <u>always be contacted</u> — the smartphone may beep each time they get a work <u>e-mail</u>. This can be <u>stressful</u> for employees who feel they can never really <u>switch off</u> from work.

4) Face-to-face <u>social interaction</u> can be neglected as more of our social lives move online. This is made worse by having the Internet on mobile devices — it's now almost possible to ignore real life completely.

Cyberbullying and **Trolling** are a problem on **Social Media**

Cyberbullying

- <u>Cyberbullying</u> is when somebody uses social media to deliberately <u>harm</u> someone else.
- This includes trying to <u>intimidate</u> or <u>insult</u> someone, or trying to <u>humiliate</u> or <u>defame</u> them (damage their reputation).
- Cyberbullying can cause serious <u>distress</u> — people have been driven to suicide because of these attacks.

Trolling

- <u>Trolling</u> is when somebody tries to cause <u>public arguments</u> with others online.
- For example, the <u>troll</u> may take part in a political discussion online, but only to make comments which would <u>frustrate</u> the other members of the discussion. Trolls normally do this for their own <u>amusement</u> or to gain <u>attention</u>.

1) Problems like cyberbullying and trolling may be a result of the <u>anonymity</u> that the Internet gives people. They say things online that they wouldn't say if talking to someone face-to-face.

2) The Internet has made it easier for children to access <u>inappropriate material</u>, like pornography, drugs and gambling. <u>Parents</u> and <u>schools</u> can use <u>parental-control software</u> to try to stop children seeing it.

3) <u>Sexting</u> (sending sexually explicit messages or images to other people) is more common as smartphones and <u>video messaging</u> applications have become more popular. Sexting can be <u>dangerous</u> as the person receiving the images might not be trustworthy — social media allows them to forward someone else's images onto anyone they want. There are now <u>laws</u> which try to prevent this.

Technology has enabled a lot of anti-social behaviour...

These are all sensitive topics, but they're worth mentioning in the exam if they're relevant to the question. The problems on this page can have a damaging impact on the mental wellbeing of the victim — if you ever experience any of them, the best thing to do is to tell someone about it.

Ethical and Cultural Issues

Overuse of technology isn't just dangerous to mental health — it can also cause physical conditions.
But as it becomes more and more central to our lives, these problems can be harder to avoid...

Using technology too much can cause **Health Problems**

1) <u>Eyestrain</u> can be caused by looking at a device's screen for too long.
   This is a particular problem if the device is used in <u>bad lighting</u>,
   the screen is <u>flickering</u> or there is <u>sunlight glare</u> on the screen.

   > Eyestrain can be prevented by using suitable lighting, keeping the screen a <u>good distance</u> away from your eyes and taking <u>regular breaks</u> from using your device.

2) <u>Repetitive Strain Injury</u> (RSI) is when parts of the body (normally <u>fingers</u> and <u>wrists</u>)
   become damaged as a result of <u>repeated movements</u> over a long period time,
   such as typing on a keyboard.

   > RSI can be prevented by having a correct <u>posture</u>,
   > arranging your <u>desk</u> appropriately and taking regular breaks.

3) Sitting at a computer too long can cause <u>back problems</u>.
   Back pains are normally caused by <u>poor posture</u>.

   > You can prevent back pains by using an <u>adjustable chair</u>, a foot rest and/or an adjustable monitor, and ensuring that you aren't sitting at an awkward angle.

Technology and the Internet have shaped our **Culture**

> <u>Selfies</u> (photos we take of ourselves) have become really <u>popular</u> because smartphone cameras and social media allow us to take them and share them easily. But could they be seen as a sign that social media is gradually making people more <u>attention-seeking</u> and <u>self-obsessed</u>...

> <u>Viral</u> is a word used to describe videos, images or messages on the Internet which have <u>rapidly spread</u> over social media and have been seen by <u>millions</u> of people. Companies, politicians, celebrities and charities all try to use images and videos in their <u>promotional campaigns</u> in the hope that they will go viral.

> <u>Social media</u> and <u>blogging</u> websites allow people to publish writing, art or other media. This can give a voice to groups of people who might have been ignored by mainstream media.

REVISION TASK

There are benefits and problems with all technologies...

Pick a new technology that you know quite a lot about. Think about what opportunities and conveniences it can give to its users. Try and come up with some issues that it can cause as well — think about the effects of overusing it, or of people abusing it. Are there any groups of people that are affected, other than the company behind it and the end user? What issues do they face?

Ethical and Cultural Issues

Computers have had a tremendous impact on our culture — it's difficult to imagine some of the things we do today without them. Just remember that many people have been left behind by this technological revolution.

New technology is changing how we do **Business**

1) Music and television <u>streaming</u> services have allowed their customers to listen and watch media for less money, usually through a <u>subscription service</u>. But some people aren't happy about it — e.g. musicians who feel streaming companies don't pay them enough money to use their music.

2) The <u>sharing economy</u> is the name given to services which use new technology to let people make money from things they already own — e.g. Uber lets you turn your car into a taxi service, and Airbnb uses the Internet to let you rent out a room in your house to tourists.

3) These services are <u>cheap</u>, but they <u>draw customers away</u> from taxi firms and hotel owners. Also, they may be more <u>risky</u> for sharers and customers. E.g. the sharer may not know the <u>safety regulations</u> they should follow, and may find their <u>insurance policy</u> won't cover them if there's <u>damage or theft</u>.

Unequal access to technology has caused a **Digital Divide**

1) The <u>digital divide</u> is created by the fact that some people have <u>greater access</u> to technology than others. E.g. people can use the <u>Internet</u> to apply for jobs or university courses, access a range of services from banking to retail, and keep in touch with friends. People who have a limited access to the Internet are therefore at a heavy <u>disadvantage</u>.

CAUSES OF THE DIGITAL DIVIDE

- Some people don't have enough <u>money</u> to buy new devices like smartphones and laptops, which can be very <u>expensive</u>.

- <u>Urban</u> areas are likely to have greater <u>network coverage</u> than <u>rural</u> areas.

- Some people <u>don't know</u> how to use the Internet and other new technologies, and so are shut out of the opportunities they offer. This is a problem for many <u>older people</u> who haven't grown up with computers and so have little experience with them.

2) The <u>global divide</u> is created by the fact that the level of access to technology is different in different <u>countries</u>. People in richer countries tend to have greater access to technology than people in poorer countries. The Internet and other technologies have created lots of opportunities for the people with access to them, so this has <u>increased</u> the inequality between poorer and richer countries.

3) Projects have been set up to <u>combat</u> the digital and global divides. There are several British community projects aimed at improving Internet coverage in rural areas. One Laptop Per Child is a charity which provides laptops to children in Africa, Central Asia and South America.

These issues have got my fingers arguing — it's a digital divide...

Technology doesn't just affect those who use it — it affects everyone, including the people who can't use it. In the exam, think about how new technology might contribute to the digital divide, as well as all the other issues covered in this section. There's often loads you can say, so don't focus too much on one single issue.

Warm-Up and Worked Exam Questions

You're probably already aware of some of the issues on these pages, but it's worth going back over any that are new to you. The more you can remember, the more marks you'll be able to bank in the exam.

Warm-Up Questions

1) Tick one box in each row to show whether it concerns censorship or surveillance.

	Censorship	Surveillance
A business monitors what their employees view online.		
A country's government blocks access to Facebook®.		
A government agency intercepts emails containing certain words.		
A school restricts access to harmful websites.		
An Internet Service Provider collects data on browsing habits.		

2) Give an example of a physical health risk caused by extended use of technology, and suggest one way that it could be prevented.

3) What is meant by the 'digital divide'?

Worked Exam Question

1   Jasmine uses several social media websites. She was recently a victim of cyberbullying.

   a) Define the terms cyberbullying and trolling.

   Cyberbullying: _The use of social media to deliberately harm someone else._

   Trolling: _Causing arguments or provoking anger and frustration online._

   [2 marks]

   b) Suggest **two** reasons why cyberbullying and trolling have become a problem on social media.

   1. _Social media can give people greater anonymity than they would have in real life._

   2. _There is often no punishment if somebody behaves badly online._

   [2 marks]

   c) Social media has also had a positive impact on how we communicate.
   Describe **one** way in which social media benefits its users.

   Social media allows friends to keep in touch over a long distance,

   which helps maintain and even improve our social lives.

   It also allows potentially cheap communication, and easy sharing of media such as photos.   *[2 marks]*

Exam Questions

2 A supermarket replaces all of their staffed checkouts with electronic self-service checkouts that provide a faster service. The owners of the supermarket notice an increase in profits, but employees who work on the checkouts lose their jobs.

For each group of people below, state whether the supermarket's decision would affect them positively or negatively, giving a reason for your answer.

<u>Owners of the supermarket</u>

The effect on this group was: Positive / Negative

Reason: ....

<u>Employees</u>

The effect on this group was: Positive / Negative

Reason: ....

[2 marks]

3 Raed works for a smartphone company. He is stressed as he feels he can't switch off from work.

a) Explain how new technology could have allowed work to intrude into other areas of Raed's life.

....

....

[2 marks]

b) Raed's company releases a new smartphone every year.
Outline the social pressures that can be created by the regular release of new technology.

....

....

[2 marks]

c) Raed's neighbour, Jerry, is also stressed because he is finding it difficult to apply for jobs. All the companies he wants to apply to only accept online applications, and he has limited access to the Internet. Explain **one** reason why a person's Internet access might be limited.

....

....

[2 marks]

4 In many factories robots have replaced humans for routine tasks such as cutting and joining materials together and retrieving products stored in a warehouse.

Discuss the impact of robots replacing humans to carry out routine tasks in factories.
In your answer you might consider the impact on: factory staff, technology and ethical issues.

[8 marks]

Try to talk about both positive and negative effects that the robots might have.

Environmental Issues

Devices all have an environmental impact. Take a smartphone — it's made of materials that are mined from the Earth, it consumes energy when used, and when it's thrown away it could end up on a landfill site.

When we **Make** devices we use up **Natural Resources**

1) Electronic devices contain lots of <u>raw materials</u>.

2) <u>Plastics</u> (which are used for casing and other parts) come from <u>crude oil</u>.

3) Devices also contain many <u>precious metals</u> like gold, silver, copper, mercury, palladium, platinum and indium. Many of these metals only occur naturally in <u>tiny quantities</u>.

4) Extracting these materials uses lots of <u>energy</u>, creates <u>pollution</u> and depletes scarce <u>natural resources</u>.

When we **Use** devices we use **Energy**... lots of it

All the billions of devices in the world today are consuming energy in the form of <u>electricity</u> — a lot of it.

1) Most electricity is made using <u>non-renewable</u> resources like coal, oil and gas. <u>Extracting</u> these resources and <u>producing electricity</u> in power stations causes lots of <u>pollution</u> including greenhouse gases.

2) All computers generate <u>heat</u> and require cooling. The powerful <u>servers</u> used by businesses and the Internet are a particular problem. They're very <u>power hungry</u> and require special <u>air-conditioned</u> rooms to keep them cool. That means using even more energy and more pollution.

3) Devices also <u>waste</u> a lot of energy. Servers normally only use a <u>small proportion</u> of their <u>processing power</u>. People often leave their desktops, laptops and smartphones <u>idle</u>. This means these devices are using a lot of energy without actually doing <u>anything</u>.

4) There are several ways to <u>reduce</u> the amount of energy wasted by devices:

- <u>Virtual servers</u> are <u>software-based</u> servers rather than real machines. Multiple virtual servers can run on one physical server, so the physical server can run at <u>full capacity</u>.

- Most modern devices include <u>sleep</u> and <u>hibernation</u> modes to reduce their power consumption when they are <u>idle</u>.

- <u>Don't</u> leave electronic devices (TVs, laptops, etc.) on <u>standby</u>.

When we **Throw Away** devices we create loads of **E-waste**

1) <u>E-waste</u> is a huge problem — the world creates <u>20-50 million tonnes</u> of e-waste every year. Modern devices have a very <u>short life</u> before they're discarded — either because they <u>break</u> or because people want to <u>upgrade</u>.

2) <u>Device manufacturers</u> and <u>retailers</u> are part of this problem. They provide short <u>warranties</u> (e.g. 1 year), use <u>marketing</u> to convince people to upgrade and have pricing policies that make it <u>cheaper to replace</u> than to repair.

3) The Waste Electric and Electronic Equipment (<u>WEEE</u>) directive was created to tackle the e-waste problem. The WEEE has rules for disposing of e-waste <u>safely</u>, to promote <u>reuse</u> (e.g. refurbishing broken devices to use again) and <u>recycling</u> (e.g. extracting the devices' <u>precious metals</u>).

4) To <u>cut costs</u> a lot of e-waste is sent to certain African and Asian countries where regulations are less strict. Here, most of it ends up in <u>landfill</u> and can be a hazard — toxic chemicals can leak into the <u>ground water</u> and harm wildlife.

Don't (e-)waste your time — use your energy to learn this page...

From manufacture right through to when they're thrown away, our devices put a strain on the environment. But it's not all bad — they let us communicate without having to travel long distances in pollution-spouting vehicles, and reduce our need for paper. However, whether these make enough of a difference is debatable.

Computer Legislation

There are now lots of different laws related to computing, but fortunately you only have to learn about a few.

The **Data Protection Act** controls the use of personal data

1) The Data Protection Act 2018 gives rights to data subjects (people whose personal data is stored on computer systems). The Act has six principles, as shown here.

2) Before collecting personal data an organisation must register with the government, saying what data they'll collect and how they'll use it.

3) The Act gives data subjects the right to see, amend and delete the personal data an organisation holds about them.

4) There are exceptions to this, e.g. organisations don't have to disclose any data that could affect national security, or the outcome of a court case.

5) Another important part of the Act is accountability. It is the responsibility of the organisation to make sure that they follow the rules — if not, they could face large fines.

Data must only be used in a fair, lawful and transparent way.

Data should be kept safe and secure.

Data must only be used for the specified purpose.

Data Protection Act

The 6 Principles

Data should not be kept longer than is necessary.

Data should be adequate, relevant and not excessive for the specified use.

Data must be accurate and kept up to date.

The **Copyright, Designs and Patents Act** protects innovation

1) The Copyright, Designs and Patents Act 1988 was introduced to protect intellectual property — anything someone has created, e.g. a novel, a song, piece of software, a new invention.

2) Copyright covers written or recorded content, e.g. books, music, films, software, video games.

3) The Act makes it illegal to share copyrighted files without the copyright holder's permission, use unlicensed software or plagiarise (copy) somebody else's work. Copyright holders can make money by granting permission to use the material for a fee.

4) Patents cover new inventions — they protect ideas and concepts rather than actual content. E.g. a patent may protect a new method of charging smartphone batteries.

In computing, patents mostly apply to pieces of hardware.

5) The Internet has made it harder to protect copyrighted content due to the ease of file sharing. It's also difficult to enforce copyright if content is held on servers in countries with more relaxed copyright laws.

6) A lot of illegal file sharing takes place over peer-to-peer networks (p.37) using the BitTorrent® protocol to share files directly between devices. Cloud-based (p.43) file-hosting websites are also used — copyrighted content is uploaded to the website where anyone with an account can download it.

7) It's a grey area as to how much responsibility the website owners have for content that users upload. However many popular websites used for illegal sharing have been prosecuted and forced to shut down.

The **Computer Misuse Act** prevents illegal access to files

The Computer Misuse Act 1990 was introduced to stop hacking and cyber crime. It added three new offences:

1) Gaining unauthorised access to a private network or device, e.g. through hacking (just accessing a network could get you a fine or prison sentence).

2) Gaining unauthorised access to a network or device in order to commit a crime, like stealing data or destroying the network.

3) Unauthorised modification of computer material — e.g. deleting or changing files. The Act also makes it illegal to make, supply or obtain malware.

REVISION TIP

The law has to keep up to date with developing technology...

You don't need to memorise the exact wording of the six data protection principles given above, but the more you know about each principle, the more detail you'll be able to give in the exam.

Open Source and Proprietary Software

A software licence is an agreement that allows one or more individuals to legally use a piece of software. Licences and copyright laws (see p.59) control whether a piece of software can be modified or shared.

Open Source software is given away with its Source Code

1) Open source software is software where the source code is made freely available. Users may legally modify the source code to create their own spin-off software, which can be shared under the same licence and terms as the original software.

2) Well-known examples include Apache HTTP server™ (runs web servers), GIMP (image editing), Mozilla® Firefox® (web browser), and VLC media player.

3) Linux® is a hugely successful open source OS released in 1991. Hundreds of Linux®-based OSs have been developed and shared over the years. The most popular include UBUNTU, Debian and Android™.

4) Popular open-source software is always supported by a strong online community (forums of users sharing ideas and solving problems). Users actively help to improve software — anyone can play with the source code and suggest bug fixes and improvements to the original developers.

Source code is the actual programming code behind the software. It shows exactly how the software was made.

Advantages of Open Source Software	Disadvantages of Open Source Software
• It is (usually) free.	• Small projects may not get regular updates...
• Made for the greater good, not profit — it benefits everyone, encourages collaboration, sharing of ideas.	• ...and so could be buggy
	• ...or have unpatched security holes.
• Software can be adapted by users to fit their needs.	• There may be limited user documentation.
• Wide pool of collaborators can be more creative and innovative than the programmers of one company.	• No warranties if something goes wrong.
	• No customer support (although community forums will often make up for this).
• Popular software is very reliable and secure — any problems are quickly solved by the community.	• Companies using open-source code to make custom software may not want competitors to see their source code, but they have no choice.

Proprietary Software is Closed Source Software

1) Proprietary software is software, usually paid for, where only the compiled code is released. The source code is usually a closely-guarded secret. Proprietary software licenses restrict the modification, copying and redistribution of the software.

2) Businesses often use proprietary software instead of open source as it tends to have better customer support options. Companies producing proprietary software include Microsoft® (Office®, Windows®, Outlook®, etc.) and Adobe® (Photoshop®, Illustrator®, etc.).

Compiled code is the final file (e.g. .exe file) that runs — it doesn't tell you how the program was made.

Advantages of Proprietary Software	Disadvantages of Proprietary Software
• Comes with warranties, documentation, and customer support.	• Can be expensive.
• Should be well-tested and reliable as the company's reputation depends on this. Fixes and updates will come regularly (open source will vary more).	• Software may not exactly fit a user's needs, and they can't do anything about it.
• Usually cheaper for companies than developing their own custom-built software.	• Software companies may not maintain older software after warranties expire — they'll want people to buy their latest product.

Learn the definitions of open source and proprietary software...

... as well as the pros and cons of each. Just talking about cost is unlikely to get you full marks in the exam.

Warm-Up and Worked Exam Questions

Make sure you know those laws inside out — it'd be easy to mix them up and drop some marks. Once you're confident with the last few pages, try out these questions — then go back over anything that slips you up.

Warm-Up Questions

1) Which of the following are materials used to create electronic devices?

   copper   jupiter   platinum   plastic   cedar wood   potato   mercury   mithril   gold   silver

2) State which law the following issues relate to:

   a) A hospital holds the medical records of its patients so they can be treated.

   b) A criminal hacks into a broadband company's network and steals its customers' account details.

   c) A company is found to be using unlicensed software on all of their work computers.

   d) A polling company holds data on members of the public for a survey it is conducting.

   e) An employee accesses their manager's network account and deletes company data.

3) Which of the following are examples of open source software?

Android™	Linux®	Adobe® Photoshop®	Microsoft® Word
Microsoft® PowerPoint®		VLC media player	Mozilla® Firefox®

Worked Exam Questions

1   The average household can spend almost £100 a year on wasted electricity.

   a)   Identify **two** ways that electronic devices waste electricity.

   1.   <u>Users sometimes leave devices idle / on standby.</u>

   2.   <u>Devices generate excess heat due to inefficiency.</u>

   [2 marks]

   b)   Explain how hardware manufacturers can limit the amount of electricity wasted by devices.

   <u>Manufacturers can include sleep or hibernation modes in new devices</u>

   <u>to reduce their energy consumption when they are idle.</u>

   [2 marks]

2   The Data Protection Act 2018 gives rights to data subjects.

   a)   Define the term data subject.

   <u>Someone whose personal data is stored on somebody else's computer system.</u>

   [1 mark]

   b)   State **two** principles of the Data Protection Act.

   Any of the six principles would be fine here.

   1.   <u>Data must only be used in a fair and lawful way.</u>

   2.   <u>Data should be kept safe and secure.</u>

   [2 marks]

Exam Questions

3 Hayley is creating a website with information on her local town and its sports teams.

   a) Define the term copyright.

....

[1 mark]

   b) Hayley wishes to use a photograph that she has found on another website. The image has been copyrighted. Outline what Hayley needs to do if she wishes to use the photograph legally.

....

....

....

....

[3 marks]

4 The average smartphone is only used for two years before it is discarded.
Outline the problems that the short life span of electronic devices has on the environment.

....

....

....

....

[4 marks]

5 A marketing company has the same, paid-for, proprietary software on all of its computers.
The software provides facilities for word processing, presentations, spreadsheets and databases.

   a) Describe what is meant by proprietary software.

....

....

[2 marks]

   b) Give **two** advantages to the company of using proprietary software.

     1. ....

     2. ....

[2 marks]

6 A cinema collects information from customers who book seats to watch movies.
The cinema would like to store this information for the following reasons:
* to make it easier for customers when they book seats in the future.
* to enable the cinema to contact customers with details of future films.

Explain the measures that the cinema should take to ensure that customer data is stored legally.

Think about what legislation they might be at risk of breaking, and what they can do to avoid this.

[6 marks]

Revision Questions for Section Four

Well, that section had a lot of issues — thankfully you're not here to solve its problems, just learn its content.

- Try these questions and <u>tick off each one</u> when you <u>get it right</u>.
- When you've done <u>all the questions</u> for a topic and are <u>completely happy</u> with it, tick off the topic.

Ethical and Cultural Issues (p.51-55) ☑

1) Define each type of issue in a sentence: ethical, legal, cultural, environmental ☑
2) List five groups of people that could be affected by the actions of a technology company. ☑
3) Give two reasons why someone might give their personal details to a website. ☑
4) Give two problems with many online companies' privacy agreements. ☑
5) What can you do to make the information you share online more private? ☑
6) Explain the difference between censorship and surveillance. ☑
7) Give one argument for and one against Internet censorship. ☑
8) Give one argument for and one against governments carrying out Internet surveillance. ☑
9) Give four examples of how new technology may affect social well-being. ☑
10) What is cyberbullying? ☑
11) What is an Internet troll? ☑
12) Give two reasons why cyberbullying and trolling have become so common. ☑
13) What is sexting and why is it dangerous? ☑
14) Give three examples of health problems which can be caused by using a computer. ☑
15) Give three examples of how technology and the Internet have shaped our culture. ☑
16) Give three reasons for why a digital divide exists. ☑

Environmental Issues (p.58) ☑

17) Give three examples of natural resources which are used to make computers. ☑
18) Explain how a device's need for energy impacts the environment. ☑
19) Give three ways to reduce the amount of energy devices waste. ☑
20) What is e-waste and why do we generate a lot of it? ☑
21) Describe an environmental danger caused by e-waste left in landfill sites. ☑

Computer Legislation and Software Licences (p.59-60) ☑

22) What are the six principles of the Data Protection Act 2018? ☑
23) What is intellectual property? ☑
24) Why do we use copyright? ☑
25) Give three things that the Copyright, Designs and Patents Act 1988 makes illegal. ☑
26) What were the three new offences introduced by the Computer Misuse Act 1990? ☑
27) What is a software licence? ☑
28) Which type of software licence does not allow access to the software's source code? ☑
29) Give three advantages and three disadvantages of open-source and proprietary software. ☑

Computational Thinking

Computational thinking is all about the steps you take to find the best solution to a complex problem.

Three Key Techniques for Computational Thinking

DECOMPOSITION — breaking a complex problem down into smaller problems and solving each one individually.

Computational Thinking

ABSTRACTION — picking out the important bits of information from the problem, ignoring the specific details that don't matter.

ALGORITHMIC THINKING — a logical way of getting from the problem to the solution. If the steps you take to solve a problem follow an algorithm then they can be reused and adapted to solve similar problems in the future.

These techniques are all used in Real-Life...

Computational thinking is something you'll do all the time without even noticing.

For example, when deciding which film to watch at the cinema with your family:

Decomposition	Abstraction	
Things to look at	Details to ignore	Details to focus on
What type of films are on?	Plot details, actors and director.	Film genre and age rating.
What times are the films on?	Days other than the date you're going.	Start and end times on the date you're going.
What are the reviews like?	In depth analysis of the characters and plot.	Ratings

Algorithmic thinking may involve coming up with some logical steps to reach a decision. E.g. listing all of the films that are showing, then deleting all the age restricted films and ones with poor ratings. Getting each family member to vote for their favourite, then picking the film with the most votes.

If the family went to see a film the following week they could use the same processes of decomposition, abstraction and algorithmic thinking, but they would have to do the research and make the decisions again.

... and the Same Skills can be used in Computer Science

Computer scientists rely on decomposition, abstraction and algorithmic thinking to help them turn a complex problem into small problems that a computer can help them to solve.

Imagine the task is to sort a list of product names into alphabetical order:
See p.70-72 for more on sorting algorithms.

- One part of the decomposition might decide what alphabetical order means — letters are straightforward but what if some entries in the list contain numbers and punctuation?

- Another part of the decomposition might look at comparing the entries — this could be decomposed further into how you could compare two entries, three entries, etc.

- Abstraction will help the programmer focus on the important bits — it doesn't matter what the entries are and what they mean. The important information is the order of the characters in each entry.

- Algorithmic thinking will put the tasks into a step by step process. For example, you might compare the first two entries and order them, then compare the third entry to each of the first two and put it in the correct place, then compare the fourth entry to each of the first three, etc.

Break your big problems down into small manageable tasks...

Think about a recent decision you've made, or a problem you've solved. How did you decompose the problem? What information did you ignore/focus on? How did you reach the final solution?

Writing Algorithms — Pseudocode

Algorithms are just sets of instructions for solving a problem. In real-life they can take the forms of recipes, assembly instructions, directions, etc. but in computer science they are often written in pseudocode.

Algorithms can be written using **Pseudocode**

1) Pseudocode is not an actual programming language but it should follow a <u>similar structure</u> and <u>read like one</u> (roughly). The idea is that pseudocode clearly shows an algorithm's steps without worrying about the <u>finer details</u> (syntax) of any particular programming language.

2) It is <u>quick to write</u> and can be <u>easily converted</u> into any programming language.

3) There are different ways to write pseudocode — they are all <u>equally correct</u> as long as the person reading the code can <u>follow it</u> and <u>understand</u> what you mean.

Pseudocode should be more 'wordy' than a formal programming language, but easier to understand.

EXAMPLE: **Write an algorithm using pseudocode to calculate the salary of a worker after a 10% pay increase.**

A <u>simple solution</u> to the problem would be:

```
Take worker's current salary
Multiply the salary by 1.1
Display the answer
```

This solution is perfectly adequate as the problem has been <u>split down</u> into steps and it is <u>obvious</u> to the reader what to do at <u>each stage</u>.

A more <u>useful solution</u> is shown here:

```
input salary
newSalary = salary × 1.1
output newSalary
```

This solution is better as the <u>words</u> and <u>structure</u> resemble a real <u>programming language</u>. It can be more <u>easily adapted</u> into real code.

Make sure your pseudocode isn't **Too Vague**

Even though pseudocode isn't a formal <u>programming language</u> you still need to make sure it's <u>readable</u>, <u>easy to interpret</u> and not too <u>vague</u>.

EXAMPLE: **When registering on a website, a user's password should be more than 6 characters long and it must be different from their username. Write an algorithm to check if the password is valid. If it's invalid it should say why.**

```
IF the length of the password is less than or equal
to 6 characters long OR password is the same as the
username THEN it is invalid ELSE the password is valid
```

This code is <u>too vague</u> and <u>unstructured</u>. It won't give reasons why the password is invalid and doesn't give any input variables (see p.79).

The pseudocode asks the user to <u>input</u> a username and password.

The code gives <u>different outputs</u> depending on why the password is <u>invalid</u>.

The <u>indentation</u> of the pseudocode makes it more <u>readable</u>.

```
input username
input password
if length of password <= 6 then
    output "Password is too short.
else
    if password matches username then
        output "Password is the same as username."
    else
        output "Password is valid."
    endif
endif
```

The first IF statement checks to see if the password is <u>too short</u> and the second checks if it's the <u>same as the username</u>.

See p.83 for more on IF statements.

Pseudocode isn't always everything it appears to be...

EXAM TIP

Pseudocode is a great way to write an algorithm in the exam if you're not told how to give your answer. Some questions in Paper 2 (Section B) will specify to use a formal programming language — either the OCR Exam Reference Language (see section 6) or a high-level language you've studied.

Writing Algorithms — Flowcharts

Algorithms can also be shown using a flowchart, and just like for pseudocode, there are different ways to write the same algorithm. You do get to draw some different shapes though, so things are looking up.

Flowcharts use **Different Boxes** for different **Commands**

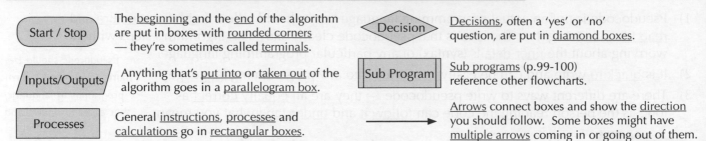

Start / Stop — The <u>beginning</u> and the <u>end</u> of the algorithm are put in boxes with <u>rounded corners</u> — they're sometimes called <u>terminals</u>.

Inputs/Outputs — Anything that's <u>put into</u> or <u>taken out</u> of the algorithm goes in a <u>parallelogram box</u>.

Processes — General <u>instructions</u>, <u>processes</u> and <u>calculations</u> go in <u>rectangular boxes</u>.

Decision — <u>Decisions</u>, often a 'yes' or 'no' question, are put in <u>diamond boxes</u>.

Sub Program — <u>Sub programs</u> (p.99-100) reference other flowcharts.

<u>Arrows</u> connect boxes and show the <u>direction</u> you should follow. Some boxes might have <u>multiple arrows</u> coming in or going out of them.

Algorithms can be written as **Flowcharts**

Flowcharts can show <u>sequences</u>, <u>selections</u>, <u>iterations</u> or a combination of them.

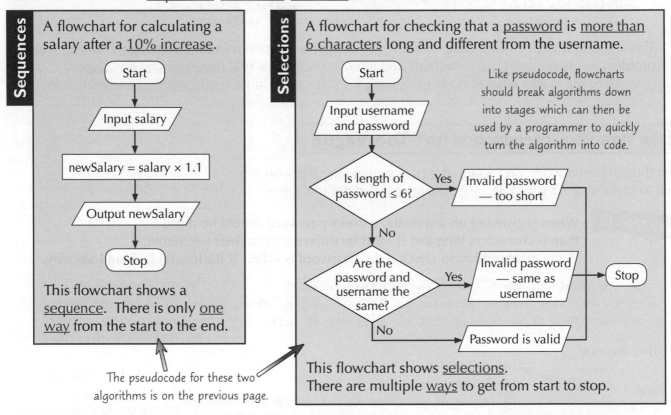

Sequences

A flowchart for calculating a salary after a <u>10% increase</u>.

This flowchart shows a <u>sequence</u>. There is only <u>one way</u> from the start to the end.

The pseudocode for these two algorithms is on the previous page.

Selections

A flowchart for checking that a <u>password</u> is <u>more than 6 characters</u> long and different from the username.

Like pseudocode, flowcharts should break algorithms down into stages which can then be used by a programmer to quickly turn the algorithm into code.

This flowchart shows <u>selections</u>. There are multiple <u>ways</u> to get from start to stop.

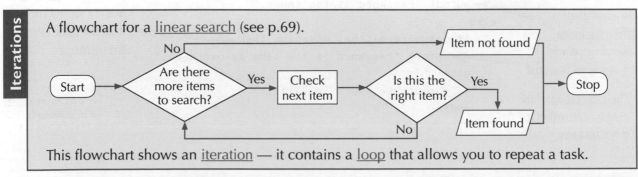

Iterations

A flowchart for a <u>linear search</u> (see p.69).

This flowchart shows an <u>iteration</u> — it contains a <u>loop</u> that allows you to repeat a task.

EXAM TIP

Flowcharts should show the general flow of the algorithm...

You don't need to pack flowcharts with all the details. If you get a flowchart question in your exam, make sure you use the correct boxes and that all paths in your diagram lead to the end.

Warm-Up and Worked Exam Questions

Now it's time to practise your computational thinking, pseudocode and flowchart skills.
Work through these warm-up questions then have a go at the exam questions.

Warm-Up Questions

1) Give the names of the three key techniques used for computational thinking.

2) What is meant by an 'algorithm'?

3) Which of these statements are true?

> A: Pseudocode is a formal programming language.
>
> B: There are lots of different ways to write pseudocode.
>
> C: The more vague that pseudocode is the better.
>
> D: Indentation helps to make pseudocode easier to follow.

4) Draw lines matching the commands below to the correct flowchart symbol.

Start   Output   Decision   Sub Program   Process

Worked Exam Question

1   The flowchart below shows how to convert miles to kilometres.

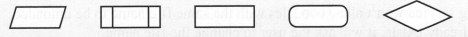

INPUT miles → kilometres = miles × 8/5 → OUTPUT kilometres

a) Identify **one** problem with this flowchart.

Think about what is missing from the flowchart.

    There are no boxes for starting and stopping.
[1 mark]

b) State the distance in kilometres of 10 miles.

    kilometres = 10 × 8 ÷ 5 = 16

               16   km
[1 mark]

c) Refine the flowchart to do the following:
   - Use a more accurate conversion factor of 1.6093 instead of 8/5.
   - Ask the user if they wish to convert another distance.
     If they do, perform the new calculation, otherwise, the flowchart ends.

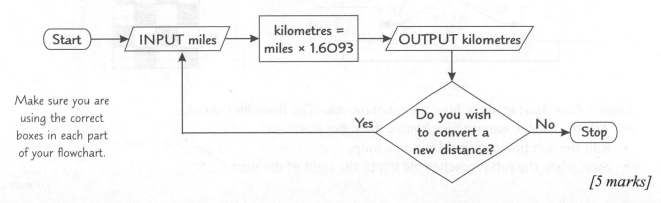

Make sure you are using the correct boxes in each part of your flowchart.

[5 marks]

Exam Questions

2 Bernard has written the algorithm on the right using pseudocode.

```
input height
input width
area = height × width
output area
```

a) Describe what Bernard's algorithm does.

Describe what is happening on each line.

....

....

....

[3 marks]

b) State the value of `area` if `height = 5` and `width = 10`.

....

[1 mark]

3 A file uploading service won't allow two files with the same file name to be uploaded. If a file name already exists, it will ask the user to change the file name.

a) Describe with examples how abstraction can help decide how to compare the files.

....

....

....

[3 marks]

b) Describe with examples how decomposition could be used to help program this task.

....

....

....

[3 marks]

4 A robot moves on the 4 × 4 square grid shown below. A sub program, SqMove, is part of a flowchart that tells the robot how to move.

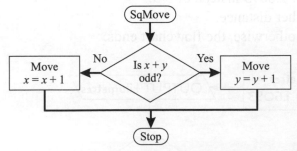

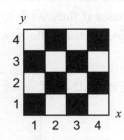

Draw a flowchart to show how the robot moves. The flowchart should:
- Ask the user to enter which square the robot starts on.
- Run the sub program SqMove on a loop.
- Stop when the robot reaches the top or the right of the grid.

This is when x = 4 or y = 4

[6 marks]

Search Algorithms

Computers need to follow search algorithms to find items in a list — the ones you'll need to know about are binary search and linear search. Now, if only someone could make a search algorithm to find my keys.

A **Binary Search** looks for items in an **Ordered List**

BINARY SEARCH ALGORITHM

1) Find the <u>middle item</u> in the ordered list. ← *To find the <u>middle item</u> in a list of n items do (n + 1) ÷ 2 and round up if necessary.*

2) If this is the item you're looking for, then <u>stop</u> the search — you've found it.

3) If not, <u>compare</u> the item you're <u>looking for</u> to the <u>middle item</u>. If it comes <u>before</u> the middle item, get rid of the <u>second half</u> of the list. If it comes <u>after</u> the middle item, get rid of the <u>first half</u> of the list.

4) You'll be left with a list that is <u>half the size</u> of the original list. Repeat steps 1) – 3) on this <u>smaller list</u> to get an even smaller one. Keep going until you find the item you're looking for.

EXAMPLE: Use the binary search algorithm to find the number 99 in the following list.

| 7 | 21 | 52 | 59 | 68 | 92 | 94 | 99 | 133 |

There are 9 items in the list so the middle item is the (9 + 1) ÷ 2 = 5th item. The 5th item is 68 and 68 < <u>99</u> so get rid of the **first half** of the list to leave:

| 92 | 94 | 99 | 133 |

There are 4 items left so the middle item is the (4 + 1) ÷ 2 = 2.5 = 3rd item. The 3rd item is 99. You've found the item you're looking for so the search is complete.

A **Linear Search** can be used on an **Unordered List**

A linear search checks <u>each item</u> of the list in turn to see if it's the correct one. It stops when it either <u>finds the item</u> it's looking for, or has <u>checked every item</u>.

LINEAR SEARCH ALGORITHM

1) Look at the <u>first item</u> in the unordered list.

2) If this is the item you're looking for, then <u>stop</u> the search — you've found it.

3) If not, then look at the <u>next item</u> in the list.

4) Repeat steps 2) – 3) until you find the item that you're looking for or you've checked <u>every item</u>.

EXAMPLE:

Use a linear search to find the number 99 from the list above.

Check the first item: 7 ≠ 99
Look at the next item: 21 ≠ 99
Look at the next item: 52 ≠ 99
Look at the next item: 59 ≠ 99
Look at the next item: 68 ≠ 99
Look at the next item: 92 ≠ 99
Look at the next item: 94 ≠ 99
Look at the next item: 99 = 99

You've found the item you're looking for so the search is complete.

1) A linear search is much <u>simpler</u> than a binary search but not as <u>efficient</u>. A linear search can be used on <u>any type</u> of list, it doesn't have to be ordered. Due to it being <u>inefficient</u>, a linear search is often only used on <u>small lists</u>.

2) Once the list has been <u>ordered</u>, a <u>binary</u> search is much <u>more efficient</u> than a <u>linear</u> search. In general a binary search takes fewer steps to find the item you're looking for, which makes it more suitable for <u>large lists</u> of items.

Write out every step of a search algorithm, don't skip ahead...

The binary and linear search algorithms might seem like a faff for you to follow when you can just look at a list and pick out the item you want. Sadly computers are more systematic and they need to follow every step of an algorithm — in your exam you'll need to show every step too.

Sorting Algorithms

I'm sure you all know how to sort things into numerical or alphabetical order but try telling a computer that. You'll need to be able to follow and carry out the three sorting algorithms on the next three pages.

A **Bubble Sort** compares **Pairs** of items

The <u>bubble sort algorithm</u> is used to sort an unordered list of items.
The algorithm is <u>very simple</u> to follow but can often take a while to actually sort a list.

BUBBLE SORT ALGORITHM

1) Look at the <u>first two items</u> in the list.
2) If they're in the <u>right order</u>, you don't have to do anything.
   If they're in the <u>wrong order</u>, <u>swap them</u>.
3) Move on to the <u>next pair</u> of items (the 2nd and 3rd entries) and repeat step 2).
4) Repeat step 3) until you get to the <u>end</u> of the list — this is called one <u>pass</u>.
   The <u>last item</u> will now be in the correct place, so <u>don't include</u> it in the next pass.
5) Repeat steps 1) – 4) until there are <u>no swaps</u> in a pass.

Each pass will have one less comparison than the one before it.

EXAMPLE: **Use the bubble sort algorithm to write these numbers in ascending order.**

| 66 | 21 | 38 | 15 | 89 | 49 |

First pass:

66 21 38 15 89 49	Compare 66 and 21 — swap them.
21 66 38 15 89 49	Compare 66 and 38 — swap them.
21 38 66 15 89 49	Compare 66 and 15 — swap them.
21 38 15 66 89 49	Compare 66 and 89 — no swap.
21 38 15 66 89 49	Compare 89 and 49 — swap them.
21 38 15 66 49 89	End of first pass.

After the <u>2nd pass</u> the order of the numbers will be: 21 15 38 49 66 89
After the <u>3rd pass</u> the order of the numbers will be: 15 21 38 49 66 89
There are <u>no swaps</u> in the 4th pass so the list has been sorted: 15 35 51 62 79 105

The bubble sort is considered to be one of the simplest sorting algorithms as it only ever focuses on <u>two items</u> rather than the whole list of items.

Pros
- It's a <u>simple algorithm</u> that can be easily implemented on a computer.
- It's an <u>efficient way</u> to <u>check</u> if a list is <u>already in order</u>. For a list of *n items* you only have to do one pass of *n* – 1 comparisons to check if the list is ordered or not.
- Doesn't use very much <u>memory</u> as all the sorting is done using the <u>original list</u>.

Cons
- It's an <u>inefficient</u> way to <u>sort a list</u> — for a list of *n items*, the <u>worst case scenario</u> would involve you doing $\frac{n(n-1)}{2}$ comparisons.
- Due to being <u>inefficient</u>, the bubble sort algorithm does not cope well with a <u>very large list</u> of items.

In the bubble sort, items bubble up to the end of the list...
A common mistake is to forget the final pass because you realise that the list is already in order. Always show a pass, even if <u>nothing changes</u>, to complete the algorithm as a computer would.

Sorting Algorithms

The next sorting algorithm you'll need to learn is the merge sort — it splits a list apart and then magically merges it back together in the correct order. I really hope you're ready to see something special.

A **Merge Sort Splits** the list apart then **Merges** it back together

The merge sort algorithm is an example of a <u>divide-and-conquer</u> algorithm and takes advantage of two facts:

- Small lists are <u>easier to sort</u> than large lists.
- It's easier to merge <u>two ordered lists</u> than two unordered lists.

> **MERGE SORT ALGORITHM**
>
> 1) <u>Split</u> the list in <u>half</u> (the smaller lists are called <u>sub-lists</u>) — the second sub-list should start at the <u>middle item</u> (see p.69).
> 2) Keep repeating step 1) on each sub-list until <u>all the lists</u> only contain <u>one item</u>.
> 3) <u>Merge pairs</u> of sub-lists so that each sub-list has twice as many items. Each time you merge sub-lists, <u>sort the items</u> into the right order.
> 4) Repeat step 3) until you've merged <u>all the sub-lists</u> together.

EXAMPLE: **Use the merge sort algorithm to write these letters in alphabetical order.**

1) <u>Split</u> the original list of 8 items into <u>two lists</u>, the second list should start at the (8 + 1) ÷ 2 = 4.5 = <u>5th item</u>.

2) Carry on <u>splitting</u> the sub-lists until each list only has <u>one item</u> in it.

3) <u>Merge</u> and <u>order</u> sub-lists back together. E.g.

> Compare <u>F</u> and <u>A</u> — <u>move A</u> to the new list.
> Compare <u>F</u> and <u>L</u> — <u>move F</u> to the new list.
> Compare <u>P</u> and <u>L</u> — <u>move L</u> to the new list.
> <u>P</u> is the <u>last item</u> in the new list.

Note that merging is always performed on <u>two ordered lists</u> and is <u>very simple</u> to do.

4) Keep <u>merging</u> sub-lists until you only have <u>one list</u>.

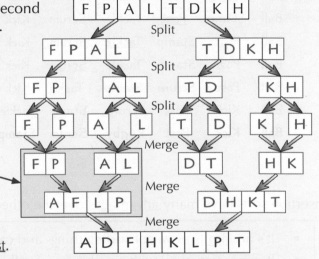

You'll often be unable to <u>split</u> or <u>merge</u> lists <u>evenly</u>. For example, sometimes you'll have to merge a list containing <u>two items</u> with a list containing <u>one item</u> to make a list of <u>three items</u>.

Pros	Cons
• In general it's much <u>more efficient</u> and <u>quicker</u> than the bubble sort (p.70) and insertion sort algorithms (p.72) for <u>large lists</u>. • It has a very <u>consistent running time</u> regardless of how ordered the items in the original list are.	• It's slower than other algorithms for <u>small lists</u>. • Even if the list is <u>already sorted</u> it still goes through the whole <u>splitting</u> and <u>merging</u> process. • It uses <u>more memory</u> than the other sorting algorithms in order to create the separate lists.

Due to its efficiency the merge sort algorithm or variations of it are used in many programming languages such as Java™, *Python*® and Perl® as the primary sorting algorithm.

To do the merge sort, split things down before sorting them...

When doing a merge sort it's important that you show the splitting process <u>and</u> the merging process — if you only show the merging process then you've only shown half the algorithm.

Sorting Algorithms

Here it comes, the final sorting algorithm you'll need to know for your exams.
It's called the insertion sort — have a look below to see how it's done.

An **Insertion Sort** orders the items as it goes

The insertion sort algorithm is the <u>simplest sorting algorithm</u> to understand — it just takes each item in turn and puts it in the right place using the first item in the list as a starting point.

INSERTION SORT ALGORITHM

1) Look at the <u>second item</u> in a list.

2) Compare it to <u>all items</u> before it (in this case just the first item) and <u>insert</u> the number into the <u>right place</u>.

3) Repeat step 2) for the third, fourth, fifth, etc. items until the <u>last number</u> in the list has been <u>inserted</u> into the <u>correct place</u>.

EXAMPLE: **Use the insertion sort algorithm to write these words in alphabetical order.**

Ball	Stamp	Post	Tackle	Scrum	Kick	Rugby

Make sure you write out the list at every step — even if there is no insertion.

Ball	<u>Stamp</u>	Post	Tackle	Scrum	Kick	Rugby	No insertion.
Ball	Stamp	<u>Post</u>	Tackle	Scrum	Kick	Rugby	Insert <u>post</u> between ball and stamp.
Ball	Post	Stamp	<u>Tackle</u>	Scrum	Kick	Rugby	No insertion.
Ball	Post	Stamp	Tackle	<u>Scrum</u>	Kick	Rugby	Insert <u>scrum</u> between post and stamp.
Ball	Post	Scrum	Stamp	Tackle	<u>Kick</u>	Rugby	Insert <u>kick</u> between ball and post.
Ball	Kick	Post	Scrum	Stamp	Tackle	<u>Rugby</u>	Insert <u>rugby</u> between post and scrum.
Ball	Kick	Post	Rugby	Scrum	Stamp	Tackle	All items are sorted into the correct order so the sorting is complete.

Insertion sorts have many <u>advantages</u> over the other sorting algorithms:

- It's an <u>intuitive</u> way of sorting things and can be <u>easily coded</u>.
- It copes very well with <u>small lists</u> — for this reason, an <u>insertion</u>/<u>merge</u> hybrid sort is often used to take advantage of the <u>strengths</u> of each algorithm.
- All the sorting is done on the <u>original list</u> so, like the bubble sort, it doesn't require very much <u>additional memory</u>.
- It's very <u>quick</u> to add items to an already <u>ordered list</u>.
- It's also very quick at <u>checking</u> that a list is <u>already sorted</u>.

However, like the bubble sort, its main <u>disadvantage</u> is that it doesn't cope well with <u>very large lists</u>. For a list containing *n* items:

- Best case scenario (when the list is already ordered) requires $n - 1$ comparisons.

- Worst case scenario requires $\frac{n(n-1)}{2}$ comparisons.

Take the items one by one and put them into the right position...

You now know about two search algorithms (binary and linear) and three sorting algorithms (bubble, merge and insertion). These algorithms might be given to you as flowcharts or code — the code for the algorithms may use IF statements (see p.83) and loops (see p.84-85) to compare all of the items in the list.

Warm-Up and Worked Exam Questions

There are lots of searching and sorting algorithms for you to learn, so here are some questions to test your knowledge. Start off with the warm-up questions then have a go at the exam questions.

Warm-Up Questions

1) Here is a list of the ages of Julie's sons and daughters:

| 3 | 6 | 8 | 11 | 13 | 15 | 18 |

   a) Use a binary search to find "8" in the list.
   b) Use a linear search to find "11" in the list.

2) Describe how a bubble sort works.

3) Here are the names of the four pupils who attend chess club.

| Chris | Beth | Dalia | Ahmed |

   a) Show the steps of a bubble sort to put the names in ascending alphabetical order.
   b) Show the steps of a merge sort to put the names in descending alphabetical order.
   c) Show the steps of an insertion sort to put the names in ascending alphabetical order.

4) Which sorting algorithm is best to use on large lists of items?

Worked Exam Questions

1 Nicola has a list of numbers: 2, 3, 7, 5, 13, 11.

   a) She says, "I can't use a binary search to find 13." Why is this the case?

   A binary search only works on ordered data.

   [1 mark]

   b) Show the steps of a linear search to find 13 in the list above.

   Check the first item: 2 ≠ 13.
   Check the second item: 3 ≠ 13.
   Check the third item: 7 ≠ 13.
   Check the fourth item: 5 ≠ 13.
   Check the fifth item: 13 = 13.
   Stop searching as the item has be found.

   The linear search is straightforward but make sure you show every single step of the algorithm to get full marks.

   [2 marks]

2 Use the insertion sort algorithm to put these European cities into alphabetical order.

Underlining the item that you're looking at will help you keep track of where you're up to.

Riga	Paris	Oslo	Baku	Minsk
Paris	Riga	Oslo	Baku	Minsk
Oslo	Paris	Riga	Baku	Minsk
Baku	Oslo	Paris	Riga	Minsk
Baku	Minsk	Oslo	Paris	Riga

[4 marks]

Exam Questions

3 Sonia has a sorted list of ice cream flavours that she sells in her shop.

a) Show the stages of a binary search to find the word 'butterscotch' in the list below.

butterscotch	chocolate	mint	strawberry	vanilla

Always check that lists are ordered before doing a binary search.

[4 marks]

b) Give **one** advantage of using a binary search over a linear search.

....

....

[1 mark]

4 Kim has a hand of playing cards, all of the same suit: 3, 7, 6, 2, 5.
Arrange the cards in order from highest to lowest using:

a) An insertion sort.   **b)** A merge sort.

[4 marks]   *[4 marks]*

5 The code on the right performs a sorting
algorithm on an array of 5 items called items.

a) Explain what the code inside the FOR loop does.

....

....

....

[2 marks]

b) Identify the sorting algorithm that the code represents.

....

[1 mark]

```
array items[5]
items = [4, 2, 1, 8, 6]
sorted = false
while sorted == false
   sorted = true
   for i = 0 to 3
     if items[i] > items[i + 1] then
        x = items[i]
        items[i] = items[i + 1]
        items[i + 1] = x
        sorted = false
     endif
   next i
endwhile
```

This code is written in OCR Exam Reference Language — it's covered in Section 6.

Section Five — Algorithms

Revision Questions for Section Five

Well that's algorithms all done and dusted. Or so you thought — just wait until you start Section 6.
- Try these questions and <u>tick off each one</u> when you <u>get it right</u>.
- When you've done <u>all the questions</u> for a topic and are <u>completely happy</u> with it, tick off the topic.

Computational Thinking (p.64) ☑

1) What is meant by: a) decomposition?   b) abstraction? ☑

2) Why is using algorithmic thinking useful when solving a problem? ☑

3) Outline the decomposition, abstraction and algorithmic processes for choosing a film at the cinema. ☑

Pseudocode and Flowcharts (p.65-66) ☑

4) What is pseudocode? Give three features of well-written pseudocode. ☑

5) What are the benefits of writing algorithms in pseudocode rather than a programming language? ☑

6) Draw the five box types used on flowcharts and say what each one is used for. ☑

7) What do sequences, selections and iterations look like on a flowchart? ☑

8)* Draw a flowchart to check if a new username is valid. Usernames should be at least
5 characters long and unique. If it's invalid, the algorithm should give the reason why
and get the user to enter another username. ☑

Search Algorithms (p.69) ☑

9) What are the four steps of the binary search algorithm? ☑

10) What are the four steps of a linear search algorithm? ☑

11)* Here's a fascinating list of British towns and cities:

| Ashington | Brecon | Chester | Dagenham | Morpeth | Usk | Watford |

 a) Use a binary search to find "Morpeth" in the list above.
 b) Now do the same using a linear search. ☑
12) What are the benefits and drawbacks of using a linear search over a binary search? ☑

Sorting Algorithms (p.70-72) ☑

13) a) What are the five steps of the bubble sort algorithm?
 b)* Use the bubble sort algorithm to sort these fruit into alphabetical order:

| Orange | Banana | Apple | Peach | Grape | Lime | ☑

14) What are the four steps of the merge sort algorithm? ☑

15) And the three steps of the insertion sort algorithm? ☑

16)* Here is a list of numbers: | 8   7   5   1   3   6   4   2 |

 a) Use the merge sort algorithm to sort this list into descending order.
 b) Use the insertion sort algorithm to sort this list into ascending order. ☑

17) Outline the strengths and weaknesses of the following sorting algorithms:
 a) bubble sort   b) merge sort   c) insertion sort ☑

Programming Basics — Data Types

*It's been a long wait of 76 pages, but **finally** we've got to the headline act, the **programming** section...*

Everything we cover in this section will work slightly differently in different programming languages, but the <u>principles</u> are the same and <u>that's</u> what you need to learn for the exam.

In this section, examples of code will be given in these boxes and will be written in OCR Exam Reference Language.

The output of the code will be shown in this box.

Programming languages have **Five Main Data Types**

1) Programming languages store data as different <u>types</u>. You need to learn the ones in this table...

Data type	Code	Characteristics	Examples
Integer	int	Whole numbers only.	0, 6, 10293, –999
Real (or float)	real	Numbers that have a decimal part.	0.15, –5.87, 100.0
Boolean	bool	Can only take one of two values, usually true or false.	True/False, 1/0, yes/no
Character	char	A single letter, number, symbol.	"A", "k", "5", "–", "$"
String	string	Used to represent text, it is a collection of characters.	"FsTmQ2", "$money$"

2) Each data type is allocated a different amount of <u>memory</u>.

3) Using the correct data types makes code more <u>memory efficient</u>, <u>robust</u> (hard to break) and <u>predictable</u>.

Programming languages can be <u>weakly typed</u> or <u>strongly typed</u>.

- Weakly typed languages will try to <u>convert</u> data types to <u>avoid errors</u>, however this can lead to <u>unpredictable results</u>.

- Strongly typed languages won't try to convert data types and so will produce <u>more errors</u> but more <u>predictable results</u>.

Data type	Typical amount of memory taken up
Integer	2 bytes or 4 bytes.
Real	4 bytes or 8 bytes.
Boolean	1 bit is needed but 1 byte is usually used.
Character	1 byte
String	1 byte for every character in the string.

Using the **Correct Data Type** for different **Variables**

You should be able to choose the best data type to use in different situations.

**EXAMPLE:**   **Give the appropriate data type for each of the categories in this registration form.**

Initial of first name:	N
Surname:	Chapman
Age (in whole years):	27
Height (in metres):	1.64
Male or Female:	Female

Initial of first name should be stored as a character.

Surname should be stored as a string.

Age (in whole years) should be stored as an integer.

Height (in metres) should be stored as a real data type.

Male or Female could be stored as boolean.

Using the wrong data type can lead to unexpected results...

Using the correct data types is a fundamental part of programming — sometimes a piece of data could take different data types and you'll have to decide which is best based on the context of the question.

Programming Basics — Casting and Operators

A mixed bag coming up on this page. First up is casting, which allows you to convert from one data type to another. Then it's arithmetic operators — you'll already be familiar with most of them from maths.

Casting is used to change the Data Type

1) Languages have <u>functions</u> (p.99) that let you manually convert between data types — this is known as <u>casting</u>. This can be done using the <u>int()</u>, <u>real()</u> (or <u>float()</u>), <u>bool()</u> and <u>str()</u> commands.

`int("1")` ◄— Converts the <u>string "1"</u> to the <u>integer 1</u>.

`real(1)` ◄— Converts the <u>integer 1</u> to the <u>real 1.0</u>.

`bool(1)` ◄— Converts the <u>integer 1</u> to the Boolean value <u>True</u>.

`str(True)` ◄— Converts the <u>Boolean value</u> True to the <u>string "True"</u>.

2) It's important to realise that the <u>integer 1</u>, the <u>real 1.0</u> and the <u>strings "1"</u> and <u>"1.0"</u> are all different.

3) You can also find the <u>ASCII number</u> (see p.27) of <u>characters</u> and vice versa using the <u>ASC()</u> and <u>CHR()</u> functions.

`ASC(b)` ◄— Converts the <u>character 'b'</u> into its <u>ASCII number 98</u>.

`CHR(98)` ◄— Converts the <u>ASCII number 98</u> into its equivalent <u>character 'b'</u>.

The Basic Arithmetic Operators are straightforward

1) The arithmetic operators take <u>two values</u> and perform a maths <u>function</u> on them.

2) <u>Addition</u>, <u>subtraction</u>, <u>multiplication</u> and <u>division</u> operators do what you'd expect.

3) The <u>exponentiation</u> operator is used to raise a number to a <u>power</u>.

4) The <u>DIV operator</u> returns the <u>whole number part</u> of a division and the <u>MOD operator</u> gives the <u>remainder</u>.

Dividing integers might behave oddly in some programming languages, e.g. 5 / 2 may give the answer 2 instead of 2.5...

...using DIV and MOD can avoid these issues.

Function	Typical Operator	Example	Result
Addition	+	5 + 5	10
Subtraction	–	3 – 10	–7
Multiplication	*	4 * 8	32
Division	/	42 / 6	7
Exponentiation	^ or **	$2 \wedge 3 \ (= 2^3)$	8
Quotient	DIV	20 DIV 3	6
Remainder (modulus)	MOD or %	20 MOD 3	2

5) These operators work on <u>integers</u> and <u>real</u> data values or a combination of the two.

6) Computers follow the rule of <u>BODMAS</u> (Brackets, Other, Division, Multiplication, Addition & Subtraction) — so <u>take care</u> when using operators to make sure your code is actually doing what you want it to. E.g. 2 + 8 * 2 will give 18. To do the addition first, use brackets: (2 + 8) * 2 will give 20.

REVISION TIP

Arithmetic Operators only work on integers and reals...

Get your head around these basic things now and you'll have a better chance of understanding the trickier stuff later on. The DIV and MOD operators might seem strange but they're really useful.

Programming Basics — Operators

*Programming languages have other types of operator too —
this page covers the assignment operator and the comparison operators.*

The **Assignment Operator**

The <u>assignment operator</u>, =, is used to <u>assign values</u> to <u>constants</u> or <u>variables</u> (see next page).

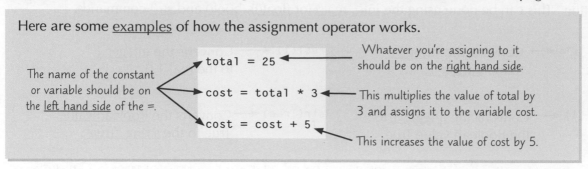

Here are some <u>examples</u> of how the assignment operator works.

The name of the constant
or variable should be on
the <u>left hand side</u> of the =.

Whatever you're assigning to it
should be on the <u>right hand side</u>.

```
total = 25
cost = total * 3
cost = cost + 5
```

This multiplies the value of total by
3 and assigns it to the variable cost.

This increases the value of cost by 5.

The **Comparison Operators**

<u>Comparison operators</u> compare the expression on their <u>left hand side</u> to the
expression on their <u>right hand side</u> and produce a <u>Boolean value</u> (either true or false).

Comparison operator	What it means	Evaluates to True	Evaluates to False
==	Is equal to	5 == 5	5 == 8
<> or !=	Is not equal to	6 != 7	6 != 6
<	Is less than	4 < 10	3 < 2
>	Is greater than	15 > 9	10 > 12
<=	Is less than or equal to	7 <= 8	11 <= 10
>=	Is greater than or equal to	3 >= 3	9 >= 12

Don't get mixed up between **= and ==**...

1) A common mistake is to get the <u>assignment operator</u> = and the <u>comparison operator</u> == mixed up.

2) You'll know you've used them <u>incorrectly</u> because your code won't behave as intended.

3) Have a look at the examples below to see the <u>impact</u> using
the <u>wrong operator</u> in an IF statement (p.83) can have.

```
if age = 25 then
```

This piece of code just <u>assigns</u> 25 to the
variable "age" — the IF statement will
consider this condition as <u>always true</u>.

```
if age == 25 then
```

This piece of code checks if
<u>age is equal to 25</u> and will only
run if the condition is true.

REVISION TASK

Comparison operators are used to compare two expressions...

Knowing what all the different operators are and what they do is essential to learning how to
write simple programs. Close the book and see if you can write down all the arithmetic and
comparison operators, explain what each operator does and give an example of it being used.

Constants and Variables

Now that you know about the different data types and operations it's time to look at constants and variables. As you can probably tell by the names, constants remain the same and variables can be changed.

Data Values can be **Constants** or **Variables**

1) Data values can be stored as constants or variables.

2) The name of the constant or variable is linked to a memory location that stores the data value. The size of the memory location depends on the data type (see p.76).

3) A constant is assigned a data value at design time that can't be changed. If you attempt to change the value of a constant in a program then the interpreter or compiler (see p.112) will return an error.

```
const distance = 40
```
Constants are assigned using the "const" command.

4) Variables on the other hand can change value which makes them far more useful than constants.

5) In some languages, like OCR Exam Reference Language, the data type is assumed when it is assigned a value:

'pressure' has an integer data type (as 30 is an integer) →
```
pressure = 30
temperature = 20.5
```
← *20.5 has a decimal part, so 'temperature' has a real data type*

6) In other languages, data types must be declared before you can use them:

These lines of code do exactly the same as the lines above. →
```
int pressure = 30
real temperature = 20.5
```

To make code easier to follow, programmers usually follow standard naming conventions for constants and variables. E.g. 'lower case for the first letter, followed by a mixture of letters, numbers and underscores.' Variable names must not contain spaces or start with a number.

Identifying **Constants** and **Variables** in Programs

In a multi-event athletics competition, athletes get 5 points for winning an event and 2 points for coming second. Otherwise they get 0 points. This program calculates the total number of points that an athlete has.

```
firsts = input("Number of 1st places.")
seconds = input("Number of 2nd places.")
print(5 * firsts + 2 * seconds)
```

a) **Rewrite the program so that all the variables have initial values.**

The two variables are firsts and seconds. As integer values have been assigned, both of the variables are assumed to be integers. →
```
firsts = 0
seconds = 0
firsts = input("Number of 1st places.")
seconds = input("Number of 2nd places.")
print(5 * firsts + 2 * seconds)
```
← *The initial value of each variable is set to 0.*

b) **Give two reasons for assigning the values 5 and 2 to constants.**

• They don't need to be changed during the running of the program.

• If the points awarded for each event was changed you'd only need to change the value given when assigning the constant.

This is an example of improving the maintainability (p.105) of the program.

A constant, a variable... and finally a constant. Time starts now...

You can't change the data type of a variable, only the value. But as you saw on p.77 you can use a casting function to return a different data type, which you can then assign to a new variable:

```
cost = 50
costString = str(cost)
```

Strings

Remember from page 76 that strings are a data type made up of characters — these characters are **alphanumeric** *(letters, numbers, spaces, symbols, etc.). Now you'll see how you can manipulate them.*

Strings are written inside **Quotation Marks**

Strings are usually written inside <u>double quotation marks</u> ", but sometimes <u>single quotes</u> are used '.

```
string1 = "Print me, I'm a string."
print(string1)
```
```
Print me, I'm a string.
```

Strings can be <u>joined together</u> to form new strings — this is called <u>concatenation</u>. It's often done using the <u>+ operator</u>.

```
string1 = "My favourite colour is"
string2 = "purple."
newString = string1 + " " + string2
print(newString)
```
```
My favourite colour is purple.
```

The + operator joins the strings together.

A space character has been added between the two strings.

Programs let you **Manipulate Strings** in a variety of ways

1) Before getting started on string manipulation you should know that the <u>characters</u> in a string are usually numbered <u>starting at 0</u>.

```
0 1 2 3 4 5
S P Y I N G
```

2) Here are some common <u>string manipulation</u> functions that you'll need to learn for your exam.

Typical function	Operation	Effect on x = "Hello"
x.upper	Changes all characters in string x to upper case.	HELLO
x.lower	Changes all characters in string x to lower case.	hello
x.length	Returns the number of characters in string x.	5
x.left(i)	Extracts the first i characters from string x.	x.left(2) = "He"
x.right(i)	Extracts the last i characters from string x.	x.right(3) = "llo"
x.subString(a, b)	Extracts a string starting at position a with length b from string x.	x.subString(3, 2) = "lo"

upper, lower, length, left, right and subString are special functions called <u>methods</u>. They act on a particular object (in this case strings) and are called using the object's name followed by a dot "." and the method's name.

**EXAMPLE:**
An electricity company generates a customer's 7 character username from:
- **the first 3 letters of their town as uppercase letters.**
- **the customer's age when they sign up (2 digits).**
- **the first and last letters of the customer's surname as lowercase letters.**

Write an algorithm to generate a username for any customer given that their data is stored under the variables town, age and surname.

Start by working out how to <u>extract</u> the information from <u>each variable</u>...

1) `town.left(3).upper`

This extracts the <u>first 3 characters</u> from the customer's town and makes them uppercase. You could also write 'town.subString(O, 3).upper'.

2) `str(age)` <u>Casts</u> (p.77) the customer's age as a <u>string</u>.

subString, left and right are examples of 'slicing' — where part of a string is extracted and returned as a new string.

3)
```
letters = surname.left(1) + surname.right(1)
letters = letters.lower
```

Finds the relevant letters by finding the <u>first</u> and <u>last characters</u> of the surname. It then makes them <u>lowercase</u>.

... then combine the code into a <u>single algorithm</u> at the end.

```
letters = surname.left(1) + surname.right(1)
username = town.left(3).upper + str(age) + letters.lower
```

Even for simple algorithms like this one, there are many possible ways of doing it.

EXAM TIP

I hope you don't just think I'm stringing you along...

It's important that you know the string manipulations on this page — the examiners might throw some different ones at you in the exam. Luckily they'll also show you exactly how they work.

Warm-Up and Worked Exam Questions

That's the first part of programming done — have a go at these questions to see how much you've understood.

Warm-Up Questions

1) What is the most appropriate data type for each of these items?
   a) The nickname of your best friend.
   b) The number on a rolled dice.
   c) The exact length of a car in metres.
   d) The answer to a yes/no question.

2) Work out the results of the following arithmetic operations:
   a) `5 * 8`
   b) `10 MOD 3`
   c) `28 DIV 6`
   d) `3 + 2 * 8`

3) Will the following pieces of code return true or false?
   a) `6 <= 10`
   b) `5 == 5`
   c) `14 > 15`
   d) `12 < 8 + 5`

4) What's the difference between a variable and a constant?

5) Given that `animal = "lobster"`, state what would be returned from the following methods:
   a) `animal.length`
   b) `animal.right(3)`
   c) `animal.upper`
   d) `animal.subString(2, 3)`

Worked Exam Questions

1 The program below calculates the cost of a burger in pounds at a fast food restaurant.
A standard burger costs £6.50 with additional costs for toppings and eating in the restaurant.

```
const standard = 6.5
toppings = 0
eatIn = false
toppings = input("How many toppings?")
eatIn = input("Are they eating in?")
if eatIn == "Yes" then
    print(standard + 0.5*toppings + 1)
else
    print(standard + 0.5*toppings)
endif
```

a) List **all** the variables in this program.

toppings and eatIn

[2 marks]

b) How much extra does it cost to eat your burger inside the restaurant?

£1

[1 mark]

c) The restaurant manager says that 0.5 should have been declared as a constant.
Give **two** reasons for declaring this value as a constant.

1. It doesn't need to be changed as the program is running.

2. Updating the value of a constant once will update it everywhere in the program.

You could also mention that giving the value a name,
e.g. toppingsCost will make the code more meaningful.

[2 marks]

2 A digital radio stores the date as a string under the variable name `date`. The radio is broken and
stuck on the date: `8 January 2016`. State the output from each of the following pieces of code:

a) `date.left(1) + date.subString(10,4)`

"8" + "2016"   They are strings so use string
concatenation instead of adding them.

82016

[1 mark]

b) `date.subString(2,3).upper`

JAN

[1 mark]

Exam Questions

3 A pedestrian crossing uses a button to request the traffic to stop. State the data type that you would use to record each of these variables and give a reason for your answer.

    a) A variable to record whether the button has been pressed or not.

        Data type: ....

        Reason: ....

        [2 marks]

    b) A variable to record how many whole seconds it's been since the button was pressed.

        Data type: ....

        Reason: ....

        [2 marks]

4 The program below calculates the value of an investment at the end of one year.
Identify **two** problems with the constants or variables in the program.

```
const investment = input("Enter investment.")
rate = "0.2"
for x = 1 to 12
   interest = rate * investment
   investment = investment + interest
next x
print(investment)
```

1. ....

....

2. ....

....

[2 marks]

5 A juice company generates a product ID for each of its fruit juices. The product ID is generated using string concatenation on the first three letters of the fruit (in uppercase) and the volume of fruit juice in ml. E.g. a 500 ml carton of apple juice would be APP500.

    a) Define what is meant by string concatenation.

        ....

        [1 mark]

    b) What would the product code be for a 2000 ml carton of orange juice?

        ....

        [1 mark]

    c) Complete the algorithm below so that line 03 reassigns the uppercase name of the fruit to the `fruit` variable and line 04 assigns the final product ID to the `prodID` variable.

```
01  fruit = input("Enter the name of the fruit.")
02  volume = input("Enter the volume of the juice.")

03  fruit = ............................................................

04  prodID = ..........................................................
05  print(prodID)
```

[3 marks]

Program Flow

The flow of a program is the order that the steps are carried out in. You can control the program flow using ***selection statements*** *— there are two types that you need to learn, IF statements and SWITCH statements.*

IF Statements usually have an IF-THEN-ELSE structure

1) IF statements allow you to check if a <u>condition</u> is true or false, and carry out different actions depending on the outcome. You can think about them as a <u>flowchart</u>.

2) Here is a program that can verify if the user knows a certain passcode before granting access.

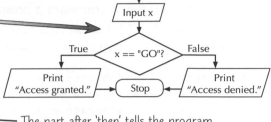

The first part of the <u>IF statement</u> is the condition that must be checked. →

Indenting the actions for each condition makes the code more readable.

```
x = input("Enter the passcode.")
if x == "GO" then
    print("Access granted.")
else
    print("Access denied.")
endif
```

The part after 'then' tells the program what to do if the condition is true.

The part after 'else' tells the program what to do if the condition is false.

3) If there is <u>nothing</u> for the program to do when the <u>condition is false</u>, <u>leave out</u> the '<u>else</u>' part.

Nested IF Statements allow multiple outputs

1) More complex IF statements can be made by putting one IF statement <u>inside</u> another one — this type of selection statement is called a <u>nested IF statement</u>.

2) Nested IF statements allow you to <u>check more conditions</u> once you've established that the <u>previous condition</u> is <u>true</u>.

If the <u>first condition</u> is <u>true</u>, it will check the <u>second condition</u>...

If the <u>first condition</u> is <u>false</u>, it will run this <u>else statement</u> — all access is denied.

<u>Indentation</u> lets the reader see where each IF statement begins and ends.

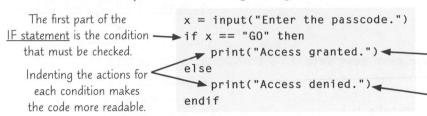

```
x = input("Enter the passcode.")
if x == "GO" then
    if usertype == "Teacher" then
        print("Unrestricted access granted.")
    else
        print("Restricted access granted.")
    endif
else
    print("Access denied.")
endif
```

If the <u>second condition</u> is <u>true</u> then unrestricted access is allowed.

If the second condition is <u>false</u> then restricted access is allowed.

3) <u>IF-ELSEIF statements</u> can also be used to check <u>multiple conditions</u>. They are different from nested IF statements as they only <u>check more conditions</u> if the <u>previous condition</u> is <u>false</u>.

The conditions are all indented to the <u>same level</u>.

If <u>all conditions</u> are <u>false</u> then access is denied

```
if usertype == "Teacher" then
    print("Unrestricted access.")
elseif usertype == "Parent" then
    print("Level 1 restricted access.")
elseif usertype == "Pupil" then
    print("Level 2 restricted access.")
else
    print("Access denied.")
endif
```

The <u>first condition</u> is always checked — if it's <u>true</u> then unrestricted access is allowed.

The <u>second condition</u> is checked if the <u>first condition</u> is <u>false</u> — if it's <u>true</u> then level 1 restricted access is allowed.

The <u>third condition</u> is checked if the <u>first</u> and <u>second conditions</u> are <u>false</u> — if it's <u>true</u> then level 2 restricted access is allowed.

If you understand IF statements then make yourself a brew...

One good thing about IF-ELSEIF statements is they're very neat, everything is indented to the same line.
Lots of nested IF statements with many levels of indentation can cause readability problems in your code.

Program Flow

Here are the SWITCH statements and the first type of iteration statement — FOR loops.

SWITCH Statements check the value of a **Variable**

1) Instead of checking to see if a statement is true or false, SWITCH (or CASE SELECT) statements can check if a <u>variable</u> has <u>specific values</u>.

2) They're used when you want a program to perform <u>different actions</u> for <u>different values</u> of the <u>same variable</u>.

3) Here is a program that can be used to <u>count votes</u> in an election.

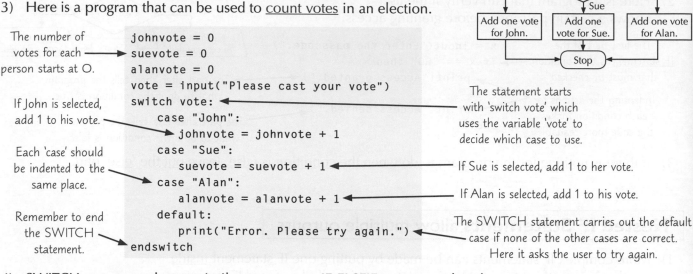

The number of votes for each person starts at 0.

```
johnvote = 0
suevote = 0
alanvote = 0
vote = input("Please cast your vote")
switch vote:
    case "John":
        johnvote = johnvote + 1
    case "Sue":
        suevote = suevote + 1
    case "Alan":
        alanvote = alanvote + 1
    default:
        print("Error. Please try again.")
endswitch
```

If John is selected, add 1 to his vote.

Each 'case' should be indented to the same place.

Remember to end the SWITCH statement.

The statement starts with 'switch vote' which uses the variable 'vote' to decide which case to use.

If Sue is selected, add 1 to her vote.

If Alan is selected, add 1 to his vote.

The SWITCH statement carries out the default case if none of the other cases are correct. Here it asks the user to try again.

4) SWITCH statements have a <u>similar structure</u> to IF-ELSEIF statements but they give a <u>neater</u> way to test <u>different values</u> of a variable — this makes them easier than ELSEIF statements to <u>maintain</u>.

5) The <u>drawback</u> of SWITCH statements is that they can <u>only check</u> the value of <u>one variable</u>. IF-ELSEIF statements can check if <u>multiple conditions</u> are true.

FOR Loops are an example of a **Count-Controlled Loop**

1) <u>FOR loops</u> will repeat the code inside them a fixed number of times. The number of times that the code repeats will depend on an <u>initial value</u>, <u>end value</u> and the <u>step count</u>.

2) For example, for k = 1 to 10 step 3 will count up from 1 to 10 in steps of 3, so k = 1, k = 4, k = 7 and k = 10. If no step count is given the count will <u>increase by 1</u> each time.

The FOR loop repeats the code between 'for' and 'next'.

3) The <u>number of times</u> the loop repeats can also be set as the <u>program runs</u> — e.g. for k = 1 to x, where x is a variable.

4) FOR loops can also use the count <u>within the loop</u> — in the example on the right, k is used to keep track of how many votes have been cast.

```
johnvote = 0
suevote = 0
alanvote = 0
for k = 1 to 100
    vote = input("Please cast your vote.")
    switch vote:
        case "John":
            johnvote = johnvote + 1
        case "Sue":
            suevote = suevote + 1
        case "Alan":
            alanvote = alanvote + 1
        default:
            print("Error. Please try again.")
    endswitch
    print(str(k) + " votes have been cast.")
next k
```

Allows 100 votes to be cast.

Many programming languages don't use the 'next' keyword in FOR loops.

The value of k can be used anywhere within the loop.

Use FOR loops when you know the number of repetitions...

EXAM TIP

A SWITCH statement should include a "default:" case, as it tells the program what to do if none of the other cases are correct. Therefore it can help to make SWITCH statements more robust.

Program Flow

Here are a couple of other loops that you need to know about — the DO UNTIL loop and the WHILE loop. Like FOR loops, they are both **iteration statements** *— they repeat a part of the program.*

Both of these **Loops** are controlled by **Conditions**

<u>DO UNTIL</u> and <u>WHILE</u> loops are easy to get mixed up — they're very similar but with subtle differences that you need to know:

You might also see a <u>REPEAT UNTIL loop</u> — this does the same thing as a <u>DO UNTIL loop</u>.

DO UNTIL Loops

- Controlled by a condition at the <u>end of the loop</u>.
- Keep going <u>until</u> the condition is <u>true</u> (i.e. while it is false).
- <u>Always run</u> the code inside them <u>at least once</u>.
- You get an <u>infinite loop</u> if the condition is <u>never true</u>.

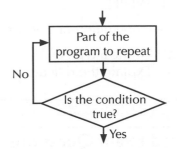

WHILE Loops

- Controlled by a condition at the <u>start of the loop</u>.
- Keep going <u>while</u> the condition is <u>true</u> (i.e. until it is false).
- <u>Never run</u> the code inside them if the condition is initially <u>false</u>.
- You get an <u>infinite loop</u> if the condition is <u>always true</u>.

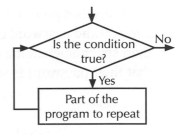

Condition-Controlled Loop Example

EXAMPLE: **Write an algorithm that someone could use to check if they have reached their savings target and also print the amount of excess money they have saved.**

You could use either of the loops shown above — the code before and after the loop is exactly the same.

DO UNTIL Loop:
```
total = 0
target = input("Enter target")
do
  funds = input("Enter funds")
  total = total + funds
until total >= target
excess = total - target
print("Excess is: " + str(excess))
```

The loop starts at '<u>do</u>' and ends when the '<u>until</u>' condition is <u>true</u> — when the total is greater than or equal to the target.

WHILE Loop:
```
total = 0
target = input("Enter target")
while total < target
  funds = input("Enter funds")
  total = total + funds
endwhile
excess = total - target
print("Excess is: " + str(excess))
```

The loop starts by checking the '<u>while</u>' condition is <u>true</u> and keeps repeating until it is <u>false</u> — when the total is greater than or equal to the target.

Both of these loops work exactly the same when target > 0.
If the target is 0, the WHILE loop won't expect funds to be input, whereas the DO UNTIL loop will.

Some languages have a <u>DO WHILE</u> loop. DO WHILE loops keep going <u>while</u> the condition (at the end of the loop) is <u>true</u> and <u>always run</u> the code inside them at least once.

Keep looping through this page until it's stuck in your head...

As well as learning what each loop does, you should learn the differences between the different loops. The key thing is recognising exactly when the loop will start or stop.

Warm-Up and Worked Exam Questions

Time to see if all that information is sinking in. Have a go at these warm-up questions then read through the worked exam questions before having a go at the questions on the next page yourself.

Warm-Up Questions

1) For each of the following, say if it is selection or iteration:
   a) DO UNTIL
   b) IF-THEN-ELSE
   c) SWITCH
   d) WHILE
   e) IF-ELSEIF

2) Give one difference between a SWITCH statement and an IF-ELSEIF statement.

3) a) Name a type of a count-controlled loop and a type of condition-controlled loop.
   b) Explain the difference between the two loops given in part a).

Worked Exam Questions

1 Salik needs a program that will ask users to create a password and then check if the password contains at least six characters. If it contains fewer than six characters the user must try again, otherwise the user is informed that their password is valid. Write an appropriate program for Salik.

```
do
        password = input("Please enter a password")
until password.length >= 6
print("Your password is valid")
```

Using a DO UNTIL loop will mean that the code in the loop always runs through at least once.

[3 marks]

2 In a basketball arcade game a player gets 10 shots to score as many baskets as they can. The code on the right keeps track of a player's score.

```
score = 0
basket = false
for x = 1 to 10
    basket = input("Did they score?")
    if basket == true then
        score = score + 1
    endif
next x
print(score)
```

a) Explain why a count-controlled loop has been used instead of a condition-controlled loop.

The player always gets the same number of shots, so you don't need to check a condition, just repeat the loop 10 times.

[2 marks]

b) Describe how you would adapt the code so that a player could specify the amount of shots that they want to take.

Introduce a new variable that the user enters, such as shots, and have the FOR loop go from 1 to this variable. E.g. for x = 1 to shots.

[2 marks]

Exam Questions

3 Jasminda has written the following program to convert minutes into hours and minutes.

```
minutes = input("Enter a number of minutes.")
hours = minutes DIV 60
mins = minutes MOD 60
print(str(hours) + " hours and " + str(mins) + " minutes")
```

a) Which programming construct has been used in this program?
Tick the correct box.

Sequence ☐   Selection ☐   Iteration ☐

[1 mark]

b) What would the program print if the input was 150?

....

[1 mark]

4 An electric heater has four temperature settings (0, 1, 2 and 3).
The code below controls the temperature of the heater.

```
setting = input()
if setting == "3" then
    temperature = 50
elseif setting == "2" then
    temperature = 30
elseif setting == "1" then
    temperature = 20
else
    temperature = 0
endif
```

a) Rewrite this program to use a SWITCH statement.

[3 marks]

b) Give **two** reasons why a SWITCH statement is appropriate for this program.

1. ....

2. ....

[2 marks]

5 Karl and John are playing snap. Write an algorithm that:
• Asks for the name of the winner of each game.
• After ten games checks who has won more and displays
  the winner's name or tells them that it's a draw.

You must use either:
• OCR Exam Reference Language, **or**
• a high-level programming language that you have studied.

You'll need variables to keep track of the winner of each game and the number of games each player has won.

[6 marks]

Boolean Logic

*Each Boolean operator (**NOT, AND** and **OR**) has its own logic gate. Logic gates take binary information and give an output based on the Boolean operation — the same principles can be used in your programs (see p.90).*

Logic Gates apply Boolean Operations to Inputs

1) Logic gates are special circuits built into computer chips.
   They receive <u>binary data</u>, apply a <u>Boolean operation</u>, then <u>output</u> a binary result.

2) Logic <u>diagrams</u> are often drawn to show logic gates and circuits.
   Each type of logic gate is shown by a different <u>symbol</u>.

3) Each type of logic gate also has a corresponding <u>truth table</u>.
   Truth tables show <u>all</u> possible input combinations of 1s and 0s, and the corresponding <u>outputs</u>.

NOT gate

1) NOT gates take a <u>single input</u> and give a <u>single output</u>.

2) The output is always the <u>opposite</u> value to the input.
   If <u>1</u> is input, it outputs <u>0</u>. If <u>0</u> is input, it outputs <u>1</u>.

It can help to think of 1s as TRUE and 0s as FALSE.

<u>NOT gate symbol</u>

Input ——————▷o—— Output

<u>NOT truth table</u>

Input	Output
0	1
1	0

AND gate

1) AND gates take <u>two inputs</u> and give <u>one output</u>.

2) If both inputs are 1, the output is <u>1</u>,
   <u>otherwise</u> the output is <u>0</u>.

<u>AND gate symbol</u>

Input A ——————┐
              ├D—— Output
Input B ——————┘

<u>AND truth table</u>

Input A	Input B	Output
0	0	0
0	1	0
1	0	0
1	1	1

OR gate

1) OR gates take <u>two inputs</u> and give <u>one output</u>.

2) If <u>one or more</u> inputs are 1, then the output is <u>1</u>,
   <u>otherwise</u> the output is <u>0</u>.

<u>OR gate symbol</u>

Input A ——————┐
              ├D—— Output
Input B ——————┘

<u>OR truth table</u>

Input A	Input B	Output
0	0	0
0	1	1
1	0	1
1	1	1

REVISION TIP

Logic isn't as scary as it looks...

These basic logic gates are the building blocks for bigger logic circuits. You should be able to draw each logic gate and the corresponding truth table — you'll also need to learn the equivalent expression and notation from this table:

Gate	Expression	Notation
NOT	NOT A	$\neg A$
AND	A AND B	$A \wedge B$
OR	A OR B	$A \vee B$

Boolean Logic

*You can make more interesting logic diagrams by **combining** logic gates. If you know the truth tables from the previous page you'll be able to create truth tables for much more complicated logic diagrams.*

Logic Gates are Combined for More Complex Operations

1) <u>Multiple</u> logic gates can be added to the <u>same</u> logic circuit to carry out different operations.

2) You can work out the <u>truth tables</u> by working through each gate in order.
For every <u>input</u> combination, follow them through each gate <u>step-by-step</u>, then write down the <u>output</u>.

3) By using brackets and the terms AND, OR and NOT, circuits can be written as <u>logical statements</u>, like NOT(A AND B) below. Operations in <u>brackets</u> should be completed <u>first</u>, just like in normal maths.

This circuit shows <u>AND</u> followed by <u>NOT</u>.

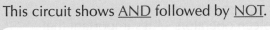

The <u>truth table</u> looks like this:

A	B	A AND B	P = NOT(A AND B)
0	0	0	1
0	1	0	1
1	0	0	1
1	1	1	0

This circuit shows <u>OR</u> followed by <u>NOT</u>.

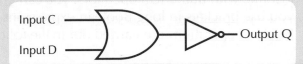

The <u>truth table</u> looks like this:

C	D	C OR D	Q = NOT(C OR D)
0	0	0	1
0	1	1	0
1	0	1	0
1	1	1	0

4) The two logic circuits shown above are examples of <u>two-level logic circuits</u> — they require the inputs to pass through a <u>maximum</u> of <u>two</u> logic gates to reach the output.

Logic Circuits can have More than Two Inputs

This is a <u>two-level logic</u> circuit with <u>3 inputs</u>.

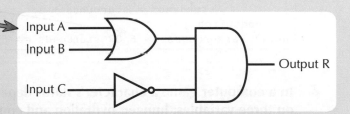

Using Boolean operators, this circuit can be written as <u>R = (A OR B) AND (NOT C)</u>. (This is an example of <u>Boolean algebra</u>).

To cover <u>every</u> input combination, extra rows are needed in the truth table. There are <u>3</u> inputs and each can take one of 2 values, so $2 \times 2 \times 2 = \underline{8}$ rows are needed.

In general, the number of rows is 2^n, where n is the number of different inputs.

A	B	C	A OR B	NOT C	R = (A OR B) AND (NOT C)
0	0	0	0	1	0
0	0	1	0	0	0
0	1	0	1	1	1
0	1	1	1	0	0
1	0	0	1	1	1
1	0	1	1	0	0
1	1	0	1	1	1
1	1	1	1	0	0

To be OR NOT to be — literally covering all forms of being...

Once you've learned each gate's truth table, you can work out the truth tables of much more complicated circuits. If you take the inputs through each gate one step at a time you'll be fine — it's only logical...

Boolean Logic

You can also use Boolean operators in programs that use Boolean values to produce a Boolean answer.

AND, OR and NOT are the only Boolean Operators you'll need

1) It doesn't make sense to use the arithmetic operators on things that are either <u>true or false</u> so instead you use the Boolean operators <u>AND</u>, <u>OR</u> and <u>NOT</u>.

Boolean operator	Examples that return true	Examples that return false
AND	3 < 5 AND 2 > 1	4 <= 5 AND 10 > 20
OR	1 > 8 OR 2 == 2	1 == 8 OR 2 < 2
NOT	NOT(5 > 8)	NOT(10 > 6)

In some code you might see AND written as &&, OR written as || and NOT written as !

2) Just like with numerical operators, you can <u>combine Boolean operators</u> — it's important that you use <u>brackets</u> in long Boolean expressions to let the computer know which part to do <u>first</u>. <u>Boolean operations</u> are carried out in the following <u>order</u>: brackets, NOT, AND then OR.

Boolean Operators can be used in Conditions

Boolean operators can be used to make all the different selection statements and iteration statements (p.83-85) more <u>efficient</u> and <u>versatile</u>.

1. **Karen and Stu are playing a 'best out of 10' game. The game should end when one of them wins 6 rounds or they both win 5 rounds. Write an algorithm to keep score in the game.**

```
karenrounds = 0
sturounds = 0
do
    roundwinner = input("Enter winner's name.")
    switch roundwinner:
        case "Karen":
            karenrounds = karenrounds + 1
        case "Stu":
            sturounds = sturounds + 1
    endswitch
until karenrounds == 6 OR sturounds == 6 OR (karenrounds == 5 AND sturounds == 5)
```

There is a SWITCH statement within the loop. This is where good indentation in your code is key.

The DO UNTIL loop stops when one of these three conditions is met.

2. **In a computer game a character's status depends on three variables: hunger, hydration and comfort. If any of the conditions on the right are met then the character dies, otherwise they are alive.**

- Any of the variables are equal to 0.
- Any two of the variables are less than 20.
- All three of the variables are less than 40.

Write an algorithm to work out the status of the character.

```
if hunger == 0 OR hydration == 0 OR comfort == 0 then
    alive = false
elseif (hunger < 20 AND hydration < 20) OR (hunger < 20 AND comfort < 20)
        OR (hydration < 20 AND comfort < 20) then
    alive = false
elseif hunger < 40 AND hydration < 40 AND comfort < 40 then
    alive = false
else
    alive = true
endif
```

The Boolean operators are AND, OR and NOT...

Using Boolean operators can save lots of work by letting you check lots of conditions at the same time.

Random Number Generation

Random numbers are really useful when you don't want your programs to do the same thing every time. They can be used to simulate random real-life events, e.g. rolling a dice, picking raffle tickets, etc.

Random Numbers are useful when making Games

1) Random numbers can be used in <u>simple games</u> when the programmer wants a number to be <u>unknown</u> — even the programmer themselves won't know what it's going to be.

2) Most programming languages have functions to <u>generate random numbers</u> — for example, OCR Exam Reference Language uses this <u>function</u> that generates a <u>random</u> number <u>between x and y</u>.

```
random(x, y)
```

3) If the values of x and y are <u>integers</u> then a <u>random integer</u> will be generated, whereas if x and y are <u>real</u> numbers then a <u>random real</u> number is generated.

```
random(1, 6)
```
Generates a random integer between 1 and 6 (including 1 and 6).

4) Here is an example of how random numbers can be used to simulate a roll of a <u>6-sided dice</u>.

Will randomly generate either 1, 2, 3, 4, 5 or 6 and assign it to the variable 'roll'.

Here, the number it has randomly generated is 2.

```
roll = random(1, 6)
print(roll)
```
```
2
```

```
random(1.0, 6.0)
```
Generates a random real number between 1.0 and 6.0 (including 1.0 and 6.0).

5) <u>FOR loops</u> can be used when you want to generate a <u>whole bunch</u> of random numbers.

This FOR loop will generate three random integers from 1 to 10.

```
for i = 1 to 3
    roll = random(1, 10)
    print(roll)
endfor
```

The output will look something like...

```
4
9
4
```

Note that the same integer can be randomly generated more than once.

You can use Random Numbers to make Random Selections

1) Instead of outputting the random number that you generated, you can use it to randomly generate <u>another event</u>.

2) Suppose you want to <u>simulate a coin toss</u> — there are two outcomes, <u>heads</u> or <u>tails</u> — we can simplify this in programming terms to 0 and 1 (where 0 = heads, 1 = tails).

```
number = random(0, 1)
if number == 0 then
    print("Heads")
elseif number == 1 then
    print("Tails")
endif
```

Randomly generates either 0 or 1.

Technically, you could have an ELSE statement at the bottom without the condition, because there are only two possible outcomes.

3) Random numbers are really handy to use with <u>arrays</u> (see p.94-95). You can generate a <u>random number</u> then pick the element in that <u>position</u> of the array.

Randomly generates either 0, 1, 2 or 3.

Uses the random number to select a piece of fruit from the array.

```
number = random(0, 3)
chosenFruit = fruits[number]
print(number)
print("Today you should eat a " + chosenFruit)
```

```
array fruits[4]
fruits[0] = "Mango"
fruits[1] = "Banana"
fruits[2] = "Pear"
fruits[3] = "Peach"
```

The random number generated was 3, so the fruit that was chosen was 'Peach'.

```
3
Today you should eat a Peach
```

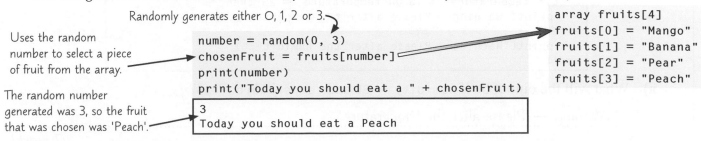

Use random numbers to make your program more unpredictable...

The random numbers that are generated in a programming language are called pseudo-random numbers because they aren't completely random, they just look like they are. They are usually generated by following a complex algorithm which means that they will have a pattern — it's just very hard to see it.

Warm-Up and Worked Exam Questions

Try these warm-up questions on logic and random numbers — if there is anything you're unsure about, have a look back through the previous four pages before having a go at the exam questions on the next page.

Warm-Up Questions

1) Look at the three logic expressions in the box below:

| (NOT A) AND B | C OR (NOT D) | (E AND F) OR G |

a) Draw a logic circuit for each expression.
b) Construct a truth table for each expression.

2) Decide whether the following Boolean expressions are true or false:
a) 12 > 4 AND 8 == 5
b) NOT(11 == 3)
c) 12 <= 4 OR 10 != 5
d) NOT(9 > 4 AND 5 < 2)

3) List all the values that could be generated by random(3, 8).

Worked Exam Questions

1 A logic gate can be written as P = A AND B.

a) State the value of input B when input A is 1 and output P is 0.

B = ...0..........
[1 mark]

b) A NOT logic gate is placed after the AND logic gate to make the logic diagram below. State the input values when output P is 0.

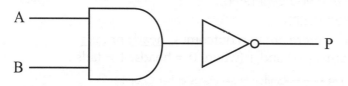

For the NOT gate to output O, the input of the NOT gate must be 1.

A = ...1.......... B = ...1..........
[1 mark]

2 A garden centre has a climate monitoring system that gives warnings if the temperature and humidity aren't at suitable levels. The climate monitoring system contains this algorithm.

```
if humidity == 50 AND (temperature > 16 AND temperature < 25) then
    print("Humidity and temperature at acceptable levels.")
elseif temperature <= 16 OR temperature >= 25 then
    print("Warning — Please alter the temperature.")
else
    print("Warning — Please alter the humidity.")
endif
```

a) What will the output be if humidity = 30 and temperature = 16?

"Warning — Please alter the temperature."
[1 mark]

b) What will the output be if humidity = 30 and temperature = 20?

"Warning — Please alter the humidity."
[1 mark]

Exam Questions

3   A series of transistors make the two-level logic circuit (NOT A) AND (B AND C).

a) Complete the truth table below.

A	B	C	NOT A	B AND C	(NOT A) AND (B AND C)
0	0	0			
0	0	1			
0	1	0			
0	1	1			
1	0	0			
1	0	1			
1	1	0			
1	1	1			

[3 marks]

b) Draw the logic diagram that represents (NOT A) AND (B AND C).

Have a look at p.88 for a reminder
of what the gates should look like.

[3 marks]

4   A tumble dryer will only be allowed to start if all of the following conditions are met:
- the real variable `weight` is more than 1.5 and less than 15.0
- the boolean variable `doorClosed` is true.

Write an algorithm that checks these conditions before allowing the tumble dryer to start.

[3 marks]

5   A developer has written the following code as part of a card game app. It is used to show
5 random playing cards from a standard deck (which is stored in an array called deck):

```
for x = 1 to 5
    randNum = random(0, 51)
    drawnCard = deck[randNum]
    print(drawnCard)
next x
```

Explain one problem with the way this code uses random number generation to draw cards.

....

....

....

[2 marks]

Arrays

When you need to store data within a program you can do it using variables. But if you have lots of similar data to store, then using variables for each one is inefficient and that's where arrays come in.

Arrays are used to store multiple **Data Values**

1) An array is a <u>data structure</u> that can store a collection of data values all under <u>one name</u>.

2) Each piece of data in an array is called an <u>element</u> — each element can be <u>accessed</u> using its <u>position</u> (or <u>index</u>) in the array.

3) Arrays are <u>most helpful</u> when you have lots of <u>related data</u> that you want to store and it doesn't make sense to use <u>separate variables</u> — e.g. the names of pupils in a class, marks in a test, etc.

A data structure is a format for storing data — other data structures include records, files and databases.

4) Just like variables, some languages require you to <u>declare arrays</u> before you use them.

One-Dimensional Arrays are like **Lists**

The easiest way to get your head around <u>one-dimensional arrays</u> is to picture them as <u>lists</u>. Different languages have lots of fancy ways to <u>create</u> and <u>update arrays</u>. Here are the ones you'll need to learn for your exam:

1) Creating arrays — the first line of the code on the right creates the array 'rowers' and makes it <u>size 4</u> (it can only contain <u>4 elements</u>). The other lines assign the strings "<u>Ivan</u>", "<u>Adam</u>", "<u>Pavni</u>" and "<u>Tobias</u>" in positions <u>0</u>, <u>1</u>, <u>2</u> and <u>3</u>.

```
array rowers[4]
rowers[0] = "Ivan"
rowers[1] = "Adam"
rowers[2] = "Pavni"
rowers[3] = "Tobias"
```

2) Retrieving elements from an array can be done by using the <u>name</u> of the array and the <u>element's position</u>. Remember that positions are numbered <u>starting at 0</u>.

```
print(rowers[0])
print(rowers[2])
```
```
Ivan
Pavni
```

3) Changing elements is done by reassigning the array position to a different data value.

Replaces the rower in position O with "Tamal".

```
rowers[0] = "Tamal"
print(rowers)
```
```
["Tamal", "Adam", "Pavni", "Tobias"]
```

Notice that "Ivan" has been completely removed from the array.

Combining these <u>array functions</u> with <u>FOR loops</u> (see p.84) will give you a <u>systematic way</u> of accessing and changing all of the <u>elements</u> in an array. Amongst other things, FOR loops can be used to <u>search</u> for specific elements, or make a similar change to <u>lots of elements</u>.

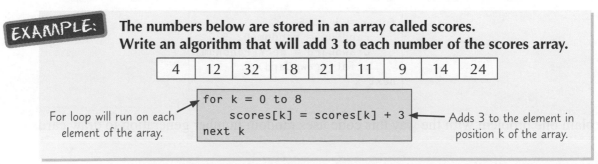

EXAMPLE: The numbers below are stored in an array called scores.
Write an algorithm that will add 3 to each number of the scores array.

4	12	32	18	21	11	9	14	24

```
for k = 0 to 8
    scores[k] = scores[k] + 3
next k
```

For loop will run on each element of the array.

Adds 3 to the element in position k of the array.

Think of one dimensional arrays as lists of similar objects...

In some languages (e.g. C, C++, Java™) you'll find that arrays can only store one data type and that you can't change their size once they've been declared. For the programming language you're using, check if it uses arrays and look at what properties they have in that language.

Arrays

Now that you've covered one-dimensional arrays, the only way is up — that's right, two-dimensional arrays. Arrays can have even more dimensions, but luckily the examiners have decided that two is enough for now.

Two-Dimensional Arrays are like a List Of Lists

You can think of two-dimensional arrays as <u>one-dimensional arrays</u> where <u>each element</u> is also a <u>one-dimensional array</u>.

```
trees = [["oak", "ash"], ["beech", "cedar"], ["pine", "elm"]]
```

You can visualise arrays as tables or grids.

	0	1
0	oak	ash
1	beech	cedar
2	pine	elm

The <u>position</u> of an element is usually written as [a, b] or [a][b], where <u>a</u> represents the position of the one-dimensional list that the element is in and <u>b</u> represents its position within that one-dimensional list.

```
print("Ceara's favourite tree is" + trees[0, 0])
print("Shaun's favourite tree is" + trees[2, 1])
```
```
Ceara's favourite tree is oak
Shaun's favourite tree is elm
```

You can also <u>change elements</u> in exactly the same way as you saw for <u>one-dimensional arrays</u> (p.94).

EXAMPLE: The 'scores' array has been used to store four test scores for five pupils, as shown. E.g. scores[2, 0] will return the test 2 score for pupil 0, which is 5.

		Pupils				
		0	1	2	3	4
Tests	0	15	5	13	12	7
	1	2	14	11	14	9
	2	5	4	12	7	13
	3	6	8	18	19	15

a) **What will each of these return?**

(i) **scores[1, 3]**

The entry in row 1 and column 3 is 14.

(ii) **scores[3, 2] / scores[1, 0]**

scores[3, 2] = 18 and scores[1, 0] = 2 so scores[3, 2] / scores[1, 0] = 18/2 = 9

b) **Write an algorithm to count the total score of any given pupil.**

As there aren't very many scores you could just add them together. E.g. for pupil 0 you could do scores[0, 0] + scores[1, 0] + scores [2, 0] + scores [3, 0]. But it's <u>better practice</u> to use a <u>loop</u> as it is easier to edit.

```
total = 0
pupil = input("Enter the number of the pupil.")
for i = 0 to 3
    total = total + scores[i, pupil]
next i
print(total)
```

c) **The pass mark on every test was 9 or above. Write an algorithm to count the number of passes in the original array.**

The passtotal variable keeps track of <u>how many values</u> are passes.

The <u>i FOR loop</u> searches each row and the <u>j FOR loop</u> searches each column.

The IF statement checks if the value in position [i, j] is a pass and <u>adds 1</u> to passtotal if it is.

Finally <u>passtotal</u> is printed.

This is an example of a nested FOR loop.

```
passtotal = 0
for i = 0 to 3
    for j = 0 to 4
        if scores[i, j] >= 9 then
            passtotal = passtotal + 1
        endif
    next j
next i
print(str(passtotal) + " marks were passes.")
```

Two-dimensional arrays are really just an array of arrays...

Two-dimensional arrays can be used to store information about a digital image — each pixel's information can be stored as an element in the array. Programmers can then manipulate the image using array commands, e.g. changing the values of pixels, cutting rows and columns out of the image, etc.

File Handling

File handling is all about how a program can access data and change data stored in an external file.

Always start by **Opening** the **External File**

1) Before you can do anything with a file you need to underline it.
This is done by using an open command and assigning it to a variable.

This page will focus on how text is stored and accessed from ".txt" files. Other text files that are commonly used are ".csv" and ".dat".

This is the name of the file you want to open. Sometimes you'll have to give the whole file path.

```
file = open("file.txt")
```

Some programming languages have separate modes for reading and writing — so they require you to say which mode you are in.

2) You can also create a new text file using this command:
However, after you have created the file, you still need to open the file using the 'open()' command.

```
newFile("myfile.txt")
```

This creates a new text file called "myFile.txt".

Read or **Write** to a file after it is **Opened**

1) After you have opened a file you can read or write to it.

2) You can write lines of text to a file using writeLine().
writeLine() will always write to the end of the text file.

The writeLine command is called on the variable that stores the external file.

```
winners = open("victory.txt")
array names[4]
names = ["Jenny", "Carlos", "Matty", "Anna"]
for i = 0 to 3
    winners.writeLine(str(i) + " " + names[i])
next i
winners.close()
```

The text file will look like this.

```
0 Jenny
1 Carlos
2 Matty
3 Anna
```

The writeLine command will automatically write a new line to the end of the file.

3) You can read lines of text from a file using readLine(). The program will start reading from the beginning of the file and will keep its place in the file (think of it like a cursor).

Reads the first line of the text file as programs always start reading from the start of the file. After this command is called, the 'cursor' will be at the beginning of the second line.

```
winners = open("victory.txt")
firstLine = winners.readLine()
secondLine = winners.readLine()
winners.close()
```

Reads the second line of the file as that's where the program is up to. After this command is called, the 'cursor' will be at the beginning of the third line.

4) endOfFile() is another useful command that you'll have to know for your exams. It returns TRUE when the 'cursor' is at the end of the file. It's main use is to signify when a program should stop reading a file (like in this example).

```
array champions[]
n = 0
winners = open("victory.txt")
while NOT winners.endOfFile()
    champions[n] = winners.readLine()
    n = n + 1
endwhile
winners.close()
print(champions)
```

```
["0 Jenny", "1 Carlos", "2 Matty", "3 Anna"]
```

5) When you're finished reading or writing to a file you should always close it using the close() command. If you forget to close it then the file can remain locked and prevent others from editing it.

Learning to read and write, it's like being back at primary school...

Data is stored externally so that it's not lost when the program is closed. E.g. a computer game will save your progress externally — if it was saved internally you'd lose your progress when the game was closed.

Storing Data

Records aren't just those big black round things that look like burnt CDs, they're also a useful data structure...
*All of the code on this page is **pseudocode**, not OCR Exam Reference Language.*

Records can contain **Different Data Types**

1) A <u>record</u> is a type of data structure (like an array — see p.94), which means that it is used to store a collection of data values.

In the context of a database table, a record is just a row of data (see next page).

2) One of the things that makes records so useful is that, unlike arrays, they can store values with <u>different data types</u> (see p.76), such as strings, integers and Booleans.

3) Each item in a record is called a <u>field</u>, and each field is given a <u>data type</u> and a <u>field name</u> when the record is created. The field name can help to <u>describe</u> the data stored in that field of the record.

4) Records are <u>fixed in length</u>, which means that you <u>can't add extra fields</u> to them once they've been created.

Different programming languages have slight variations on record data structures. E.g. Python® has dictionaries, and C has structures.

Records can keep **Related Information** in one place

1) When you create a record structure, you can assign a <u>data type</u> and a <u>name</u> to each field:

Each field has its own data type.

```
record recipes
    int recipeNumber
    string recipeName
    bool tested
    int score
endrecord
```

The record is called 'recipes'.

'recipeNumber', 'recipeName', 'tested' and 'score' are the <u>fields</u> of the record.

2) Once you've created the structure of your record, you can <u>assign it</u> to variables:

'recipe1', 'recipe2' and 'recipe3' are all <u>variables</u> with the 'recipes' <u>record structure</u>.

```
recipe1 = recipes(1, "Chocolate Cake", True, 3)
recipe2 = recipes(2, "Lemon Slice", False, 0)
recipe3 = recipes(3, "Coconut Cookies", True, 8)
```

The data in each field needs to have the correct data type. E.g. the last one, 'score', should be an integer.

3) You can use the <u>variable name</u> to access a <u>whole record</u>. Alternatively, you can use the <u>variable name</u> along with a <u>field name</u> to access a <u>particular item</u> of a record.

```
print(recipe1)
print(recipe3.recipeName)
```
```
(1, "Chocolate Cake", True, 3)
Coconut Cookies
```

Individual items in a record can be accessed and changed.

```
recipe2.tested = True
recipe2.score = 6
print(recipe2.recipeName + " has a
       score of " + str(recipe2.score))
```
```
Lemon Slice has a score of 6
```

Arrays are handy if you want to **Group Records** together

If you have multiple variables with the <u>same record structure</u>, you can collect them in an array.

```
array recipeBook = [recipe1, recipe2, recipe3]
for i = 0 to 2
    if recipeBook[i].score >= 7 then
        print(recipeBook[i].recipeName)
    endif
next i
```
```
Coconut Cookies
```

This will print the names of all recipes with a score ≥ 7.

You can visualise the recipeBook array as a table:

	recipe Number	recipe Name	tested	score
0	1	Chocolate Cake	True	3
1	2	Lemon Slice	True	6
2	3	Coconut Cookies	True	8

Well, we got through all that in record time...
You might see records presented differently to this, but the key concepts will be the same.
You'll still need to understand what records and fields are, and how they are used in programming.

Searching Data

Structured Query Language (SQL) can be used to search tables (usually in a database) for specific data. When we talk about the records and fields of a database table we just mean the rows and columns.

SELECT and FROM are the most important keywords

In SQL, the <u>SELECT</u> keyword is followed by the names of the <u>fields</u> (columns) you to want to <u>retrieve</u> and <u>display</u>. Then the <u>FROM</u> keyword is followed by the name of the <u>table</u> (or <u>tables</u>) you want to search.

Table: hotels

ID	hotelName	hotelRating	rooms	bathroom	priceInPounds
1	Water Lodge	2.3	50	En-suite	42
2	Fire Inn	4.2	64	Shared	42
3	Earthen House	4.4	215	En-suite	39
4	Windy Hotel	3.5	150	Shared	57
5	River Hotel	3.8	180	Shared	46

```
SELECT hotelName
FROM hotels
```
This returns hotelName for all the records in the table hotels.

```
SELECT hotelName, hotelRating
FROM hotels
```
This returns hotelName and hotelRating for all the records in the table hotels.

```
SELECT *
FROM hotels
```
If you want to return all the fields, you can use * as a wildcard.

You can use WHERE to filter the results

1) The <u>WHERE</u> statement is used to specify <u>conditions</u> that a record must satisfy before it is returned.

```
SELECT * FROM hotels WHERE hotelRating >= 4.1
```
This condition looks for records with a hotelRating greater than or equal to 4.1.

* is the wildcard character and will return all the fields.

Look in the table hotels.

ID	hotelName	hotelRating	rooms	bathroom	priceInPounds
2	Fire Inn	4.2	64	Shared	42
3	Earthen House	4.4	215	En-suite	39

2) The boolean operators <u>AND</u> and <u>OR</u> can be used with <u>WHERE</u> to make more <u>specific searches</u>.

```
SELECT hotelName FROM hotels WHERE bathroom = "En-suite" AND priceInPounds < 45
```

Will only select the hotelName.

Look in the table hotels.

This condition uses a Boolean operator to check if a hotel room has an en-suite bathroom AND is less than £45.

hotelName
Water Lodge
Earthen House

EXAMPLE:

1. Stacey is searching for a hotel that has more than 100 rooms. Write a search query for Stacey that returns the name and the number of rooms of the hotels that match her requirements.

Read the question carefully to decide which fields need to be returned.

```
SELECT hotelName, rooms FROM hotels WHERE rooms > 100
```

This condition finds hotels with more than 100 rooms.

hotelName	rooms
Earthen House	215
Windy Hotel	150
River Hotel	180

2. Stacey decides that the hotel needs to have a rating of 4.0 or above, as well as having 100 rooms. Write a search query for Stacey that returns the name and price of the hotels that match her requirements.

```
SELECT hotelName, priceInPounds FROM hotels
WHERE rooms > 100 AND hotelRating >= 4.0
```

hotelName	priceInPounds
Earthen House	39

This condition finds hotels with more than 100 rooms AND a rating of 4.0 or above.

There is only one hotel that satisfies her conditions, so only one hotel is returned.

Tables of data can be searched using SQL...

EXAM TIP

In the exam you'll only have to know how to use the SELECT, FROM and WHERE keywords. Fortunately the commands and syntax in SQL are relatively easy, so you'll pick it up in no time.

Sub Programs

Sub programs can be used to save time and to simplify code. By now you'll definitely have come across procedures and functions even if you don't know what they are yet — all is explained on the next two pages.

Procedures and Functions help to avoid Repeating Code

1) <u>Procedures</u> are <u>sets of instructions</u> stored under <u>one name</u> — when you want your program to do the whole set of instructions you only need to <u>call the name</u> of the procedure.

2) <u>Functions</u> are similar to procedures — the main difference is that functions always <u>return a value</u>.

3) Procedures and functions are very useful when you have sets of instructions that you need to <u>repeat</u> in different places within a program. They give your program more <u>structure</u> and <u>readability</u> whilst cutting down on the <u>amount of code</u> you actually need to write.

4) High-level programming languages (see p.112) have <u>common</u> procedures and functions <u>built into them</u>. If you want one that does something <u>more specific</u> you can <u>create them</u> yourself.

5) In most sub programs you'll encounter <u>parameters</u> and <u>arguments</u> so it's important that you know what they are and the <u>difference</u> between them:

> • <u>Parameters</u> are special variables used to pass values into a sub program. For each parameter you can specify a <u>name</u>, a <u>data type</u> and a <u>default value</u>.
> • <u>Arguments</u> are the <u>actual values</u> that the <u>parameters</u> take when the sub program is called.

Procedures carry out a Set Of Instructions

1) Procedures don't have to take <u>parameters</u>...   ...but they <u>sometimes will</u>.   *'name' is a parameter.*

```
procedure welcome()
    print("Hello and welcome.")
    print("Let's learn about procedures.")
endprocedure
```

```
procedure betterWelcome(name)
    print("Hello " + name + " and welcome.")
    print("Let's learn about procedures.")
endprocedure
```

2) Procedures are called by <u>typing their name</u> (and giving an <u>argument</u> if necessary).

```
welcome()
```
```
Hello and welcome.
Let's learn about procedures.
```

```
betterWelcome("Pablo")
```
```
Hello Pablo and welcome.
Let's learn about procedures.
```
The betterWelcome procedure requires one argument.

3) Note that procedures <u>don't</u> return a value.

Functions will always Return a Value

1) Functions take <u>at least one parameter</u> and they must always <u>return a value</u>.

2) When a function is called it should be <u>assigned</u> to a <u>variable</u> or used in a <u>statement</u> otherwise the value that it returns will not be stored anywhere and will be lost.

 **Write a function to join two strings together with a space between them and show it working on the strings "computer" and "science".**

See p.80 for a reminder on string manipulation.

A function should always return a value.

The result is stored as the variable 'subject'.

```
function joinStrings(x, y)
    return x + " " + y
endfunction
subject = joinStrings("computer", "science")
print(subject)
```
```
computer science
```
x and y are parameters.

"computer" and "science" are the arguments.

Functions will always return a value, procedures will not...

Even though they're similar, it's important that you don't get mixed up between functions and procedures.

Sub Programs

Make sure that you know your procedures from your functions and your parameters from your arguments.

Sub Programs can contain anything covered in this Section

 **EXAMPLE:** Orla has been given a maths problem to add together all of the numbers between two integers (including the integers themselves) and work out if the total is divisible by 7. Write a sub program that Orla could use to solve the maths problem for any pair of integers.

The sub program is a function as it returns a value. ⟶

x and y are the parameters of the function. ⟵

The variable 'total' is defined inside the function so it's a local variable (see below).

The FOR loop is used to add up all the integers from x to y.

The IF statement checks if the total is divisible by 7. Remember MOD will give the remainder of a division (p.77).

The variable 'divisible' is set to True or False depending on the outcome of the IF statement.

```
function addIntegers(x, y)
    total = 0
    for i = x to y
        total = total + i
    next i
    if total MOD 7 == 0 then
        divisible = True
    else
        divisible = False
    endif
    return divisible
endfunction
```

Variables can be Local or Global

1) All variables have a <u>scope</u> (either local or global) — the scope of a variable tells you <u>which parts</u> of the program the variable can be used in.

All parameters have local scope to the sub program.

> <u>Local variables</u> can only be used <u>within the structure</u> they're declared in — they have a <u>local scope</u>.
> <u>Global variables</u> can be used <u>any time</u> after their declaration — they have a <u>global scope</u>.

2) Variables declared inside a <u>sub program</u> are <u>local variables</u>. They are <u>invisible</u> to the rest of the program — this means that they can't be used <u>outside</u> the function.

3) The <u>advantage</u> of local variables is that their scope only extends to the sub program they're declared in. They <u>can't affect</u> and are <u>not affected</u> by anything outside of the sub program. It also doesn't matter if you use the <u>same variable name</u> as a local variable defined elsewhere in the program.

4) Variables in the <u>main body</u> of a program can be made into global variables using the 'global' keyword — these variables can then be used anywhere in the program. It can be difficult to keep track of the <u>value</u> of global variables in <u>larger programs</u>.

5) The example below shows how <u>global variables</u> are used to store data outside of the sub program.

x and y are defined <u>globally</u> — if they were declared inside the sub program then they'd <u>reset to 0</u> each time the sub program was called.

The sub program is a <u>procedure</u> as it <u>doesn't</u> return a value.

The <u>parameters</u> a and b are added to the <u>global variables</u> x and y.

The program <u>keeps track</u> of the position after the first move and then applies the second move from that position.

a and b are parameters so they have <u>local scope</u> to this procedure — they're <u>invisible</u> elsewhere in the program.

```
// A sub program to keep track of a character's x and y position.
global x = 0
global y = 0
procedure move(a, b)
    x = x + a
    y = y + b
    print("You're in square (" + str(x) + ", " + str(y) + ").")
endprocedure
move(3, 5)
move(4, 7)
```

```
You're in square (3, 5).
You're in square (7, 12).
```

It's considered good practice to use local variables wherever possible...

You should be able to identify the local and global variables in a program and use them in your own programs.

Warm-Up and Worked Exam Questions

That's all the learning done for the programming section — perfect time for some practice. Here are some warm-up questions to get you started, followed by a whole bunch of exam questions on the next two pages.

Warm-Up Questions

1) Explain what the following commands will do with the array `footballers`.
   a) `player = footballers[3]`
   b) `footballers[5] = "Pele"`

2) Write some program code that will:
   a) Open a file.
   b) Create a new file.
   c) Close a file.
   d) Read a line of text from a file.

3) Give two reasons why a programmer may choose to use a record to store data.

4) Explain what each of these SQL keywords should be immediately followed by:
   a) SELECT
   b) FROM
   c) WHERE

5) Give three benefits of using sub programs when you are writing code.

Worked Exam Question

1 Frances has written a list of jobs she has to do and stored it in the ToDoList.txt file shown on the right.

> 1. Clean my room.
> 2. Computer Science homework.
> 3. Organise my stamp collection.

a) Describe what each line of the code below does.

open(), readLine() and close() are three commands you'll need to be familiar with for your exams.

```
01  myList = open("ToDoList.txt")
02  print(myList.readLine())
03  myList.close()
```

Line 01 ....Opens the file and stores it under the variable myList.........................

Line 02 ....Prints the first line of the file, i.e. "1. Clean my room."......................

Line 03 ....Closes the file..

[3 marks]

Frances writes the following code to replace the first job on her list.

```
myList = open("ToDoList.txt")
myList.writeLine("1. Make lunch for parents.")
myList.close()
```

You'll also need to know what the writeLine() command does.

b) Explain why the code Frances has written will not work as intended.

....The writeLine command will start writing from the end of the file, so this text will be........

....added to the end of the file instead of overwriting the first line as Frances intended.........

[2 marks]

Exam Questions

2 Write a function that takes an integer as a parameter and returns the difference between the integer's cube and its square.

[3 marks]

3 A 2D array is used to store the names of the top 3 pupils in each event of a sports day.

a) What data type should each element of the array be assigned?

....

[1 mark]

b) Give **three** reasons for using a 2D array to store this data.

1. ....

2. ....

3. ....

[3 marks]

4 The cars table below shows some data on the used cars that a car dealership has in stock.

CarID	Registration	Make	Type	Price	EngineSize
1	NF09 APY	Stanton	Hatchback	2500	1.4
2	SZ15 LUY	Fenwick	Saloon	4800	1.8
3	FQ55 ALW	Stanton	Hatchback	1700	2.1
4	SQ57 TTW	Fenwick	Estate	2300	2.8
5	NZ12 MBE	Stanton	Saloon	5200	1.8

a) How many records does this table have?

....

[1 mark]

b) Explain the difference between a record and a field.

....

....

....

[2 marks]

c) Draw a table showing what would be returned by the following SQL command:
`SELECT Make, Type FROM cars WHERE EngineSize = 1.8`

[2 marks]

Exam Questions

5 John and three of his friends are training to run a marathon. John records how many miles he and three friends ran each day last week. John stores the data in a 2D array called `distanceRun`.

		Days of the week						
		0	**1**	**2**	**3**	**4**	**5**	**6**
Runner	**0**	9	10	8	12	0	6	9
	1	10	12	15	15	0	0	10
	2	15	14	13	16	0	8	9
	3	6	8	9	10	12	12	0

The distance run on day 0 by runner 2 is given by `distanceRun[0, 2]`.

a) Write the code to display the distance run on day 4 by runner 3.

....

[1 mark]

b) Write an algorithm that takes a runner number as an input and outputs the total number of miles that they ran over the week.

[4 marks]

c) John has written the function `milesConvert()` which takes a distance in miles and returns the equivalent distance in km. E.g. `milesConvert(5)` would return 8. Write an algorithm to convert all distances in the array to km.

[3 marks]

6 Omar has written an adventure story in the file adventure.txt.
Write some program code that allows a user to print Omar's adventure story one line at a time.
- Each time the user presses the "y" key the next line of the story should be printed.
- The program should end when it's at the end of the text file.

   You'll need to use the endOfFile() command. *[5 marks]*

7 Noel has written the function `rollTwo(n)`, which simulates the outcome of two random rolls of an n-sided dice, returning the results as an array. E.g. `rollTwo(6)` might return `[5, 3]`.

a) Noel has declared a local variable inside the function.
Explain **two** reasons why it is good practice to use local variables.

1. ....

....

2. ....

....

[4 marks]

b) Noel wants to use his function in a dice game where two identical dice are rolled together.
- The player can choose the number of sides that the dice have.
- The player's score is the number of rolls it takes until both dice land on the same number.

Write a sub program that takes the number of sides of the dice as a parameter, uses the `rollTwo` function to simulate a game, and returns a player's score.

[5 marks]

Revision Questions for Section Six

Well, that just about wraps up the programming section, perfect time to try some revision questions I think.

- Try these questions and tick off each one when you get it right.
- When you've done all the questions for a topic and are completely happy with it, tick off the topic.

Data Types, Operators, Constants, Variables and Strings (p.76-80) ☑

1) Define the following data types: integer, real, boolean, character and string. ☑

2) a) What does casting mean?
   b) Explain what each of these functions do:
      (i) int()   (ii) real()   (iii) str()   (iv) ASC()   (v) CHR() ☑

3) What do each of these operators mean?
   a) ==   b) !=   c) <=   d) =   e) ^ ☑

4) What is meant by: a) a constant?   b) a variable? ☑

5) a) Define string concatenation and give an example of it being used.
   b) Explain what the following string manipulation methods do:
      (i) x.upper   (ii) x.length   (iii) x.left(i)   (iv) x.subString(a, b) ☑

Program Flow, Boolean Logic and Random Numbers (p.83-91) ☑

6) In 20 words or less, outline what each of these statements does:
   a) IF statement   b) SWITCH statement. ☑

7) What is the main difference between IF-ELSEIF statements and nested IF statements? ☑

8) Compare the features of the two condition-controlled loops, DO UNTIL and WHILE. ☑

9) For each of the three main logic gates: a) Draw its symbol.   b) Draw its truth table. ☑

10)* Write an algorithm that outputs the number of Mondays in a 30-day month
     when the user inputs the day of the week that the month started on. ☑

11)* Write an algorithm to simulate 100 rolls of an 8-sided dice and print the result of each roll. ☑

Arrays (p.94-95) ☑

12) Why are arrays useful? ☑

13)* Write commands to perform the following operations on this array. The name of the array is 'chars'.
    ["3", "T", "P", "2", "M", "e", "4", "q", "s", "3"].
    a) Print the character "M".
    b) Replace every element in the chars array with an "N". ☑

14)* Write an algorithm to create a two-dimensional array with 10 rows and 10 columns where each
     element is an integer and its value is given by the row number multiplied by the column number.
     (Hint: Remember that rows and columns are numbered starting at 0.) ☑

File Handling, Storing Data and Searching Data (p.96-98) ☑

15) Briefly describe what each of the following functions do:
    a) open()   b) newFile()   c) endOfFile()   d) writeLine()   e) readLine() ☑

16) In programming, data can be stored in records:
    a) What is a record?   b) Give two differences between a record and an array. ☑

17)* Outline what this SQL query will do: `SELECT * FROM worldRecords WHERE sport = "athletics"` ☑

Sub Programs (p.99-100) ☑

18) What is the difference between a function and a procedure? ☑

19) Define these terms:
    a) parameter   b) argument   c) local variable   d) global variable ☑

*Answers on p.146

Structured Programming

On p.99-100 you saw how sub programs could be used to store a whole set of instructions under one name. Well, a single program will typically use lots of sub programs that each perform specific and simple tasks.

Structure Diagrams make Creating Programs Easier

1) <u>Structure</u> (or modular) diagrams show the smaller tasks of a larger program.

2) They are made by <u>decomposing</u> (see p.64) the program that you want to write into <u>manageable modules</u>. Each of those <u>modules</u> is then decomposed even further into <u>smaller modules</u> and eventually into modules that perform <u>individual tasks</u>.

You may see program modules referred to as the <u>subsections</u> of a program.

3) Simple <u>sub programs</u> can be written to carry out each individual task. Then the <u>bigger modules</u> and <u>main program</u> can be written using these <u>sub programs</u>.

4) For example, to design a program simulating a game of noughts and crosses you might have:

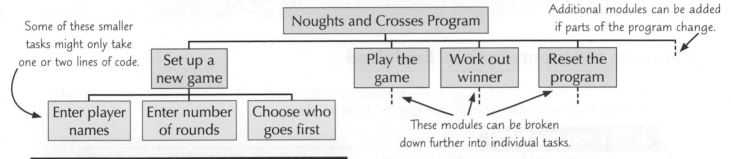

Some of these smaller tasks might only take one or two lines of code.

Additional modules can be added if parts of the program change.

These modules can be broken down further into individual tasks.

Advantages of using Structure Diagrams

- Coding is <u>easier</u> because you're only writing code to carry out very <u>simple tasks</u>.
- Lots of programmers can work on one program as each module can be written <u>independently</u>.
- It's <u>easier to test</u> structured programs as each module can be <u>tested individually</u> (see p.107).
- Individual sub programs and modules can be <u>fixed</u> and <u>updated without affecting</u> the rest of the program.
- You will be able to <u>reuse</u> the sub programs and modules in programs you write <u>in the future</u>.

Your program should be Easy To Maintain

1) When using structured programming, it's important that your code is <u>well-maintained</u>.

2) A well-maintained program makes it <u>easy</u> for other programmers to understand what the code does. They should also be able to <u>change</u> parts of the source code without the risk of causing problems elsewhere in the code (e.g. knock on effects).

3) The following features can <u>improve</u> the maintainability of source code:

- <u>Comments</u> (usually written after // or #) are useful for <u>explaining</u> what the <u>key features</u> of a program do — <u>well written</u> and <u>clear</u> comments are fundamental for helping other programmers <u>understand your programs</u>.

  Too many comments can leave your programs looking cluttered and unreadable.

- <u>Indentation</u> can be used to separate <u>different statements</u> in a program. This allows other programmers to see the flow of the program more <u>clearly</u> and pick out the <u>different features</u>.

- <u>Variables</u>, <u>sub programs</u> and <u>parameters</u> should be named so that they refer to what they actually are. This helps programmers to understand what they do, and makes it easier to keep track of them. It's also important that they follow the <u>standard naming conventions</u> (see page 79).

- Using <u>sub programs</u> can make it easier for other programmers to see how <u>different parts</u> of a program <u>work</u>, which can help them understand the <u>overall program faster</u>.

Keep your revision notes well-maintained, too...

Keeping code well-maintained isn't rocket science but sometimes programmers can get lazy and their code ends up in a bit of a mess. Have a look back at some code you've written. Write down some ways that you could have improved the maintainability of your code.

Defensive Design

On p.45 you saw that insecure databases can be a security threat — unfortunately, every program that interacts with a user can be a risk. To keep programs safe from tampering you need to use defensive design.

Defensive Design helps to ensure programs Function Properly

1) When programs are functioning correctly they should never break or produce errors. In practice this is difficult to achieve — even big software companies need to update and patch their programs regularly.

2) Programmers try to protect their programs through defensive design. They will try to:

- Anticipate how users might misuse their program, then attempt to prevent it from happening.
- Ensure their code is well-maintained (see p.105).
- Reduce the number of errors in the code through testing (see p.107-108).

Misuse refers to the user doing things that you don't expect them to.

Make sure the Inputs can't be Exploited

1) The easiest way for a user to accidentally or intentionally misuse a program is when entering data. You can try to prevent this from happening by using validation.

INPUT VALIDATION

Checking if data meets certain criteria before passing it into the program. E.g. checking that an email address contains an @ symbol and has a suitable ending (.com, .co.uk, etc).

2) Here are a few types of input validation check you can use:

3) Programs can use a mixture of input validation checks to verify that the inputted data has an acceptable format before passing it into the program.

Range check	Checks the data is within a specified range.
Presence check	Checks the data has actually been entered.
Format check	Checks the data has the correct format (e.g. a date).
Look-up table	Checks the data against a table of acceptable values.
Length check	Checks the data is the correct length.

Authentication can help Protect your programs

1) Authentication can confirm the identity of a user before they're allowed to access certain pieces of data or features of the program. A common way that programs do this is using passwords.

2) Passwords are usually associated with a username. When someone tries to access a protected part of the program, it should ask them for their password to check that they are who they claim to be.

3) Here are some common ways to increase the security of a password-based authentication system:

- Force users to use strong passwords (see p.46) and get them to change their passwords regularly.
- Limit the number of failed authentication attempts before access to an account is lost.
- Ask for a random selection of characters from the password on each authentication.

4) It's important that programmers get the level of authentication correct — too much authentication can affect a program's functionality and put people off using it.

Authentic revision materials, available to all users of this book...

When you write programs, you should ensure the data is valid. However, too many restrictions can make your program hard to use. When validation and authentication start to affect the functionality of the program or impact the user's experience then you know you've gone too far with your defensive design.

Testing

When you're writing programs, remember that the testing is just as important as the programming itself.
Have a look at these pages to test your knowledge of testing — they'll prepare you for being tested in the tests.

Programming Errors can be **Syntax Errors** and **Logic Errors**

1) It's quite typical for a program to contain <u>errors</u> during its development
— these errors need to be <u>found</u> and <u>corrected</u> as soon as possible.

2) The first task is to figure out what <u>type of error</u> has occurred:

> SYNTAX ERRORS — when the compiler or interpreter <u>doesn't understand</u> something
> you've typed because it doesn't follow the <u>rules</u> or <u>grammar</u> of the programming language.
>
> LOGIC ERRORS — when the compiler or interpreter is able to <u>run the program</u>,
> but the program does something <u>unexpected</u>.

3) <u>Syntax errors</u> can be <u>diagnosed</u> by compilers and interpreters (see p.112) — they'll be unable to
turn the <u>source code</u> into <u>machine code</u> and a syntax error (with its location) will be returned.

4) <u>Logic errors</u> are more <u>difficult to diagnose</u> and <u>track down</u> — compilers and interpreters
<u>won't</u> pick them up. Logic errors are found through general use of the program
and by systematically <u>testing</u> it using a <u>test plan</u> (see p.108).

5) Once you have <u>identified</u> the errors in a program, you can then <u>refine</u> your code to <u>fix them</u>.

Jerry has written the following function. It multiplies a given positive integer by all the positive integers less than it (e.g. if the integer was 5 it should do 1 × 2 × 3 × 4 × 5). Identify two logic errors in Jerry's function and suggest how he should fix them.

Error 1: In line 3 the count variable is declared (and set to 1)
<u>within the loop</u>, so each time the loop repeats,
the count value will be set back to 1. The declaration
of the count variable should be moved <u>before the loop</u>.

Error 2: In line 4 the count variable is multiplied by n,
whereas it should be multiplied by i.
It should read count = count * i.

```
function multiplier(n)
    for i = 1 to n
        count = 1
        count = count * n
    next i
    return count
endfunction
```

Shreena is designing a program that she can use to create a database of file names. She has written the following function to check an inputted file name.

a) **Explain what the function nameCheck() does.**

It checks if the file name has any
exclamation marks and returns "Rejected"
if it does or "Accepted" if it does not.

b) **Identify one syntax error in her
function and explain how to fix it.**

There is no 'endwhile' command to end
the WHILE loop. This should be added
before the 'return' statement (and indented in
line with the start of the while loop).

```
function nameCheck(file)
    x = 0
    status = "Accepted"
    while x < file.length
        if file.subString(x, 1) == "!" then
            status = "Rejected"
        endif
        x = x + 1
    return status
endfunction
```

This is an example of input validation.

There are more testing times ahead...

Syntax errors are usually easy to fix as the compiler should point you to the exact line that contains the error.
On the other hand, it's often difficult for computers to help you out with logic errors — as far as they're
concerned, if the program is running, everything is hunky-dory and working as it should.

Testing

So now that you know why programs are tested and what you're actually looking for, it's time to have a closer look at how they're tested. Often testing is planned out before development is even begun.

Testing can happen at **Different Points** in **Development**

1) There are <u>two main types</u> of testing:

> • <u>Iterative testing</u> — the program is tested <u>while it is being developed</u>. Often a programmer will test a <u>module</u> (see p.105), <u>fix any errors</u> they find and then <u>test it again</u>. They will repeat the process until the module is <u>working correctly</u>.
>
> • <u>Final (terminal) testing</u> — the program is tested at the <u>end</u> of the development process. The <u>whole program</u> is tested at the same time to check that it's working correctly.

2) Iterative testing is used to identify and <u>fix</u> small errors, which will help <u>prevent</u> larger (and more difficult to fix) errors from occurring <u>later on</u> in the development process.

3) Final testing is also important as modules may work perfectly <u>on their own</u>, but errors may occur when the modules <u>interact</u> with each other in the program.

4) Using a <u>combination</u> of iterative testing and final testing is a good way to help <u>minimise</u> the total number of <u>errors or bugs</u> that a program has when it is released.

A **Test Plan** should be made **Before Implementation**

1) A <u>test plan</u> will outline exactly what you're going to test and how you're going to test it. It should cover all the <u>possible paths</u> through a program.

2) A <u>good test plan</u> will anticipate all of the potential issues with the program and select appropriate <u>test data</u> to test for these issues.

Possible paths are all the branches of the flowchart (p.66) for your program.

3) The <u>test data</u> that you use in your test plan should fall into one of four categories:

> • <u>Normal data</u> — things that a user is <u>likely</u> to input into the program.
> • <u>Boundary (extreme) data</u> — values at the <u>limit</u> of what the program should be able to handle.
> • <u>Invalid data</u> — inputs with a <u>correct data type</u> that should be <u>rejected</u> by the program.
> • <u>Erroneous data</u> — inputs with an <u>incorrect data type</u> that should be <u>rejected</u> by the program.

4) The table below shows an example of a test plan for setting an alarm system. Users should be able to set their own 3-5 digit alarm code.

Type of data	Test data	Reason for testing	Expected outcome
Normal	2476	To see how the alarm copes with normal usage.	Code accepted.
Normal	No input	To see if the alarm prompts an input.	Prompt to enter a code.
Boundary	000	To see if the smallest code is accepted.	Code accepted.
Boundary	99999	To see if the largest code is accepted.	Code accepted.
Invalid	12	To see if the alarm accepts inputs shorter than 3 digits.	Error: The code is too short.
Invalid	632191	To see if the alarm accepts inputs longer than 5 digits.	Error: The code is too long.
Erroneous	23aY	To see if the system accepts non-digits.	Error: The code contains non-numeric data.

5) During testing the tester can add "<u>actual outcome</u>" and "<u>pass or fail</u>" columns to the table.

Luckily for you, this page flew through its testing stage...

In the exam, you'll need to be able to design suitable testing procedures for a given scenario. This could include coming up with your own test plan and test data.

Warm-Up and Worked Exam Questions

I've designed some questions to test your knowledge about design and testing — I know, aren't I nice?
Try the warm-ups first, then if you're feeling confident, move on to the exam questions on the next page.

Warm-Up Questions

1) Suggest why a programmer may use a structure diagram when planning a program.
2) Give four features that will improve the maintainability of code.
3) Name the type of input validation check that:
   a) checks that data has been entered.   b) checks data against a table of possible values.
4) Are the following statements true or false?
   a) Syntax errors are harder to find than logic errors.
   b) Using the wrong boolean operator is a logic error.
   c) Syntax errors will prevent code from running.
   d) Logic errors will prevent code from running.
5) Describe what is meant by 'iterative testing'.

Worked Exam Questions

1 A retailer keeps a database of its loyalty card holders.
The retailer stores the following data for each card
holder: name, age, postcode and customer number.

Name	Age	Postcode	Customer No.
Carol Foreman	20	NE85 3TW	100278
Peter Taylor	55	HA55 8PZ	223327

a) Define the term input validation.

Checking data meets certain criteria before passing it through a program.

[1 mark]

b) Describe **two** suitable types of validation for an entry in the postcode field.

1. Length check to make sure the input has a valid number of characters.

2. Format check to make sure the input contains only letters and numbers.

A format check could also do things like check that the postcode ends with a number and two letters.   *[2 marks]*

2 A holiday company has written a simple program to calculate the price of its group holiday
packages. The program asks the user to input the group size — if the group size is smaller
than two or greater than 10 the program displays an error message. If not, the price (in £s)
is calculated by multiplying the group size by 50 and then adding 10.

Complete the test plan below by filling in the missing spaces.

Test Data	Expected Outcome	Reasons for test
groupSize = 4	210	Check program with data user is likely to input.
groupSize = 10	510	Check program works with values on the limit.
groupSize = 12	Display an error message	Check what happens if input too large.

Work backwards from the outcome by subtracting 10, then dividing by 50

This is an example of invalid data.

[5 marks]

Exam Questions

3 Malcolm is leading a team who are designing a program to manage a movie streaming service.
He has decomposed the program into modules, as shown on the structure diagram below.

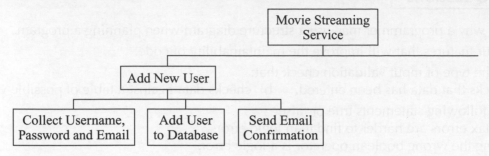

a) Add a module named 'Add New Film' to the structure diagram above.
Include **two** examples of smaller tasks within this module.

[3 marks]

b) The team decompose the program into modules to improve its maintainability.
Explain **two** other ways that the team could improve the maintainability of the program.

1. ....

....

2. ....

....

[4 marks]

4 Tiffany writes some code to check if an entered pincode is between 4 and 6 characters long.

```
pincode = input("Enter pincode")
if pincode.length >= 4 OR pincode.length <= 6 then
    print("Valid pincode"
else
    print("Not a valid pincode, please try again")
endif
```

a) Identify the syntax error in Tiffany's code and suggest how she could correct it.

Error: ....

Correction: ....

[2 marks]

b) Identify the logic error in Tiffany's code and suggest how she could correct it.

Error: ....

Correction: ....

[2 marks]

5 A website's payment form requires users to input their credit card
details, e.g. name, card number, expiration date, security code, etc.
Evaluate the benefits and limitations of using input validation to check the details.

[6 marks]

Think about problems that input validation can prevent, and those it can't.

Trace Tables

Trace tables are really useful when you're learning the fundamentals of programming.
They help you to follow a piece of code in a systematic way to see if it's doing what you expect.

Trace Tables help you to find **Logic Errors**

1) Trace tables give a simple way of testing that a piece of code is working correctly.
   They keep track of the values that certain variables take as you go through the code.

2) Their main use is to 'dry run' a sub program or algorithm to make sure there are no logic errors.

3) The columns of a trace table usually represent variables. Each row of a trace table
   represents the values that the variables take at a particular point in the algorithm.

 **EXAMPLE:**

The function on the right is used to add up all of the odd numbers up to the given number.

Complete the trace table below when the function call `sumOfOdd(5)` **is made.**

```
function sumOfOdd(num)
    total = 0
    for count = 1 to num
        if count MOD 2 == 1 then
            total = total + count
        endif
    next count
    return total
endfunction
```

Each variable that you're interested in (including parameters) should have its own column.

The initial values of the variables before you get to the FOR loop are in the first row.

num	count	total
5	—	0
5	1	1
5	2	1
5	3	4
5	4	4
5	5	9

As the count increases, values are added to the total if they are odd.

The last value of 'total' is returned — so the sum of the odd numbers up to five is 9.

If the value of variables don't change you don't need to keep writing them out — so you could have just written the values in red.

4) The columns of a trace table might not always be variables — they could be any information
   that the programmer is interested in. For example, they might have a column for the length
   of an array or for the output of the algorithm.

5) When testing a larger program, the tester will often use debugging tools — for example, breakpoints
   are used to stop the program at certain places so that you can look at the values of variables.

Use **Trace Tables** to help **Understand Programs**

Trace tables can also be used to help you figure out what a piece of code is actually doing.

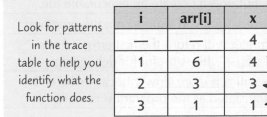 **EXAMPLE:**

The function `test` **takes an array with 4 elements as a parameter. The trace table shown below is for the function** `test([4,6,3,1])`. **Explain the purpose of the function** `test`.

Look for patterns in the trace table to help you identify what the function does.

i	arr[i]	x
—	—	4
1	6	4
2	3	3
3	1	1

x *doesn't change* when the value of arr[i] is larger than x.

The value of x only decreases.

```
function test(arr)
    x = arr[0]
    for i = 1 to 3
        if arr[i] < x then
            x = arr[i]
        endif
    next i
    return x
endfunction
```

The function returns the minimum value in the array.

 EXAM TIP

Trace tables can help you understand a program or algorithm...

If trace tables crop up in your exam, you might not be told the purpose of the algorithm you're tracing — don't worry, just work your way through the algorithm step-by-step.

Translators

For computers to process any computer language it needs to be translated into machine code.

Computer Languages can be **High-Level** or **Low-Level**

1) Most of the programming languages that you'll be familiar with (e.g. *Python*®, C++) are high-level languages. The source code is easy for humans to write, but computers need to translate it into machine code before they can read and run it.

2) On the other hand, low-level languages are tricky for humans to read and write but are easier for a computer to run. They consist of machine code and assembly languages:

`000000 00010 00011 00100 00000 100000` ⟵ Binary machine code is very tricky for humans to understand.

`ADD r4, r2, r3` ⟵ Assembly code is more readable for humans and easier to remember — the first bit (ADD) is the operation code and the rest tells you what to perform that operation on.

3) High-level languages are popular with programmers, but low-level languages have their uses too:

High-Level Languages	Low-Level Languages
• One instruction of high-level code represents many instructions of machine code.	• One instruction of assembly code usually only represents one instruction of machine code.
• The same code will work for many different machines and processors.	• Usually written for one type of machine or processor and won't work on any others.
• The programmer can easily store data in lots of different structures (e.g. lists and arrays) without knowing about the memory structure.	• The programmer needs to know about the internal structure of the CPU (see p.2-3) and how it manages the memory.
• Code is easy to read, understand and modify.	• Code is very difficult to read, understand and modify.
• Must be translated into machine code before a computer is able to understand it.	• Commands in machine code can be executed directly without the need for a translator.
• You don't have much control over what the CPU actually does so programs will be less memory efficient and slower.	• You control exactly what the CPU does and how it uses memory so programs will be more memory efficient and faster.

Translators convert programming languages into **Machine Code**

1) Computers only understand instructions given to them as machine code, so high level languages need to be translated before a computer is able to execute the instructions.

2) There are two types of translator that you need to know about: compilers and interpreters.

3) Compilers and interpreters are both used to turn high-level code into machine code.

Compiler	Interpreter
Translates all of the source code at the same time and creates one executable file.	Translates and runs the source code one instruction at a time, but doesn't create an executable file.
Only needed once to create the executable file.	Needed every time you want to run the program.
Returns a list of errors for the entire program once compiling is complete.	The interpreter will return the first error it finds and then stop — this is useful for debugging.
Once compiled the program runs quickly, but compiling can take a long time.	Programs will run more slowly because the code is being translated as the program is running.

4) The type of translator used will depend on which programming language and IDE (p.113) you're using.

5) If the program is stored over multiple source code files then a linker is used to join all of the separate compiled codes into one executable program.

"Cette page est incroyable!" — call in the translators...

You should know the key features of low-level languages, high-level languages, compilers and interpreters.

Integrated Development Environments

Integrated development environments (IDEs) provide programmers with lots of handy tools when they're coding. If there's one thing I know about programmers, it's that they'll do anything to make life a bit easier.

IDEs have lots of Features to help Programmers

An <u>integrated development environment</u> is a piece of software that provides features to help a programmer to develop their program. Most IDEs will have <u>similar features</u> — the example below shows some of the features from the Microsoft® Visual Studio® IDE:

The <u>code editor</u> is the <u>main part</u> of an IDE, it's where the code is written. Most code editors will have <u>line numbering</u> and <u>auto-colour coding</u> for things like strings, functions, variables and comments. Good code editors will also have other automatic features like <u>auto-correct</u>, <u>auto-indentation</u> and <u>auto-complete</u>.

A <u>run-time environment</u> allows the code to be run quickly <u>within the IDE</u> — this is done using a <u>start</u> or <u>run button</u>. The run-time environment can also help to identify logic errors in the program as the programmer can see which part of the code is running when errors occur.

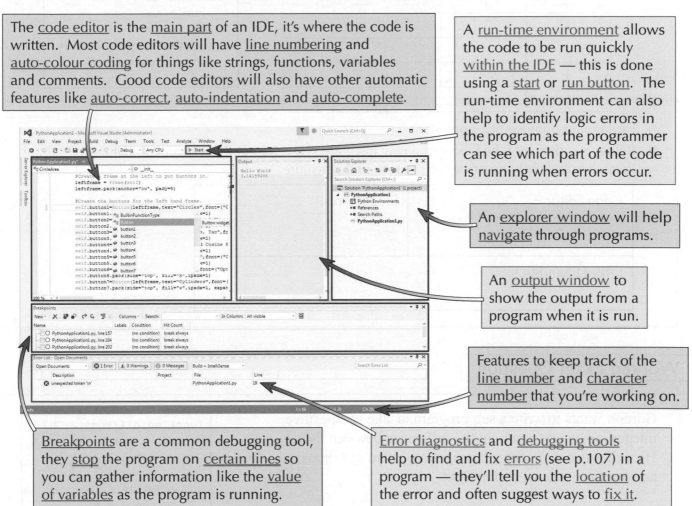

An <u>explorer window</u> will help <u>navigate</u> through programs.

An <u>output window</u> to show the output from a program when it is run.

Features to keep track of the <u>line number</u> and <u>character number</u> that you're working on.

<u>Breakpoints</u> are a common debugging tool, they <u>stop</u> the program on <u>certain lines</u> so you can gather information like the <u>value of variables</u> as the program is running.

<u>Error diagnostics</u> and <u>debugging tools</u> help to find and fix <u>errors</u> (see p.107) in a program — they'll tell you the <u>location</u> of the error and often suggest ways to <u>fix it</u>.

Here are some other <u>common features</u> of an IDE:

- A <u>translator</u> (compiler, interpreter or both) which will translate the source code into <u>machine code</u> (see p.112). If the IDE has <u>both</u> then you can take advantage of each translator's <u>best features</u>.

- <u>Auto-documentation</u> helps with the <u>maintenance</u> of programs. It can <u>extract</u> certain features of a program, like the <u>names of variables</u>, <u>names of sub programs</u> and <u>comments</u>. This information is stored in a <u>separate document</u> to give a <u>summary</u> of what the code does.

- A <u>Graphical User Interface (GUI) builder</u> helps the programmer design a user interface by building it up <u>graphically</u> rather than having to design it using source code. It allows you to <u>drag and drop</u> different <u>objects</u> and <u>customise</u> them, so you can make the interface look exactly how you want it to.

IDEs can make developing programs much quicker and easier...

Each IDE has advantages and disadvantages so it's all about choosing one that meets your needs. For example, certain IDEs will have features that support multiple programming languages and others will specialise in one programming language — both types of IDE can be helpful in different situations.

Warm-Up and Worked Exam Questions

That's the last of the stuff you have to learn, but you're not finished yet — there are a whole bunch of questions to answer. For the final time, test what you've learnt with these warm-up and exam questions.

Warm-Up Questions

1) Complete the trace table for the algorithm on the right.

i	num	subtext
—	0	—
1		
2		
3		
4		

```
num = 0
text = "antic"
for i = 1 to 4
    num = num + i
    print(num)
    subtext = text.left(i)
    print(subtext)
next i
```

2) Explain the purpose of a compiler.

3) Below is a sketch of the layout of a new Integrated Development Environment (IDE). In each box, briefly describe the purpose of that feature.

Code Editor	Breakpoints
Error Diagnostics	

Worked Exam Question

1 Gordon wants to write a sub program to take two positive integer inputs and work out the difference between them. He writes two different sub programs, called diffNums and numDiff, shown on the right.

```
function diffNums(a, b)
    while a > 0 AND b > 0
        a = a - 1
        b = b - 1
    endwhile
    return a + b
endfunction
```

```
function numDiff(a, b)
    if a > b then
        return a - b
    else
        return b - a
    endif
endfunction
```

a) Complete the trace table to show the result of diffNums(11, 4).

Each time the WHILE loop repeats, the values of a and b are each decreased by 1.

a	b
11	4
10	3
9	2
8	1
7	0

[2 marks]

b) Explain which sub program you think Gordon should use.

He should use numDiff because it returns the answer straight away regardless

of the values of a and b. diffNums would have to repeat the WHILE loop

many times if the values of a and b are both much greater than zero.

[2 marks]

Exam Questions

2 Cynthia is writing code for a tablet computer application aimed at children.
Explain how each of the following tools in the Integrated Development Environment (IDE)
could help Cynthia write her application.

Translator: ....

....

Error Diagnostics: ....

....

Code editor: ....

....

[6 marks]

3 A company specialises in writing programs using low-level languages.
a) Identify **two** reasons why some programmers might use low-level languages.

1. ....

2. ....

[2 marks]

b) Explain why programmers might prefer to use an assembly language over machine code.

....

....

[2 marks]

4 The procedure `test` takes an array as a parameter.
a) Complete the trace table below to show
the result of `test([4, 2, 7, 1, 9])`.

k	arr[k]	x	y

[4 marks]

```
procedure test(arr)
    x = 0
    y = 0
    for k = 0 to 4
        if arr[k] > x then
            y = x
            x = arr[k]
        elseif arr[k] > y then
            y = arr[k]
        endif
    next k
    print(x)
    print(y)
endprocedure
```

b) Explain the purpose of the procedure `test`.

....

....

[2 marks]

Revision Questions for Section Seven

And just like that it's the end of section seven — but before you put the book down you've got one more task.

- Try these questions and <u>tick off each one</u> when you <u>get it right</u>.
- When you've done <u>all the questions</u> for a topic and are <u>completely happy</u> with it, tick off the topic.

Structured Programming and Defensive Design (p.105-106) ☑

1) Give five advantages of using a structure diagram. ☑

2) a) Give four features of maintainable source code. ☑
   b) Explain how each feature can help other programmers to maintain your code. ☑

3) Why is it important for your programs to have a defensive design? ☑

4) Define the term input validation. ☑

5) Give five types of input validation check and explain what each check does. ☑

6)* The program below checks which year the user was born in.
   What type of input validation check has been used?

```
do
    year = input("Enter the year you were born.")
until year > 1900 AND year <= 2020
```

7) What is authentication and why is it used? ☑

8) Give three things that can be done to make a password-based authentication system more secure. ☑

Testing (p.107-108) ☑

9) Define the following terms: a) Syntax Error b) Logic Error ☑

10) Explain why logic errors are more difficult to diagnose than syntax errors. ☑

11)* This algorithm should take the user's age and always print one of the two strings.
    Find two errors in the code and suggest ways that you could fix them.

```
x = input("Enter your age")
if x > 16 then
    print("At the age of " + x + " you must be a computer science genius.")
elseif x < 16 then
    print("Practice makes perfect!")
endif
```

12) Why is testing important? ☑

13) What is meant by: a) iterative testing? b) final testing? ☑

14) What are the four different types of test data? ☑

15)* A software company is designing an anagram application. It will take a string
    of letters and return all of the words that can be spelt using all of the letters exactly once.
    Come up with five pieces of test data that the company could use to test their program. ☑

Trace Tables, Translators and IDEs (p.111-113) ☑

16) What are trace tables used for? ☑

17) Define and give an example of the following: a) Machine code b) Assembly Language ☑

18) Give six differences between high-level languages and low-level languages. ☑

19) What are the two main types of translator? Compare the functionality and uses of each. ☑

20) IDEs have lots of different features. Explain what each of these features are:
    a) Code Editor   b) Run-time environment   c) Error diagnostics
    d) GUI builder   e) Auto-documentation   f) Breakpoints ☑

*Answers on p.147

Practice Paper 1

Once you've been through all the questions in this book, you should be starting to feel prepared for the final exams. This practice paper will test you on Sections 1-4 of this book and contains a mix of short answer and longer answer questions. It also has one extended writing question.

GCSE OCR Computer Science
for exams in 2022 and beyond

Practice Paper 1
Computer Systems

Centre name				
Centre number				
Candidate number				

Time allowed:
* 1 hour 30 minutes

Surname
Other names
Candidate signature

You **may not** use a calculator

Instructions to candidates
* Write your name and other details in the spaces provided above.
* Answer **all** questions in the spaces provided.
* Do all rough work in this book. Cross through any work you do not want to be marked.

Information for candidates
* There are 80 marks available on this paper.
* The marks available are given in brackets at the end of each question.
* Quality of extended responses will be assessed in this paper in questions marked with an asterisk (*).

For examiner's use

Q	Attempt Nº		Q	Attempt Nº	
1			6		
2			7		
3			8		
4			9		
5					
		Total			

Answer **all** questions in the spaces provided

1. Annie has a three year old laptop. She is giving it a full service before selling it on.

   (a) Annie runs some 'Disk Health' utility software to check for any problems with her HDD.

      (i) Define what is meant by utility software.

      ....
      [1 mark]

      (ii) Give **two** other examples of utility software.

      1 ....

      2 ....
      [2 marks]

   (b) The utility reports that Annie's hard disk is 25% fragmented.

      (i) Explain **one** problem caused by a fragmented hard disk.

      ....

      ....
      [2 marks]

      (ii) Briefly describe the defragmentation process.

      ....

      ....

      ....
      [3 marks]

   (c) Annie also plans to perform a disk clean-up. Suggest why it could be better to do the disk clean-up before defragmentation, rather than afterwards.

      ....

      ....
      [1 mark]

   (d) Annie is considering getting a new laptop with an SSD rather than an HDD. Give **two** advantages of choosing an SSD over an HDD.

      1 ....

      2 ....
      [2 marks]

2. Karen uses cloud storage to store her holiday pictures and videos.
She decides to download an image from the cloud storage to her laptop.

(a) Define what is meant by cloud storage.

....

....

[1 mark]

(b) Karen's laptop and the cloud server have a client-server relationship.
Describe the communication that takes place between the cloud server
and Karen's laptop when she downloads the image.

....

....

....

....

[2 marks]

(c) Give **one** advantage and **one** disadvantage of Karen taking an external hard disk
drive to store her holiday photos and videos instead of using cloud storage.

Advantage: ....

....

....

Disadvantage: ....

....

....

[2 marks]

(d) The cloud storage company that Karen uses offers other cloud services.
Describe **one** other service that they might provide.

....

....

....

[2 marks]

Turn over ▶

3. A Yorkshire-based television company has two studios, one based in Leeds and the other based in York. The company's computer network is shown in the diagram below.

Leeds — Local Area Network (LAN)   York — Local Area Network (LAN)

The Leeds studio uses wired connections, while the York studio uses wireless connections.

(a) Select words from the lists to complete the sentences below:

(i) .... is a network protocol used on wired networks.

Ethernet   **Fibre optic**   **WAP**   **Coaxial**   **Bluetooth®**

[1 mark]

(ii) The Leeds studio is using a .... topology.

Bus   **Ring**   **Star**   **Mesh**

[1 mark]

(b) Describe **one** difference between a CAT5e twisted pair cable and a coaxial cable.

....

....

[2 marks]

(c) Outline the advantages and disadvantages of each LAN setup.

The Leeds studio's wired setup: ....

....

....

....

The York studio's wireless setup: ....

....

....

....

[4 marks]

(d) The studios are connected in a Wide Area Network (WAN) using fibre optic cables.

(i) State **one** advantage of using fibre optic cables rather than copper cables in a WAN.

....

[1 mark]

(ii) Identify **one** reason why the company uses leased lines for its WAN.

....

....

[1 mark]

4. **(a)** Convert the binary number 10101000 into denary.

....

....

....

[2 marks]

(b) Convert the binary number 10110101 into hexadecimal.

....

....

....

[2 marks]

(c) Calculate the sum of the binary numbers 10101000 and 10110101.

....

....

[1 mark]

(d) When a computer tried to add the binary numbers in part (c) together, an overflow error occurred. What is meant by the term 'overflow error'?

....

....

[1 mark]

Turn over ▶

5. Hardeep wants to try a new operating system on his computer.
The new operating system is optimised for use with a touchscreen.

	Hardeep's PC	OS Minimum Requirements
Processor:	2.1 GHz, 4 cores	1.0 GHz, 4 cores
RAM:	2 GB	2 GB
Storage:	256 GB, 125 MB free	19 GB free space
GPU:	Integrated 256 MB	Dedicated 512 MB

(a) Hardeep needs to upgrade some of the components in his computer before the new operating system can be installed. State which components must be upgraded.

1 ....

2 ....
[2 marks]

(b) Would you recommend that Hardeep upgrades any other components in his computer? Explain your answer.

....

....
[2 marks]

(c) Explain why an operating system requires a certain amount of RAM.

....

....
[2 marks]

(d) The new operating system's GUI is optimised for touchscreen use. Describe **two** features that a GUI may include to take advantage of touchscreen technology.

1 ....

....

2 ....

....
[4 marks]

6. Florence is a graphic designer for a publishing company. The image editing software that she uses represents each unique colour as a six digit hexadecimal code.

(a) As a power of 16, how many possible unique colours could Florence use?

....

[1 mark]

(b) Explain **one** benefit to programmers of using hexadecimal codes to represent the different colours.

....

....

....

[2 marks]

Florence saves the same image as three different file types (shown in the table below).

File Type	JPEG	PNG	TIFF
Size	0.2 MB	1 MB	0.9 MB

(c) One of the file types uses lossy compression. State and explain which file type is most likely to be an example of lossy compression.

....

....

....

[2 marks]

(d) Evaluate the impact if Florence always used lossless compression to store all her images.

....

....

....

....

....

[4 marks]

(e) Give **two** pieces of metadata that are often included in image files.

1 ....

2 ....

[2 marks]

Turn over ▶

7. Dishley Academy stores personal information about pupils, such as name, age, address and phone number, on their network.

(a) For the following actions, tick the corresponding box to show whether or not they would be allowed under the Data Protection Act 1998.

	Allowed	Not Allowed
Giving each teacher a USB flash drive containing the personal information of all the pupils who have attended the school.		
Transferring pupils' personal information to their new school when they leave.		
Putting pupils' personal information on the school website to make it easier for teachers and parents to access.		
Using pupils' personal information to get in contact with their parents.		
Backing up pupils' personal information on a drive that is stored in a locked safe.		

[5 marks]

(b) The IT technicians at the academy want to protect pupils' data against possible network attacks. Describe **two** different types of network attack, and suggest a method that could be used to protect against it.

Type of attack: ....

Description: ....

....

Method of protection: ....

Type of attack: ....

Description: ....

....

Method of protection: ....

[6 marks]

8. A company has its employees' computers spread across four floors.
The computers on each floor are connected to that floor's server in a star network.
Employees need to access files on all of the servers, so each of the four servers are connected in another star network, with a central switch located on the ground floor.

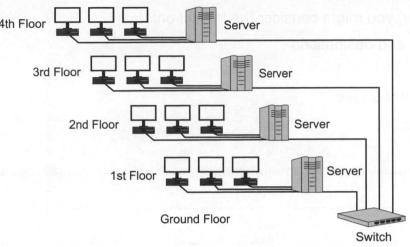

(a) Describe the effect that the central switch failing would have on the rest of the network.

....

....

[2 marks]

(b) The company decides to remove the switch from the network and instead connect the four servers in a full mesh network, as shown in this diagram.

Explain the advantages and disadvantages to the company of connecting the servers together in a full mesh network instead of a star network.

....

....

....

....

....

[4 marks]

Turn over ▶

9.* Recent years have seen the increasing use of computer technology to distribute and view digital media content (music, movies and books).

Discuss the impact of the increasing use of digital media.

In your answer, you might consider the impact on:

* consumers and businesses
* technology
* environmental issues
* legal issues

....

....

....

....

....

....

....

....

....

....

....

....

....

....

....

....

....

....

[8 marks]

END OF QUESTIONS

This practice paper will test you on Sections 5-7 of this book and features many algorithm-based questions. Section A will test your knowledge, understanding and analytical skills, while section B will test your practical programming skills and ability to create, test and refine programs.

GCSE OCR Computer Science
for exams in 2022 and beyond

Practice Paper 2
Computational Thinking, Algorithms and Programming

Centre name				
Centre number				
Candidate number				

Time allowed:
- 1 hour 30 minutes

Surname
Other names
Candidate signature

You **may not** use a calculator

Instructions to candidates
- Write your name and other details in the spaces provided above.
- Answer **all** questions in the spaces provided.
- Do all rough work in this book. Cross through any work you do not want to be marked.

Information for candidates
- There are 80 marks available on this paper.
- The marks available are given in brackets at the end of each question.

For examiner's use					
Q	Attempt Nº		Q	Attempt Nº	
1			5		
2			6		
3			7		
4					
			Total		

128

Answer **all** questions in the spaces provided

Section A

1. A petrol station needs a program to calculate the cost of fuel for each customer.

(a) For each row of the table, tick the appropriate data type to store the given data.

	Real	Boolean	String
The name of the fuel that the customer used.			
The total cost of the customer's fuel.			

[2 marks]

(b) Explain why it's important to use the correct data type to store information.

....

....

....
[2 marks]

(c) Describe, with an example, how the function `str()` might be used when printing the receipt.

....

....

....
[2 marks]

(d) The source code for the program needs to be translated into machine code. Outline **two** differences in the way a compiler and interpreter would translate the program.

1 ....

....

2 ....

....
[4 marks]

2. Lenny is writing a program using an IDE. His program is for an exercise bike that adjusts the difficulty based on information about the user.

(a) Give one specific feature of an IDE that will help Lenny write his program.

....

[1 mark]

(b) One of Lenny's sub programs takes `weight` as a parameter.

(i) Define what is meant by a 'parameter'.

....

[1 mark]

(ii) What is the scope of a parameter?

....

[1 mark]

(c) The code below appears near the start of Lenny's program.

```
global difficulty = 0
currentWeight = input("Enter weight.")
procedure setInitialDifficulty(weight)
    difficulty = 50 - (weight DIV 6)
endprocedure
```

(i) Explain what the first line of this code does.

....

....

[2 marks]

(ii) Describe what the `setInitialDifficulty` procedure does.

....

....

[2 marks]

Turn over ▶

(d) Lenny's program will adjust the difficulty based on the user's heart rate on a loop. If their heart rate is above 140, then the difficulty will decrease by 1. If their heart rate is below 90, then the difficulty will increase by 1, up to a maximum of 50. In addition, if the user's heart rate ever goes higher than 160, then the difficulty will be set to 0, a warning message will be displayed and the loop will stop.

Write an algorithm for the part of Lenny's program described above.

....

....

....

....

....

....

....

....

....

....

....

[6 marks]

3. A car uses a logic circuit to decide whether to start the engine or not.

- The car has two buttons, labelled **S** (START) and **D** (DRIVE).
  If both buttons are on, the engine will start.

- The engine also starts if the ignition switch **I** is turned on.

(a) Draw the logic circuit diagram for this system, with **Z** as an output.

[3 marks]

(b) Fill in the missing values in the truth table for the logic circuit in part (a).

S	D	I	Z
0	1		0
		0	1
1			0

[3 marks]

4. Every 5 minutes, an app on a mobile phone records the electrical current (in mA) passing through a pair of connected headphones. A sample of the readings is shown in the table below.

10	18	12	15	20

(a) Show the stages of a linear search to find the value '12' in the list above.

....

....

....

....

....

....

[2 marks]

(b) Arrange the values in order from smallest to largest using an insertion sort.

[4 marks]

Turn over ▶

5. Tony is writing a program to calculate a player's score in a dice game.
A player starts with a score of 0 and rolls a six-sided dice as many times as they want.
After each roll they add the number the dice lands on to their score. The aim is to get as close to 21 as possible. If you go over 21 you get a score of 0.

The flowchart below shows an initial design for his program.

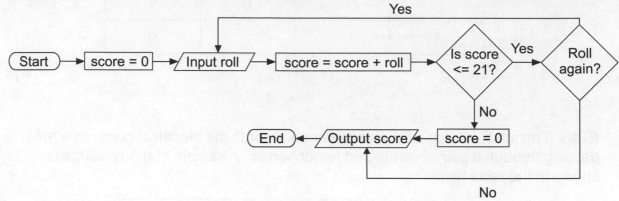

(a) Tony designs a test plan for his program.
Explain why it's important for the test plan to include erroneous test data.

....

....

[2 marks]

(b) Tony tests each of the following sequences of inputs in his program.
For each test, state the type of test data, the intended outcome,
and what the actual outcome will be with his program's current design.

(i) 5, 6, 4, 3, 2

Type of data: ....

Intended Outcome: ....

Actual Outcome: ....

[3 marks]

(ii) 5, 9, 3, 2

Type of data: ....

Intended Outcome: ....

Actual Outcome: ....

[3 marks]

(c) Identify **two** ways that Tony could use input validation in his program.

1 ....

2 ....

[2 marks]

6. A comic book shop stores information about each of its comics in records.
The table below shows two records stored in the comics table.

ID No.	Title	Date published	Length	Genre	Rating
0001	Hike of Hope	04-05-2019	82	Adventure	5
0002	Space Voyage	05-09-2019	65	Science Fiction	2

(a) Explain why the comic book shop has chosen to store this information
in records rather than an array.

....

....

....

[2 marks]

(b) Write an SQL query to return the titles of all comics with a rating of 5.

....

....

....

[3 marks]

END OF SECTION A

Turn over ▶

Section B

Any questions that require you to give your answer in OCR Exam Reference Language or a high-level programming language will have specific instructions given in the question.

7. The Prime Koalas are a band consisting of four members:
    John on guitar, Paul on bass, Cheryl on vocals and Ida on drums.

    (a) Complete the code below to generate a 2D array containing
    the names and instruments of all the band members.

    ```
    array primeKoalas[4, 2]
    primeKoalas[0, 0] = "John"
    primeKoalas[1, 0] = "Paul"
    primeKoalas[2, 0] = "Cheryl"
    primeKoalas[3, 0] = "Ida"
    ```

    [2 marks]

    (b) John wants to open the empty text file called musicians.txt and write to it.
    Each line of the file should contain a different band member and their instrument.

    Write an algorithm that uses your array in part (a) to write this information to the text file.

    You must use either:
    • OCR Exam Reference Language, or
    • a high-level programming language that you have studied.

    ....

    ....

    ....

    ....

    ....

    ....

    ....

    [3 marks]

(c) John has written a sub program, `toSpeech()`, which takes a string as a parameter, turns the string into audio data and reads it out loud.
He wants to write a procedure using `toSpeech()` that takes a file name as a parameter and reads out all the data in the file.

Complete the design of this procedure. You must use either:
- OCR Exam Reference Language, or
- a high-level programming language that you have studied.

```
procedure readAll(fileName)

.........................................................................................

.........................................................................................

.........................................................................................

.........................................................................................

.........................................................................................

.........................................................................................

endprocedure
```

[4 marks]

(d) John has written a program that helps predict the number of fans that attend each gig and how much the band will earn in ticket sales. In the program:

- `fans` is the number of fans that would buy a ticket to a gig.
- `price` is the current ticket price (in pounds) for a gig.
- `total` is the total (in pounds) that the band receives from ticket sales for a gig.
- Each repetition of the FOR loop corresponds to the band playing another gig.

```
fans = 5
price = 0
for i = 1 to 4
    fans = 2 * fans
    price = price + 2
    total = fans * price
next i
```

Complete the trace table to test this program.

i	fans	price	total
—	5	0	—
1			

[4 marks]

Turn over ▶

(e) When the band makes an album, John uses a program to enter the track names.
After entering a track name, the program asks if he wants to enter another name.
If yes, the program repeats, and if not, the program ends.
Design a flowchart that shows how the program works.

[5 marks]

(f) The array `trackNames` contains the names of the 11 tracks on the band's first album.
John uses this array in the program below.

```
inputString = input("Enter track number.")
trackNumber = int(inputString)
print(trackNames[trackNumber - 1])
```

Refine the program so that if the string "random" is entered,
the program prints a random track name from the album.
Write the refined version of the program.

You must use either:
- OCR Exam Reference Language, or
- a high-level programming language that you have studied.

....

....

....

....

....

....

....

[4 marks]

(g) John also uses the program below to create a code for each track.

```
trackName = input("Enter track name.")
letters = trackName.left(1).upper + trackName.subString(2, 3)
length = trackName.length
trackCode = letters + str(length)
```

(i) What code would be generated for the track `koalifications`?

....
[2 marks]

(ii) John wants to refine the program to not allow track names that contain spaces. He is writing a function, `noSpace()`, that takes a string as a parameter, and returns True if the string has no spaces, or False if the string contains spaces.

Complete the design of this function.

```
function noSpace(string1)

    len = ....................................................

    for i = 0 to (len - 1)

        if ....................................... == " " then

            ...........................................

        endif
    next i
    return true
endfunction
```

[3 marks]

(iii) Write some program code that uses the `noSpace()` function to carry out the validation check on a track name. The program should notify the user if an input is invalid, and ask them to re-enter it until the input is valid.

You must use either:
• OCR Exam Reference Language, or
• a high-level programming language that you have studied.

....

....

....

....

....

....
[3 marks]

END OF QUESTIONS

Section One — Components of a Computer System

Page 4 (Warm-Up Questions)

1 E.g.
   - Power supply
   - Case cooling fan
   - CPU
   - Heat sink
   - Optical drive
   - RAM
   - Hard Disk Drive/HDD
   - Graphics card/GPU
   - Motherboard

2
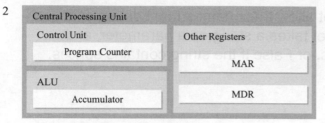

3 a) The accumulator stores the results of calculations done by the ALU.

   b) The MAR holds any memory address about to be used by the CPU.

   c) The MDR holds data or instructions that have been fetched from / are about to be written to memory.

Page 5 (Exam Questions)

3 a) A computer system built into another device. *[1 mark]*

   b) Any **two** devices, e.g.
      - Dishwasher *[1 mark]*
      - MP3 player *[1 mark]*
      - Digital thermometer *[1 mark]*
      - Washing machine *[1 mark]*
      - Manufacturing machinery *[1 mark]*
      [2 marks available in total]

   c) Any **two** benefits explained, e.g.
      - Embedded systems are far smaller than general purpose computers *[1 mark]* which means microwaves can be made more compact. *[1 mark]*
      - Embedded systems are cheaper to produce than general purpose computers *[1 mark]* which can reduce the costs / sale price of microwaves. *[1 mark]*
      - Embedded systems tend to be more reliable than general purpose computers *[1 mark]* which means that microwaves are less likely to break. *[1 mark]*
      [4 marks available in total]

4 a) Any **two** functions, e.g.
      - The control unit executes instructions. *[1 mark]*
      - It follows the fetch-execute cycle. *[1 mark]*
      - It controls the flow of data within the CPU. *[1 mark]*
      - It controls the flow of data between the CPU and other parts of the computer system (such as memory, and input and output devices). *[1 mark]*
      [2 marks available in total]

   b) E.g. The ALU carries out arithmetic operations, e.g. addition, subtraction and multiplication (using repeated addition). *[1 mark]* It performs logic operations on binary data, such as AND, NOT, and OR. *[1 mark]*

   c) E.g. The cache is extremely fast memory in the CPU. *[1 mark]* It stores regularly used data or instructions. *[1 mark]* The CPU can access data stored in the cache much faster than retrieving it from RAM. *[1 mark]*

Page 10 (Warm-Up Questions)

1 RAM is volatile memory that can be read from and written to, used to store files and applications while they are in use. ROM is non-volatile memory that can generally only be read, which contains the startup instructions for the computer.

2 A clock speed of 3 GHz means that the single-core processor can carry out 3 billion instructions per second.

3 a) Magnetic tape

   b) E.g. Solid State Drive (SSD) / USB pen drive / SD card

   c) Hard disk drive (HDD)

4 E.g.
   - Optical discs tend to have lower capacity.
   - USB pen drives have faster read/write speeds.
   - Optical discs are easily scratched.
   - USB pen drives are more reliable for repeatedly rewriting to.
   - USB pen drives are pocket-size so are easier to carry.

Page 11 (Exam Questions)

3 a) E.g.
      - Secondary storage is needed to store data and software in the long term. *[1 mark]*
      - Secondary storage is non-volatile memory, so retains data when there is no power. *[1 mark]*
      - Computers could not function without permanent data storage, as all software and data would be lost when switched off. *[1 mark]*
      - Secondary storage has a high capacity, so you can store a lot more data. *[1 mark]*
      [3 marks available in total]

   b) Any **two** advantages, e.g.
      - Optical discs have a low cost per GB. *[1 mark]*
      - They are highly portable. *[1 mark]*
      - They are durable against shock and water damage. *[1 mark]*

      Any **two** disadvantages, e.g.
      - They are very slow to write to. *[1 mark]*
      - They require an optical drive to be read / written. *[1 mark]*
      - They can be scratched easily. *[1 mark]*
      - They have a low capacity compared to other forms of storage, e.g. flash memory cards. *[1 mark]*
      [4 marks available in total]

4 a) Cache is much faster than RAM. *[1 mark]* The larger the cache, the more data can be stored for quick access by the CPU, meaning the CPU should perform better. *[1 mark]*

   b) E.g. Jackson's CPU has more cores than Will's CPU, which should mean better performance. *[1 mark]* It also has a larger cache than Will's, which should again lead to better CPU performance. *[1 mark]* On the other hand Will's CPU has a higher clock speed than Jackson's, so there is a chance that Will's may give better performance than Jackson's. *[1 mark]* Overall, it is hard to tell whether Will's CPU will offer better performance, therefore it seems unwise to buy Will's CPU, as it may be no better than Jackson's current one. *[1 mark]*
   If you'd decided that Will's CPU was the best option, you'd still get the marks as long as you'd put together a sensible argument based on comparisons of the CPU specs.

   c) E.g. Increasing the amount of RAM increases the amount of data / number of applications that the computer can hold in memory. *[1 mark]* Jackson may not use all of the current RAM in his computer, as he may use undemanding software or he may not open many programs at once *[1 mark]* so adding more RAM will not improve performance. *[1 mark]*
   [2 marks available in total]

Page 16 (Warm-Up Questions)

1

	System Software	Not System Software
Operating System	✓	
Word Processor		✓
Disk Defragmenter	✓	

2 a) Defragmentation

b) Compression

c) Anti-virus

Page 17 (Exam Questions)

2 a) Any **three** functions from:
- The OS communicates with hardware via device drivers. *[1 mark]*
- The OS provides a user interface. *[1 mark]*
- The OS provides a platform for applications to run. *[1 mark]*
- The OS allows a computer to multitask by controlling memory / CPU resources. *[1 mark]*
- The OS deals with file and disk management. *[1 mark]*
- The OS manages the security of the system. *[1 mark]*
[3 marks available in total]

b) Device drivers are pieces of software *[1 mark]* that allow the OS and hardware to communicate with each other. *[1 mark]*

3 a) Encryption software encrypts (scrambles) the data so that it cannot be read if it is stolen. *[1 mark]* The intended reader is given the 'key' that allows them to decrypt the data and turn it back into its original form. *[1 mark]*

b) Any **two** features, e.g.
- It may have anti-theft measures, like password or pin protection. *[1 mark]*
- It may allow different user accounts, giving each user access to their own personal data and desktop, which cannot be accessed by other users. *[1 mark]*
- It may include anti-virus software or a firewall to help protect against unauthorised users / software. *[1 mark]*
[2 marks available in total]

4 E.g.
- When applications / programs / files are opened, the OS moves the necessary parts to memory. *[1 mark]*
- The OS will remove unneeded data from memory, e.g. when programs or files are closed. *[1 mark]*
- The OS divides memory into segments. When different programs are used, their data is placed into different segments so that running applications can not write over or interfere with each other. *[1 mark]*
- The OS organises the movement of data to and from virtual memory. *[1 mark]*
- The OS divides CPU time between running applications / programs / processes, as it can only process one at a time. *[1 mark]*
- The OS can prioritise CPU time for different programs in order for them to be processed in the most efficient order. *[1 mark]*
[6 marks available in total — award a maximum of 4 marks for points about RAM or CPU time]

Section Two — Data Representation

Page 25 (Warm-Up Questions)

1 4

2 a) 89   b) 1000101

3 11110010

4 Overflow errors occur when binary operations produce results that have more bits than the CPU is expecting to store/process.

5 00010111

6 Multiplying the number by 2.

7 a) 30   b) 198   c) A2   d) 111101

Page 26 (Exam Questions)

3 a) Convert all the values into the same unit.
0.3 TB = 300 GB
200 000 MB = 200 GB
So the 0.3 terabyte SSD is the largest. *[1 mark]*

b) 1 GB = 1000 MB
So 250 GB = 250 × 1000 MB = 250 000 MB *[1 mark]*
250 000 ÷ 5 = 50 000 music files. *[1 mark]*

4 a) A 2 place right shift *[1 mark]* gives 00110101. *[1 mark]*

b) He is not correct.
E.g. 0001 + 0001 = 0010 is a 1 place left shift.
[2 marks available — 1 mark for not correct, 1 mark for a valid explanation]

5 a) Split bytes into nibbles and convert to hexadecimal.
0100 = 4, 0011 = 3, so 01000011 = C = 43. *[1 mark]*
0100 = 4, 0001 = 1, so 01000001 = A = 41. *[1 mark]*
0101 = 5, 0100 = 4, so 01010100 = T = 54. *[1 mark]*

b) i) D = 44 = 01000100 *[1 mark]*

ii) From CAT, 43 = C and from DOG, 44 = D and 4F = O.
E is 1 more than D (= 44) so 45 = E. *[1 mark]*
The password is CODE. *[1 mark]*

Page 31 (Warm-Up Questions)

1 ASCII uses fewer bits to represent each character but is a much smaller character set.

2 16

3 a) The file size would increase.

b) The file size would decrease.

4 10 × 50 000 × 4 = 2 000 000 bits
The sample rate is given in kilohertz but the formula uses hertz, so you need to convert the sample rate first.

5 a) The file size and quality would both increase.

b) The file size and quality would both decrease.

6 Lossy compression and lossless compression.

Page 32 (Exam Questions)

3 a) A character set is a collection of characters a computer recognises from their binary representation. *[1 mark]*

b) E.g. The keyboard sends the binary code of the character to the computer. *[1 mark]* The code is then translated using the character set. *[1 mark]*

4 a) Recording 2 would have a better sound quality *[1 mark]* because it has a higher sample rate and bit depth, both of which are indications of better overall sound quality. *[1 mark]*

b) The file size would be larger. *[1 mark]*

5 a) i) The number of pixels in a bitmap image. *[1 mark]*

ii) 200 × 100 × 32 *[1 mark]* = 640 000 bits *[1 mark]*

b) Metadata is 'data about data' / information about a file.
[1 mark] Metadata includes information about height, width, resolution etc. so the image is displayed properly. *[1 mark]*

Page 33 (Revision Questions)

4 a) 2 terabytes

b) 2 000 000 megabytes

5 a) i) 10001   ii) 10010100   iii) 11110000

b) i) 11   ii) 94   iii) F0

6 a) i) 56   ii) 159   iii) 43

b) i) 38   ii) 9F   iii) 2B

7   a) i) 74   ii) 117   iii) 217
    b) i) 1001010   ii) 1110101   iii) 11011001

8   1 (the left-most bit)

9   10001111

16 3200 bits

Section Three — Networks

Page 39 (Warm-Up Questions)

1   E.g.
    • Network Interface Controller (NIC)
    • Switch
    • Ethernet cables
    • Wireless Access Point (WAP)

2   Wi-Fi®

3   Clients send requests for data/services to the server,
    which processes the requests and then replies.

4   E.g. video calling/file sharing/etc.

5

No. of devices	Star	Partial Mesh	Full Mesh
4	Switch		
5	Switch		
6	Switch		

*For the partial mesh topology, there are lots of possible answers —
all you need is for all nodes to be indirectly linked to each other and
for there to be more than one way to get between some of the nodes.*

Page 40 (Exam Questions)

2   Switch: A switch connects devices in a local area network.
    [1 mark] Data is received by the switch and sent to the
    device with the correct MAC address. *[1 mark]*

    Router: A router transmits data between networks. *[1 mark]*
    A router can be used to connect a local area network (LAN)
    to the Internet. *[1 mark]*

    WAP: A Wireless Access Point (WAP) connects devices in
    a local area network *[1 mark]* wirelessly / using radio waves /
    using Wi-Fi®. *[1 mark]*

3   Any **one** advantage,
    E.g. If a single device or connection fails on a mesh network,
    the network still functions as data can go along a different route.
    [1 mark] In a star network, central switch failure will cause the
    whole network to fail / a single connection failure will cut that
    device off from the network. *[1 mark]*

    Any **one** disadvantage,
    E.g. Devices in a mesh network need many more connections
    than in a star network. *[1 mark]* This requires a lot of cabling
    which can be expensive / impractical for networks with a large
    number of nodes. *[1 mark]*

4   a) A Peer-to-Peer network is a group of devices connected to
        share data with each other *[1 mark]* in which all devices are
        equal / connected without a server. *[1 mark]*
        A Client-Server network is a group of devices connected
        to a central computer (server) *[1 mark]* which manages the
        network / processes requests from devices (clients) / stores files
        centrally. *[1 mark]*

    b) Any **two** benefits, e.g.
        • User files are stored centrally so resources are used more
          efficiently / files are less likely to be duplicated. *[1 mark]*
        • Software is easier to install / update because it is centrally
          stored. *[1 mark]*
        • Servers are more reliable than peer machines. *[1 mark]*
        • It is easier to backup data centrally. *[1 mark]*
        • There is greater security as anti-malware software can be
          installed centrally / user access to files can be controlled.
          [1 mark]

        Any **two** drawbacks, e.g.
        • Client-Server networks are expensive to set up. *[1 mark]*
        • The business would need to employ an IT specialist to
          maintain the server / network. *[1 mark]*
        • If the server fails then all the client computers lose access
          to their files / client computers are dependent on the server.
          [1 mark]
        [4 marks available in total]

Page 47 (Warm-Up Questions)

1

Protocol	Function
TCP	Sets rules for how devices connect on the network / splits data into packets / reassembles packets into original data / checks data is sent and delivered.
IP	Responsible for directing data packets across a network.
HTTP	Used by web browsers to access websites / communicate with web servers.
HTTPS	A more secure version of HTTP.
FTP	Used to access, edit and move files on other devices.
SMTP	Used to send emails / transfer emails between servers.
IMAP	Used to retrieve emails from a server. The user downloads a copy of the email and the server holds the original email until the user deletes it.
POP3	Used to retrieve emails from a server. The server holds the email until the user downloads it, at which point the server deletes it.

2   a) Trojan
    b) Rootkit
    c) Worm
    d) Ransomware

Pages 48-49 (Exam Questions)

2   a) The Internet is a global network of networks. *[1 mark]*
        The World Wide Web is a collection of websites hosted
        on web servers. *[1 mark]*

    b) A Domain Name Server translates a website's domain name
        into its IP address / stores domain names of websites in a
        directory. *[1 mark]*

3   a) E.g.
        • An SQL Query is entered into the input box of a website.
          [1 mark]
        • The input box was not designed for that query but it is
          permitted by the website's / database's code. *[1 mark]*
        • The inserted code runs a database query that can give
          unauthorised access to the whole or part of the database.
          [1 mark]
        [2 marks available in total]

    b) E.g.
        • A criminal calls one of the supermarket's employees and
          pretends to be a member of the supermarket's IT team.
          [1 mark]
        • The criminal gains the employee's trust through the use of
          jargon, information related to the supermarket or flattery.
          [1 mark]
        • The criminal persuades the employee to disclose their
          account details, giving the criminal access to their company
          account. *[1 mark]*
        [2 marks available in total]

4 a) E.g.
- Different user access levels prevent students from accessing the same data as teachers, including sensitive data like their peers' personal information. *[1 mark]*
- Different user access levels prevent a student from maliciously deleting or editing data. *[1 mark]*
- Different user access levels prevent students accidentally deleting or editing important files. *[1 mark]*
- Different user access levels allow network administrators to flexibly change the amount of access students and staff have to certain files. *[1 mark]*

[3 marks available in total]

b) i) A brute force attack is a type of attack on a network which uses trial and error to crack passwords *[1 mark]* by employing automated software to produce hundreds of likely combinations. *[1 mark]*

ii) Any **two** measures, e.g.
- The school can lock access to user accounts after a certain number of password attempts. *[1 mark]*
- The school can ensure that strong passwords are used / the school can ensure that passwords are long enough / the school can ensure that passwords are made of a mix of different types of character. *[1 mark]*
- The school can add additional security checks, like using a secret question or CAPTCHA test. *[1 mark]*

[2 marks available in total]

5 a) E.g.
- A MAC address is a unique identifier. *[1 mark]*
- A MAC address is assigned to the hardware of every network-enabled device. *[1 mark]*
- MAC addresses are used to direct data to the right device on a network. *[1 mark]*

[2 marks available in total]

b) i) A layer of network protocols is a group of protocols with similar functions *[1 mark]* that cover one particular aspect of network communications. *[1 mark]*

ii) Any **three** benefits, e.g.
- Layers break network communication into manageable pieces. *[1 mark]*
- Layers allow developers to focus on one area of the network without worrying about the others. *[1 mark]*
- Layers are self-contained. *[1 mark]*
- There are set rules for each layer. *[1 mark]*
- Layers allow interoperability / layers make companies produce compatible, universal hardware and software. *[1 mark]*

[3 marks available in total]

6 Points you might include:

Advantages of the cloud
- Users can access files from any location, so the company and authors can work on the same files without having to email or post manuscripts.
- Cloud storage is managed by the hosting company which will be a cheaper alternative to managing their own storage.
- The hosting company manages the security of data in the cloud, so the publishing company does not need to spend time securing its data.
- The hosting company is responsible for backing up data in the cloud, so the publishing company does not need to invest in any additional hardware to ensure data is backed up correctly.
- The publishing company could use cloud-based software rather than installing it on their machines and keeping it up to date. This could give writers access to the same software.

Disadvantages of the cloud
- An Internet connection is required to access the cloud, and maintaining a steady Internet connection can be difficult in rural areas.
- The publishing company is dependent on the hosting company for the security in the cloud, meaning the publishing company has very little control over the security of its data.
- The publishing company is dependent on the hosting company for backing up their data.
- Cloud software may require a monthly subscription which may be more expensive than buying computer licences.

How to mark your answer:
- Two or three brief points with very little explanation. *[1-2 marks]*
- Three or four detailed points covering both advantages and disadvantages. *[3-4 marks]*
- Five or more detailed points that form a well-written, balanced discussion, covering both advantages and disadvantages. *[5-6 marks]*

Make sure your answer is relevant to the situation you're given — the company in the question has particular needs and qualities which you shouldn't ignore.

7 Points you might include:

The threats posed to the firm's network
- Hackers could use rootkits, spyware and other malware to steal confidential information.
- Employees unaware of the potential dangers could be tricked into giving criminals sensitive information through social engineering.
- Disgruntled employees could use their position to attack the network, e.g. by releasing malware onto the network from a USB drive.
- Hackers with packet sniffers or other similar tools could intercept and read information entering or leaving the company's network.
- Hackers could use automated software to crack weak passwords.

Methods to ensure network security
- Automatic encryption of all data leaving and entering the network could prevent intercepted data from being read by hackers and criminals.
- Installing anti-malware and firewall software and keeping it up-to-date could prevent harmful malware from entering the network.
- Regular penetration testing to find problems in the network security.
- Educating employees on the dangers of social engineering could protect against it.
- Mandatory use of strong passwords / passwords that are changed regularly.
- Introducing an acceptable use policy that employees must sign.
- Controlling physical access to hardware / the network, e.g. using locks to prevent access to server rooms etc.
- Different user access levels given to different groups of users to limit the dangers of an attack from within the firm.

How to mark your answer:
- Two or three points with very little explanation. *[1-2 marks]*
- Three to five points with detailed explanation. *[3-5 marks]*
- Six or more detailed points that form a well-written, balanced discussion. *[6-8 marks]*

Section Four — Issues

Page 56 (Warm-Up Questions)

1

	Censorship	Surveillance
A business monitors what their employees view online.		✓
A country's government blocks access to Facebook®.	✓	
A government agency intercepts emails containing certain words.		✓
A school restricts access to harmful websites.	✓	
An Internet Service Provider collects data on browsing habits.		✓

2 E.g.
   • Eyestrain — use suitable lighting / keep a good distance from the screen / take regular breaks.
   • Repetitive Strain Injury (RSI) — ensure good posture / arrange your desk appropriately / take regular breaks.
   • Back pain — ensure good posture / use adjustable equipment / sit at a suitable angle.

3 The digital divide is the separation between people who have ready access to technology and those who don't, who tend to be at a disadvantage because of this.

Page 57 (Exam Questions)

2 Owners of the supermarket — positive because they receive increased profits and do not have to pay the staff. *[1 mark]* Employees — negative because they have lost their jobs. *[1 mark]*

3 a) E.g.
   • The Internet / social media / email mean Raed can be contacted at any time of day. *[1 mark]*
   • Raed may be expected to carry a smartphone so he can be contacted by his boss at all times. *[1 mark]*
   • Raed's smartphone may alert him when he receives work emails from clients. These can be hard to ignore. *[1 mark]*
   [2 marks available in total]

   b) E.g.
   • Companies try to influence people into using their new product, e.g. by using advertisements. *[1 mark]*
   • Many children may feel peer pressure to buy the new devices for fear of being bullied by their classmates. *[1 mark]*
   • Parents can feel pressured to buy the latest technology for their children. *[1 mark]*
   [2 marks available in total]

   c) Any **one** reason, e.g.
   • They might not have a lot of money *[1 mark]* so cannot afford to buy expensive electronic devices. *[1 mark]*
   • They might live in a rural area *[1 mark]* so could have poor network coverage. *[1 mark]*
   • They might have little knowledge of how to use the Internet or electronic devices *[1 mark]* so feel too intimidated to use them. *[1 mark]*
   [2 marks available in total]

4 Points you might include:

Factory staff
   • Workers in the manufacturing sector could become unemployed, as robots take over their jobs.
   • Introducing the robots could create extra jobs as people will be needed to monitor and repair them.

Technology
   • The hardware and software of robots may not be sophisticated enough to fully replicate the work of human employees.
   • The increased use of robots in the workplace could help improve them as problems can be identified and fixed.
   • Successful use of robots in manufacturing could lead to their application in other areas of work.

Ethical issues
   • Manufacturing businesses could leave hundreds of people without jobs in order to pursue profit.
   • There is currently a lack of awareness of the rules on using robots in the workplace.
   • By allowing robots to do the routine jobs, workers are free to do more interesting, creative and fulfilling work.
   • Robots can perform hazardous tasks, meaning there could be fewer injuries in the workplace.

How to mark your answer:
   • Two or three brief points with very little explanation. *[1-2 marks]*
   • Three to five detailed points covering at least two of: factory staff, technology and ethical issues. *[3-5 marks]*
   • Six or more detailed points that form a well-written, balanced discussion, covering all of: factory staff, technology and ethical issues. *[6-8 marks]*

Page 61 (Warm-Up Questions)

1 Copper, platinum, plastic, mercury, gold and silver.

2 a) Data Protection Act 2018
   b) Computer Misuse Act 1990
   c) Copyright, Designs and Patents Act 1988
   d) Data Protection Act 2018
   e) Computer Misuse Act 1990

3 Android™, Linux®, VLC media player and Mozilla® Firefox®

Page 62 (Exam Questions)

3 a) The legal right that gives the creator of content (e.g. books, music, films, software, video games, etc.) protection over how their content is used. *[1 mark]*

   b) Hayley needs to contact the owner of the image *[1 mark]* and request permission to use it. *[1 mark]* Hayley will have to follow the copyright holder's request / acknowledge the source of the image / may have to pay a fee. *[1 mark]*

4 E.g.
   • E-waste is sent to landfill sites *[1 mark]* where toxic chemicals can enter groundwater / harm wildlife. *[1 mark]*
   • The short life span of devices also means more natural resources have to be extracted to make new devices *[1 mark]* which causes pollution and depletes scarce resources. *[1 mark]*
   • Manufacturing devices uses up a lot of electricity *[1 mark]* which is often generated using non-renewable resources. *[1 mark]*
   [4 marks available in total]

5 a) Proprietary software is software where only the compiled code is released. *[1 mark]* Users are not allowed to modify, copy or redistribute the software. *[1 mark]*

   b) Any **two** advantages, e.g.
   • The software is likely to include customer support. *[1 mark]*
   • It should be well-tested and reliable. *[1 mark]*
   • Cheaper than the company developing its own software. *[1 mark]*
   [2 marks available in total]

6 Points you might include:
   • The cinema should ask permission from the customer before storing their data.
   • The cinema should ask the customer to sign an agreement as to how the information should be used.
   • The cinema should only use the data to make it easier for customers to book seats and for contacting them for details on future films.
   • The cinema should give customers the option to unsubscribe from their service, so that their data is removed from the cinema's computer system if they want.
   • The cinema should be active in keeping its data up to date and allow their customers to change their details.

- The cinema should not give customers' data to third party organisations unless the customer permits it.
- The cinema should ensure that customers' data is held safely and securely, e.g. by using a firewall on its computer system and encrypting the data.

How to mark your answer:
- Two or three brief points with very little explanation. *[1-2 marks]*
- Three or four detailed points that show a good understanding of the Data Protection Act. *[3-4 marks]*
- Five or more detailed points that show a good understanding of the Data Protection Act and clearly apply it to the situation. *[5-6 marks]*

Think about each principle of the Data Protection Act and apply it to this situation.

Section Five — Algorithms

Page 67 (Warm-Up Questions)

1 Decomposition, Abstraction and Algorithmic Thinking

2 An algorithm is a process or set of instructions used to solve a problem or carry out a task.

3 B and D

4
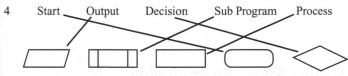

Page 68 (Exam Questions)

2 a) It asks the user to input a height and width. *[1 mark]*
       It then multiplies these values together *[1 mark]*
       to get the area and prints the value of the area. *[1 mark]*

   b) $5 \times 10 = 50$ *[1 mark]*

3 a) E.g. Abstraction is picking out important details and ignoring irrelevant ones. The file uploading service will focus on the important details like the file name and ignore the unimportant details like the contents of each file.
       [3 marks available — 1 mark for a definition of abstraction, 1 mark for an example of a detail to ignore, 1 mark for an example of a detail to focus on]

   b) E.g. Decomposition breaks the programming task down into smaller problems. A programmer might focus on 'How will the service keep track of files already uploaded?' or 'How will the service compare file names?' and try to solve each programming problem individually.
       [3 marks available — 1 mark for a definition of decomposition, 1 mark for each example of decomposition up to a maximum of 2 marks]

4 Using Start / Begin. *[1 mark]*
   Asking user to input x, y. *[1 mark]*
   Using SqMove (with correct sub program box). *[1 mark]*
   Decision box with appropriate question. *[1 mark]*
   Creating a loop to repeat SqMove. *[1 mark]*
   Using Stop / End. *[1 mark]*
   E.g.

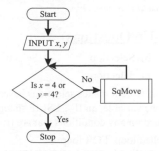

Page 73 (Warm-Up Questions)

1 a) Middle item = $(7 + 1) / 2$ = 4th item = 11
       11 is bigger than 8 so take left hand side.
       3, 6, 8
       Middle item = $(3 + 1) / 2$ = 2nd item = 6
       6 is smaller than 8 so take right hand side.
       8
       Middle item = $(1 + 1) / 2$ = 1st item = 8
       Stop searching as 8 has been found.

   b) Check 1st item: $3 \neq 11$.
       Check 2nd item: $6 \neq 11$.
       Check 3rd item: $8 \neq 11$.
       Check 4th item: $11 = 11$.
       Stop searching as 11 has been found.

2 See page 70.

3 a) *1st pass (2 swaps):*

Chris	Beth	Dalia	Ahmed
Beth	Chris	Dalia	Ahmed
Beth	Chris	Ahmed	Dalia

   2nd pass (1 swap):

Beth	Chris	Ahmed	Dalia
Beth	Ahmed	Chris	Dalia

   3rd pass (1 swap):

Beth	Ahmed	Chris	Dalia
Ahmed	Beth	Chris	Dalia

   4th pass (no swaps — list is in order):

Ahmed	Beth	Chris	Dalia

   You don't necessarily need to do the last pass — since there are four items in the list, the algorithm will only take at most three passes to get the list in order.

   b)
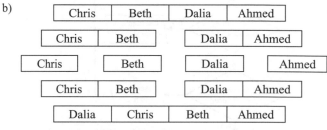

   c)

Chris	Beth	Dalia	Ahmed
Beth	Chris	Dalia	Ahmed
Beth	Chris	Dalia	Ahmed
Ahmed	Beth	Chris	Dalia

4 Merge Sort

Page 74 (Exam Questions)

3 a) Compare butterscotch to mint. *[1 mark]*
       Mint is greater so split and take the left side. *[1 mark]*
       A further comparison. *[1 mark]*
       Correct identification of butterscotch. *[1 mark]*
       E.g.
       Middle item = $(5 + 1) / 2$ = 3rd item = mint.
       Compare mint with butterscotch.
       Butterscotch comes before mint, so take left hand side.
       The list is: Butterscotch, Chocolate.
       Middle item = $(2 + 1) / 2$ = 1.5 = 2nd item = chocolate.
       Compare chocolate to butterscotch.
       Butterscotch comes before chocolate, so take left hand side.
       Middle item = $(1 + 1) / 2$ = 1st item = butterscotch.
       Stop searching as butterscotch has been found.

   b) It is much more efficient / takes fewer steps for large lists of items. *[1 mark]*
       You won't get the mark for just saying it's quicker or more efficient.

4 a)

3	**7**	6	2	5
7	3	**6**	2	5
7	6	3	**2**	5
7	6	3	2	**5**
7	6	5	3	2

[4 marks available — 1 mark for each row from rows 2-5]

b) E.g.

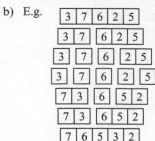

[4 marks available — 1 mark for correctly splitting the list into single items, 1 mark for each correct merging row]
The list doesn't split evenly so there is more than one way to get the right answer depending on how you split the items.

5 a) It compares the first pair of elements in the array and swaps them if the first element is bigger. *[1 mark]* It then repeats for each other pair of elements in the array. *[1 mark]*

b) Bubble sort *[1 mark]*

Page 75 (Revision Questions)

8 E.g.

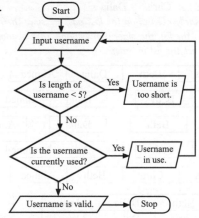

11 a) <u>Binary Search</u>:
The middle item is the 4th item, *Dagenham*, which comes before *Morpeth*. So <u>lose first half of list</u> to leave:
Morpeth, Usk, Watford
The middle item of the new list is the 2nd item, *Usk*, which comes after *Morpeth* so <u>lose second half of list</u> to leave:
Morpeth
The middle item of the new list is the 1st item, which is *Morpeth*, so you've found the correct item.
Even when there is one entry left you still have to carry on with the algorithm to check that it is the correct entry.

b) <u>Linear Search</u>:
Ashington ≠ Morpeth
Brecon ≠ Morpeth
Chester ≠ Morpeth
Dagenham ≠ Morpeth
Morpeth = Morpeth
You've found the correct item.

13 b) *1st pass (4 swaps)*:
<u>O, B</u>, A, P, G, L
B, <u>O, A</u>, P, G, L
B, A, O, <u>P, G</u>, L
B, A, O, G, <u>P, L</u>
B, A, O, G, L, P

2nd pass (3 swaps):
<u>B, A</u>, O, G, L, P
A, B, <u>O, G</u>, L, P
A, B, G, <u>O, L</u>, P
A, B, G, L, O, P

3rd pass (no swaps — list is in order):
A, B, G, L, O, P

16 a)

8	7	5	1	3	6	4	2
8	7	5	1	3	6	4	2
8	7	5	1	3	6	4	2
8	7	5	1	3	6	4	2
8	7	5	1	6	3	4	2
8	7	5	1	6	4	3	2
8	7	6	5	4	3	2	1

b) 8 *7* 5 1 3 6 4 2
7 8 *5* 1 3 6 4 2
5 7 8 *1* 3 6 4 2
1 5 7 8 *3* 6 4 2
1 3 5 7 8 *6* 4 2
1 3 5 6 7 8 *4* 2
1 3 4 5 6 7 8 *2*
1 2 3 4 5 6 7 8

Section Six — Programming

Page 81 (Warm-Up Questions)

1 a) String   b) Integer   c) Real/Float   d) Boolean

2 a) 40   b) 1   c) 4   d) 19

3 a) True   b) True   c) False   d) True

4 E.g. The value of a constant is set at design time and does not change as the program is running. The value of a variable might change as the program is running.

5 a) 7   b) ter   c) LOBSTER   d) bst

Page 82 (Exam Questions)

3 a) Boolean *[1 mark]* — the variable can only take two values, either pressed or not pressed, i.e. true or false. *[1 mark]*

b) Integer *[1 mark]* — it's measuring the number of whole seconds and whole numbers are best stored as integers. *[1 mark]*

4 Investment is declared as a constant but its value changes. *[1 mark]* The rate variable has a string type, but should have a real type. *[1 mark]*

5 a) Joining together two or more strings. *[1 mark]*

b) ORA2000 *[1 mark]*

c) 03 fruit = fruit.upper *[1 mark]*
04 prodID = fruit.left(3) *[1 mark]*
        + str(volume) *[1 mark]*
You could have used fruit.subString(0, 3) instead of fruit.left(3) in line 04.

Page 86 (Warm-Up Questions)

1 a) Iteration   b) Selection   c) Selection
d) Iteration   e) Selection

2 E.g. A SWITCH statement makes selections based solely on the value of one variable, an IF-ELSEIF statement makes selections based on any conditions that are true or false.

3 a) Count-controlled loop: FOR loop
Condition-controlled loop: E.g. DO UNTIL loop

b) A FOR loop will iterate a specified number of times.
A DO UNTIL loop will keep iterating until a specific condition is satisfied.

Page 87 (Exam Questions)

3 a) Sequence *[1 mark]*

   b) 2 hours and 30 minutes *[1 mark]*

4 a) Using a SWITCH statement. *[1 mark]*
       Using the correct cases for all settings. *[1 mark]*
       Changing the temperature correctly for each setting. *[1 mark]*
       E.g.

```
setting = input()
switch setting:
   case "3":
     temperature = 50
   case "2":
     temperature = 30
   case "1":
     temperature = 20
   default:
     temperature = 0
endswitch
```

   b) Any **two** reasons, e.g.
       • You only need to check the value of one variable. *[1 mark]*
       • The setting variable only has a set number of possible values. *[1 mark]*

5 Count controlled loop to allow 10 games. *[1 mark]*
   Asking for an input of the winner's name for each game. *[1 mark]*
   A selection statement for the winner of each game. *[1 mark]*
   Adding 1 to the winner's score. *[1 mark]*
   A selection statement to find the overall winner. *[1 mark]*
   Printing the correct message depending on the scores. *[1 mark]*
   E.g.

```
karlWin = 0
johnWin = 0
for i = 1 to 10
   winner = input("Enter the winner's name.")
   if winner == "Karl" then
     karlWin = karlWin + 1
   elseif winner == "John" then
     johnWin = johnWin + 1
   endif
next i
if karlWin > johnWin then
   print("The winner is Karl.")
elseif johnWin > karlWin then
   print("The winner is John.")
else
   print("The game is a draw.")
endif
```

To make your algorithm more robust you could have used input validation to make sure winner was either "Karl" or "John". You could also have named the variables differently so that the game could be played by any two players regardless of their name.

Page 92 (Warm-Up Questions)

1 a)

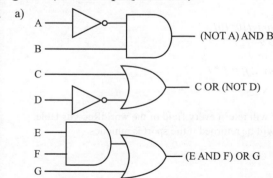

(NOT A) AND B

C OR (NOT D)

(E AND F) OR G

b)

A	B	NOT A	(NOT A) AND B
0	0	1	0
0	1	1	1
1	0	0	0
1	1	0	0

C	D	NOT D	C OR (NOT D)
0	0	1	1
0	1	0	0
1	0	1	1
1	1	0	1

E	F	G	E AND F	(E AND F) OR G
0	0	0	0	0
0	0	1	0	1
0	1	0	0	0
0	1	1	0	1
1	0	0	0	0
1	0	1	0	1
1	1	0	1	1
1	1	1	1	1

2 a) False   b) True   c) True   d) True

3 3, 4, 5, 6, 7, 8

Page 93 (Exam Questions)

3 a)

A	B	C	NOT A	B AND C	(NOT A) AND (B AND C)
0	0	0	1	0	0
0	0	1	1	0	0
0	1	0	1	0	0
0	1	1	1	1	1
1	0	0	0	0	0
1	0	1	0	0	0
1	1	0	0	0	0
1	1	1	0	1	0

[3 marks available — 1 mark for each correct column]

   b)

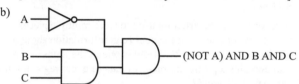

(NOT A) AND B AND C

[3 marks available — 1 mark for input A going into a NOT gate, 1 mark for inputs B and C going into an AND gate, 1 mark for outputs going into an AND gate with one output]

4 Using an appropriate selection statement. *[1 mark]*
   A Boolean condition that checks each of the conditions. *[1 mark]*
   Allowing the dryer to start if conditions are met. *[1 mark]*
   E.g.

```
weight = input("Enter weight.")
doorClosed = input("Is the door closed?")
if (weight > 1.5 AND weight < 15.0) AND doorClosed == true
then
   allowStart = true
else
   allowStart = false
endif
```

5 E.g. The random function could produce the same number more than once, which would produce the same card twice.
   [1 mark] This is not intended, as when a card is drawn it should be removed from the deck. *[1 mark]*

Page 101 (Warm-Up Questions)

1 a) Assigns the 4th element in the array to the variable 'player'.

   b) Replaces the 6th element of the array with the string "Pele".

2 a) open()   b) newFile()   c) close()   d) readLine()

3 E.g.
   • A record can store different data types.
   • Names can be given to the different fields.
   • Record structures cannot accidentally be changed later on.

4 a) SELECT — the fields you want to return.

   b) FROM — the table you want to get the data from.

c) WHERE — a condition that has to be true for a record to be returned.

5 Any **three** benefits, e.g.
- You only have to write them once so you don't have to repeat blocks of code.
- You can call them from anywhere in the program.
- You only have to debug them once.
- They will improve the readability / maintainability of the code.
- They break the program down into smaller more manageable chunks.

Pages 102-103 (Exam Questions)

2 A function that takes a single parameter. *[1 mark]*
Finding the cube and square of the parameter. *[1 mark]*
Returning the difference between the cube and square. *[1 mark]*
E.g.
function cubeSquare(numberInt)
  return(numberInt^3 – numberInt^2)
endfunction

3 a) String *[1 mark]*

b) Any **three** reasons, e.g.
- Multiple items of data need to be stored. *[1 mark]*
- All the data being stored has the same data type. *[1 mark]*
- The data is split by two categories / can be represented in a table so a 2D array is useful for storing it. *[1 mark]*
- Stores the data together under one variable name. *[1 mark]*
- Accessing the information is more efficient. A single command, e.g. *sportsDay[position, event]* can be used to access any name from the array. *[1 mark]*

  [3 marks available in total — at least one reason must specifically mention 2D arrays.]

4 a) 5 *[1 mark]*

b) A record is a data structure used to store multiple pieces of data about one thing together (e.g. information about a particular car). *[1 mark]* A field is one of the items in a record that contains a particular piece of data (e.g. car registration or car make). *[1 mark]*

Just saying that records are rows of the table and fields are columns will not be awarded any marks.

c)

Make	Type
Fenwick	Saloon
Stanton	Saloon

[2 marks available — 1 mark for each correct record]

5 a) *print(distanceRun[4, 3])* *[1 mark]*

b) Asking the user to input the runner number. *[1 mark]*
Using a FOR loop. *[1 mark]*
Adding all elements correctly. *[1 mark]*
Printing the total distance. *[1 mark]*
E.g.
totalDistance = 0
runner = input("Choose a runner number from 0-3")
for i = 0 to 6
  totalDistance = totalDistance + distanceRun[i, runner]
next i
print(totalDistance)

c) A FOR loop going from 0 to 3. *[1 mark]*
A FOR loop going from 0 to 6. *[1 mark]*
Using milesConvert() on each element of the array. *[1 mark]*
E.g.
for i = 0 to 3
  for j = 0 to 6
    distanceRun[i, j] = milesConvert(distanceRun[i, j])
  next j
next i

6 Opening the story. *[1 mark]*
A condition-controlled loop to stop at the end of the file. *[1 mark]*
Waiting for a keypress input. *[1 mark]*
Using a selection statement to check the user's input. *[1 mark]*
Printing the next line of the story. *[1 mark]*
E.g.
story = open("adventure.txt")
while NOT story.endOfFile()
  keypress = input()
    if keypress == "y" then
      print(story.readLine())
    endif
endwhile
story.close()

7 a) Any **two** reasons, e.g.
- Local variables can only be changed and accessed from within the sub program they're declared in. *[1 mark]* This prevents programmers from accidentally affecting things in different parts of a program. *[1 mark]*
- A local variable 'disappears' outside of the sub program, *[1 mark]* which means that you could declare the same variable name twice without it creating a conflict. *[1 mark]*
- A sub program with only local variables is self-contained *[1 mark]* so you could reuse it in a different program without having to declare any variables beforehand. *[1 mark]*

  [4 marks available in total]

b) A function that takes the number of sides the dice have as a parameter. *[1 mark]*
Using a condition controlled loop. *[1 mark]*
Using the rollTwo function. *[1 mark]*
Increasing the score by 1 after each roll. *[1 mark]*
Returning the score. *[1 mark]*
E.g.
function rollGame(side)
  score = 0
  do
    results = rollTwo(sides)
    score = score + 1
  until results[0] == results[1]
  return(score)
endfunction

Page 104 (Revision Questions)

10 *firstDay = input("Enter the first day of the month")*
if firstDay == "Sunday" OR firstDay == "Monday" then
  print("The month has 5 Mondays")
else
  print("The month has 4 Mondays")
endif

11 *for i = 1 to 100*
  roll = random(1, 8)
  print(roll)
next i

13 a) *print(chars[4])*

b) *for i = 0 to 9*
    chars[i] = "N"
  next i

14 *array multiply[10, 10]*
  for i = 0 to 9
    for j = 0 to 9
      *multiply[i, j] = i * j*
    next j
  next i

17 The query will return every field of the worldRecords table.
A record will be returned if the sport is athletics.

Section Seven — Design, Testing and IDEs

Page 109 (Warm-Up Questions)

1 E.g. They can make coding easier because they break the program down into modules that each only carry out a simple task. Programmers can fix and update modules without affecting the rest of the program.

2 E.g.
- Clear comments
- Indentation
- Properly named variables/sub programs
- Use of sub programs

3 a) Presence check
  b) Look-up table

4 a) False   b) True   c) True   d) False

5 Iterative testing is where the program is tested while it is being developed, so that any errors can be fixed before they cause larger problems later on in the development process.

Page 110 (Exam Questions)

3 a) E.g.

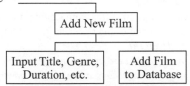

[3 marks available — 1 mark for correctly adding the module to the structure diagram, 1 mark for each suitable task within the module (up to 2 marks)]

  b) Any **two** ways with valid explanations, e.g.
- Agreeing how and when to use comments will improve the maintainability *[1 mark]* as the team will be able to understand each other's code. *[1 mark]*
- Establishing and using naming conventions will improve the maintainability *[1 mark]* as the team will easily be able to understand what variables and sub programs are for. *[1 mark]*
- Agreeing how and when to use global variables will lead to fewer errors *[1 mark]* as each person's code is more likely to work with the other developers' code. *[1 mark]*
- Agreeing how to validate inputs will reduce errors *[1 mark]* as all parts of the program will accept similar inputs. *[1 mark]*
[4 marks available in total]

4 a) Error: Missing bracket on line 3. *[1 mark]*
     Correction: *print("Valid pincode")* *[1 mark]*

  b) Error: Wrong Boolean operator in line 2. *[1 mark]*
     Correction:
     if pincode.length >= 4 AND pincode.length <= 6 then
     [1 mark]
     Tiffany's code currently allows any pincode length. Changing OR to AND makes sure only pincodes with lengths from 4 to 6 characters are allowed.

5 E.g.
- Input validation could make sure that only appropriate data was entered. *[1 mark]* E.g. only allowing numbers to be entered for the card number. *[1 mark]*
- Input validation would ensure the input data matches certain criteria or is of a certain format. *[1 mark]* E.g. it can make sure that the expiration month is between 1 and 12. *[1 mark]*
- Input validation alone will not prevent all errors. *[1 mark]* E.g. it cannot check that a customer's card number matches their name. *[1 mark]*
- Too much validation could make the form difficult to use *[1 mark]* e.g. if it rejected names that contain accents or other special characters. *[1 mark]*
[6 marks available in total]

Page 114 (Warm-Up Questions)

1

i	num	subtext
—	0	—
1	1	"a"
2	3	"an"
3	6	"ant"
4	10	"anti"

2 A compiler translates all of a program's source code into one executable file of machine code.

3 Code Editor: used for writing code.
  Breakpoints: a debugging tool that stops the program at certain points.
  Error Diagnostics: highlight errors in the program.

Page 115 (Exam Questions)

2 A translator turns the source code into machine code *[1 mark]* allowing Cynthia to run the application. *[1 mark]*

  Error Diagnostics highlight errors in the code *[1 mark]* allowing Cynthia to easily find and fix errors in her application. *[1 mark]*

  A Code editor allows the user to enter code and includes features like indenting, auto-correct, line numbering and colour coding *[1 mark]* making it a lot easier for Cynthia to write and maintain her application. *[1 mark]*

3 a) Any **two** reasons, e.g.
- They may need to have a greater control over the program in order to make a program with lower memory use. *[1 mark]*
- They may need to have a greater control over what the CPU does in order to make a program run quicker. *[1 mark]*
- They may be trying to maintain old code or hardware. *[1 mark]*
[2 marks available in total]

  b) Assembly languages are more readable for humans than machine code *[1 mark]* so can be programmed/edited more easily. *[1 mark]*

4 a)

k	arr[k]	x	y
		0	0
0	4	4	0
1	2		2
2	7	7	4
3	1		
4	9	9	7

[4 marks available — 1 mark for each column with the correct values in the correct order]
It doesn't matter if you've put spaces in different places to the table above, or if you've not got any spaces at all, as long as the values that each variable takes are correct.

  b) It finds the largest two numbers in an array of positive numbers *[1 mark]* and prints them, largest first. *[1 mark]*

Page 116 (Revision Questions)

6 Range check

11 The code doesn't do anything if the age is exactly 16. Either change the first condition to "*x >= 16*" or the second condition to "*x <= 16*".

   On line 3 of the code, the variable x should be cast as a string before being concatenated with the other strings. Instead of "*x*", it should read "*str(x)*".

15 E.g.

Test Data	Reason for Testing	Expected Outcome
"tra"	Normal usage of the program.	"art", "rat", "tar"
No input	No input is entered.	Prompt to enter something.
"stm"	Input can't be made into a word.	Returns no words.
"AtN"	Input contains upper and lower case letters.	"tan", "ant", "nat"
"2t1?"	Input contains numbers and symbols.	Error: Unknown character.

Practice Paper 1 — Computer Systems

1 a) i) Utility software is software that helps to configure, optimise or maintain a computer. *[1 mark]*

   ii) Any **two** examples of utility software, e.g.
   - Disk defragmentation software *[1 mark]*
   - System diagnostic tools *[1 mark]*
   - Anti-virus / anti-spyware *[1 mark]*
   - Backup software *[1 mark]*
   - Compression software *[1 mark]*
   - File management software *[1 mark]*
   [2 marks available in total]

   b) i) E.g. When the hard disk is fragmented, it will take longer to read/write data on the hard disk. *[1 mark]* This in turn may slow down the computer. *[1 mark]*

   ii) E.g.
   - Defragmentation software reduces fragmentation by moving files on the hard disk. *[1 mark]*
   - The empty spaces/gaps are collected together. *[1 mark]*
   - Different bits of the same file are moved to be stored together. *[1 mark]*
   - This means the read/write heads won't need to move as far across the disk, so the read/write speed should improve. *[1 mark]*
   [3 marks available in total]

   c) E.g. Disk clean-up will remove a number of files, so it will immediately leave gaps in the data stored on the hard disk, leading to fragmentation. *[1 mark]*

   d) Any **two** advantages, e.g.
   - SSDs are faster than HDDs. *[1 mark]*
   - SSDs do not need to be defragmented. *[1 mark]*
   - SSDs do not make any noise. *[1 mark]*
   - SSDs are more shock-proof than HDDs. *[1 mark]*
   [2 marks available in total]

2 a) The use of online servers, provided by a hosting company, to store data. *[1 mark]*

   b) E.g.
   - Laptop/web browser sends a request to the cloud server, to send the image. *[1 mark]*
   - The cloud server processes the request. *[1 mark]*
   - The cloud server replies with the image. *[1 mark]*
   [2 marks available in total]

   c) Any **one** advantage, e.g.
   - Karen doesn't need an Internet connection to access her photos and videos. *[1 mark]*
   - Karen has full control over the security of her photos and videos. *[1 mark]*
   - The external hard drive might be cheaper than paying a subscription fee for the cloud service in the long run. *[1 mark]*

   Any **one** disadvantage, e.g.
   - An external hard drive can be easily damaged. *[1 mark]*
   - An external hard drive can be quite bulky, so would be inconvenient to take on holiday. *[1 mark]*
   - The cost of an external hard drive may be more than the cost of using the cloud storage service. *[1 mark]*
   [2 marks available in total]

   d) Any **one** service, e.g.
   - Cloud software/applications *[1 mark]* where the hosting company runs software on their machines and clients access it remotely. *[1 mark]*
   - Cloud processing *[1 mark]* where the hosting company provides clients with extra processing power so they can perform more memory-intensive tasks. *[1 mark]*
   [2 marks available in total]

3 a) i) Ethernet is a network protocol used on wired networks. *[1 mark]*

   ii) The Leeds studio is using a star topology. *[1 mark]*

   b) Any **one** difference, e.g.
   - CAT5e twisted pair cables use four twisted copper wires *[1 mark]* whereas coaxial cable uses one single copper wire. *[1 mark]*
   - CAT5e cables prevent interference by twisting the wires together *[1 mark]* whereas coaxial cable uses a braided metallic shield to prevent interference. *[1 mark]*
   [2 marks available in total]

   c) E.g.
   The Leeds studio's wired setup:
   - Wired connections have a more reliable performance as there is no loss of signal no matter where the devices are in the building. *[1 mark]*
   - Wired connections are more restrictive as it is harder to add new devices / access the network while moving through the building. *[1 mark]*

   The York studio's wireless setup:
   - Wireless connections are easier for the employees to connect to (e.g. no need for cables to add a laptop or mobile device to the network). *[1 mark]*
   - Wireless connections can suffer from signal problems caused by building interference or interference from other wireless signals nearby. *[1 mark]*
   To get all four marks, you'll need one advantage and one disadvantage for wired connections, as well as one advantage and one disadvantage for wireless connections.

   d) i) Any **one** advantage, e.g.
   - Fibre optic cables tend to have greater bandwidth / can carry more data than copper cables. *[1 mark]*
   - Fibre optic cables can carry data over longer distances / don't suffer signal degradation or interference. *[1 mark]*
   - Fibre optic cables are easier to maintain than copper cables so cost less in the long term. *[1 mark]*
   [1 mark available in total]

   ii) E.g.
   - Laying its own cables between Leeds and York could be too expensive for the company. *[1 mark]*
   - Leased lines are likely to be more reliable and faster than other WAN connections. *[1 mark]*
   [1 mark available in total]

4 a) 10101000 = 128 + 32 + 8 = 168
   [2 marks available — 1 mark for correct working and 1 mark for correct final answer]

   b) Split 10110101 into nibbles:
   1011 = B, 0101 = 5, so 10110101 = B5
   [2 marks available — 1 mark for correct working and 1 mark for correct final answer]

   c) ```
      1 0 1 0 1 0 0 0
    + 1 0 1 1 0 1 0 1
    1 0 1 0 1 1 1 0 1   [1 mark]
              1
   ```

   d) An overflow error is where the result of a calculation requires more bits than are available and some of the data is lost. *[1 mark]*

5 a) Storage *[1 mark]*, GPU *[1 mark]*

   b) E.g. Hardeep should upgrade the RAM in his computer, *[1 mark]* as he only just has enough RAM to cover the minimum requirements, so the OS may not run very smoothly. *[1 mark]*
   *It's fine to answer 'no', as long as you've justified your answer.*
   ```

c) RAM stores applications and data that is currently in use. *[1 mark]* As operating systems are running all the time, a large amount of the OS is kept in RAM. *[1 mark]*

d) Any **two** features, e.g.
- Large buttons and icons *[1 mark]* that can be pressed to open applications and windows. *[1 mark]*
- Screens and menus *[1 mark]* that can be navigated / controlled by swiping or dragging with a finger. *[1 mark]*
- Support for finger gestures *[1 mark]* such as pinching to zoom out / tap and hold to open additional options / four finger swipes to swap between apps etc. *[1 mark]*
- Virtual on-screen keyboard *[1 mark]* to allow the user to type without attaching an external keyboard. *[1 mark]*

[4 marks available in total]

6 a) 16^6 *[1 mark]*

b) E.g. It would be easier to remember the hex code for a particular colour *[1 mark]* because the hex code would be shorter than the binary or denary equivalents. *[1 mark]*

c) JPEG is an example of lossy compression *[1 mark]* — it produces a much smaller file size than the other formats. *[1 mark]*

d) E.g.
- No data is lost when compressed *[1 mark]* so graphics can be reverted back to the original — this is essential to ensure graphics are always high quality. *[1 mark]*
- File sizes are only slightly reduced *[1 mark]* so there would be an impact on storage requirements to the company. *[1 mark]*
- Not all software is compatible with lossless file types *[1 mark]* so clients may not be able to open graphics. *[1 mark]*
- File sizes are large *[1 mark]* so the images will take longer to upload or attach to emails for clients. *[1 mark]*

[4 marks available in total]

e) Any **two** pieces of metadata, e.g.
- File format *[1 mark]*
- Height/width in pixels *[1 mark]*
- Colour depth *[1 mark]*
- Resolution *[1 mark]*
- Date created/date modified *[1 mark]*
- Creator's name *[1 mark]*

[2 marks available in total]

7 a)

	Allowed	Not Allowed
Giving each teacher a USB flash drive containing the personal information of all the pupils who have attended the school.		✓
Transferring pupils' personal information to their new school when they leave.	✓	
Putting pupils' personal information on the school website to make it easier for teachers and parents to access.		✓
Using pupils' personal information to get in contact with their parents.	✓	
Backing up pupils' personal information on a drive that is stored in a locked safe.	✓	

[5 marks available — 1 mark for each correct row]

b) Any **two** forms of network attack and a suitable method of protection, e.g.
- Passive attack *[1 mark]* — using tools such as network-monitoring devices and packets sniffers to intercept sensitive information. *[1 mark]* Can be protected against by encrypting data on the network. *[1 mark]*
- Active attack *[1 mark]* — using malware or other means to break into a network and steal data. *[1 mark]* Can be protected against by using a firewall. *[1 mark]*
- Insider attack *[1 mark]* — exploiting a person's position within the organisation to gain access to data on the network. *[1 mark]* Can be protected against by using user access levels to restrict access to people that are trusted. *[1 mark]*
- Brute force attack *[1 mark]* — using automated software and trial-and-error to find a password that will allow access to the network. *[1 mark]* Can be protected against by locking accounts after a certain number of failed attempts. *[1 mark]*

[6 marks available in total]

8 a) If the central switch fails, users will be unable to access files on other servers *[1 mark]* because there will be no connections between any of the servers. *[1 mark]*

b) E.g.
- Connecting servers in a mesh network means that if one connection fails, there are other routes to connect the servers. *[1 mark]* This means the network can still operate fully and all the computers can access data on all servers. *[1 mark]*
- Adding an extra server to a mesh network would be more complicated *[1 mark]* because it would need to be connected to all of the other servers rather than just the switch. *[1 mark]*
- Some connections would be redundant most of the time *[1 mark]* as the servers would communicate using the quickest or most direct route. *[1 mark]*

[4 marks available in total — at least one advantage and one disadvantage required for full marks]

9 Points you might include:

Consumers and businesses
- Consumers will be able to access a greater variety of books, films and music. They will be able to purchase them at their own convenience without having to go to a shop. The books, films and music should also be cheaper as the costs are much lower to produce digital copies than physical copies.
- Traditional bookshops, CD shops and film retailers will have to adapt to distributing their stock digitally or face a decline in profits.
- New businesses that distribute books, music and films digitally could flourish as they gain some of the traditional stores' market share. New business models have been founded to distribute digital media, e.g. subscription-based services or streaming services where money is made through advertising.

Technology
- Use of digital media has encouraged the development and improvement in technology. E.g. e-readers introduced a new type of display technology that looks and feels more like a printed book. In the future, displays which are even more paper-like may be used.
- The use of digital media has placed extra demands on communication networks. This creates a cycle of improvement, e.g. watching high-quality films increases demand for better broadband speeds, which in turn encourages people to watch higher quality films, increasing demand for good broadband.
- The use of digital media is changing TVs from devices that receive broadcasted transmissions to Internet-enabled devices used to stream media from the Internet.

Environmental issues
- Less use of physical media means there could be less physical waste from packaging and discarded books, CDs and DVDs.
- No need for packaging or physical media, so fewer natural resources required in the distribution of the media.
- Greater use of digital media means increased use of electricity, as well as increased e-waste if hardware is discarded.

Legal issues
- Use of digital media could increase the amount of illegal file sharing.
- It is often unclear who owns the copyright to the original piece of work, and how profit from the book / music / film should be shared. E.g. how much money should a musician receive from their music being listened to on a free streaming service.
- It is often unclear who owns the digital file. E.g. should someone be able to pass their movie files on to their children, or does the ownership over them go back to the original distributor.

How to mark your answer:
- Two or three brief points with very little explanation. *[1-2 marks]*
- Three to five detailed points covering at least two of: consumers and businesses, technology, environmental issues and legal issues. *[3-5 marks]*
- Six or more detailed points that form a well-written, balanced discussion, covering all of: consumers and businesses, technology, environmental issues and legal issues. *[6-8 marks]*

Practice Paper 2 — Computational Thinking, Algorithms and Programming

1 a)

	Real	Boolean	String
The name of the fuel that the customer used.			✓
The total cost of the customer's fuel.	✓		

[2 marks available — 1 mark for each correct row]

b) Using the correct data type will make your programs more memory efficient. *[1 mark]* It will also make your programs more robust and predictable. *[1 mark]*

c) E.g. All the different data values might be converted to strings using the str() function so string concatenation can be used to join them together on the receipt. *[1 mark]* For example the cost of fuel might be converted from a real / float to a string so it can be printed in a sentence, e.g. "The cost of fuel was £20.76". *[1 mark]*

d) Any **two** differences, e.g.
- A compiler would produce an executable file *[1 mark]* while an interpreter would not. *[1 mark]*
- A compiler would list any errors at the end of the translation *[1 mark]* while an interpreter would return the first error it found then stop. *[1 mark]*
- A compiler would translate the code all at once *[1 mark]* while an interpreter would translate and run the code line by line. *[1 mark]*
[4 marks available in total]

2 a) Any **one** feature, e.g.
- Code editor *[1 mark]*
- Run-time environment *[1 mark]*
- Output window *[1 mark]*
- Breakpoints *[1 mark]*
- Error diagnostics *[1 mark]*
- Debugging tools *[1 mark]*
- Auto-documentation *[1 mark]*
[1 mark available in total]

b) i) A parameter is a special variable that passes data into a sub program. *[1 mark]*
   ii) Parameters have a local scope to the sub program they're defined in. *[1 mark]*

c) i) Declares a new variable, difficulty, and assigns it a value of 0. *[1 mark]* The variable has global scope so it can be used anywhere in the program. *[1 mark]*
   ii) It takes weight as a parameter *[1 mark]* and sets the variable difficulty equal to 50 minus the integer (quotient) part of weight divided by 6. *[1 mark]*

d) Using a condition-controlled loop. *[1 mark]*
Using a selection statement based on heart rate. *[1 mark]*
Decreasing difficulty with correct conditions. *[1 mark]*
Increasing difficulty, up to a maximum of 50, with correct conditions. *[1 mark]*
Correct conditions for ending the loop. *[1 mark]*
Setting difficulty to 0 and outputting a suitable message. *[1 mark]*
E.g.
do
  input heartRate
  if heartRate > 140 then
    difficulty = difficulty – 1
  elseif heartRate < 90 AND difficulty < 50 then
    difficulty = difficulty + 1
  endif
until heartRate > 160
difficulty = 0
print("Warning — heart rate too high.")

3 a)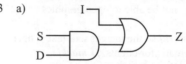

[3 marks available — 1 mark for inputs S and D going into an AND gate, 1 mark for the output of AND gate and input I going into an OR gate and 1 mark for Z being the OR gate output]

b)

S	D	I	Z
0	1	0	0
1	1	0	1
1	0	0	0

[3 marks available — 1 mark for each correct row]

4 a) Check each item in order.
Check the first item: 10 ≠ 12
Check the second item: 18 ≠ 12
Check the third item: 12 = 12.
Stop searching as the item has been found.
[2 marks available — 1 mark for starting with 10 and 1 mark for checking items in order until you find 12]

b)

10	<u>18</u>	12	15	20
10	18	<u>12</u>	15	20
10	12	18	<u>15</u>	20
10	12	15	18	<u>20</u>
10	12	15	18	20

[4 marks available — 1 mark for each row from rows 2-5]

5 a) Erroneous test data contains values that are the incorrect data type and should not be accepted by the program. *[1 mark]* Using them in testing will make sure that the program doesn't break if it receives data of a type it wasn't expecting. *[1 mark]*

b) i) Type of data: Normal *[1 mark]*
Intended Outcome: 20 *[1 mark]*
Actual Outcome: 20 *[1 mark]*

ii) Type of data: Invalid *[1 mark]*
Intended Outcome: User receives an error message, e.g. "Invalid dice score, please re-enter." *[1 mark]*
Actual Outcome: 19 *[1 mark]*
The game uses a six-sided dice, so if the user inputs a 9 they should receive an error message. However, Tony's program does not check for this.

c) Any **two** ways, e.g.
- He could make sure only integers are accepted. *[1 mark]*
- He could make sure only the numbers from 1 to 6 are accepted. *[1 mark]*
- He could ensure that the input is only one character long. *[1 mark]*
- He could make sure that only Yes/No, yes/no, Y/N, y/n, etc. are accepted for the "Roll again" prompt. *[1 mark]*

[2 marks available in total]

6 a) E.g. Storing the data in records allows the different fields to have different data types *[1 mark]* while if they used an array, they would all have to be the same data type. *[1 mark]*

b) SELECT Title *[1 mark]*
FROM comics *[1 mark]*
WHERE Rating = 5 *[1 mark]*

7 a)
```
array primeKoalas[4, 2]
primeKoalas[0, 0] = "John"
primeKoalas[1, 0] = "Paul"
primeKoalas[2, 0] = "Cheryl"
primeKoalas[3, 0] = "Ida"
primeKoalas[0, 1] = "guitar"
primeKoalas[1, 1] = "bass"
primeKoalas[2, 1] = "vocals"
primeKoalas[3, 1] = "drums"
```
[2 marks available — 2 marks for all 4 correct lines of code, otherwise 1 mark for at least two correct lines of code]

b) Opening and closing the file properly. *[1 mark]*
Using a loop. *[1 mark]*
Writing the name and instrument of each band member to the file. *[1 mark]*
E.g.
```
band = open("musicians.txt")
for i = 0 to 3
  band.writeLine(primeKoalas[i, 0] + " " + primeKoalas[i, 1])
next i
band.close()
```
Your answer must be given in OCR Exam Reference Language or a high-level programming language or award no marks.

c) Correct use of the fileName parameter. *[1 mark]*
Opening and closing the file properly. *[1 mark]*
Looping through the lines of the file. *[1 mark]*
Using the toSpeech() sub program correctly. *[1 mark]*
E.g.
```
procedure readAll(fileName)
  file = open(fileName)
  while NOT file.endOfFile()
    toSpeech(file.readLine())
  endwhile
  file.close()
endprocedure
```
Your answer must be given in OCR Exam Reference Language or a high-level programming language or award no marks.

d)

i	fans	price	total
—	5	0	—
1	10	2	20
2	20	4	80
3	40	6	240
4	80	8	640

[4 marks available — 1 mark for each row from rows 2-5]

e) Using start and stop boxes. *[1 mark]*
Asking user to input track name. *[1 mark]*
Decision box with an appropriate question. *[1 mark]*
Looping back to input with correct condition. *[1 mark]*
Ending the loop with correct condition. *[1 mark]*
E.g.

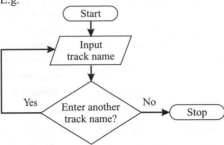

f) Generating a random integer between 1 and 11. *[1 mark]*
Using a selection statement. *[1 mark]*
Having correct conditions on the selection statement. *[1 mark]*
Assigning the correct track number depending on the conditions. *[1 mark]*
E.g.
```
inputString = input("Enter track number.")
if inputString == "random" then
  trackNumber = random(1, 11)
else
  trackNumber = int(inputString)
endif
print(trackNames[trackNumber – 1])
```
Your answer must be given in OCR Exam Reference Language or a high-level programming language or award no marks.

g) i) *Kali14*
[2 marks available — 1 mark for correct letters, 1 mark for correct length]

ii) *E.g.*
```
function noSpace(string1)
  len = string1.length
  for i = 0 to (len – 1)
    if string1.subString(i, 1) == " " then
      return false
    endif
  next i
  return true
endfunction
```
[3 marks available — 1 mark for each correct line]
The function will end as soon as it returns false, so it won't keep checking the remaining characters in the string.

iii) Using an iteration statement. *[1 mark]*
Using noSpace() with a correct Boolean condition for the iteration statement. *[1 mark]*
Notifying the user of an invalid input and asking for a new input within the iteration statement. *[1 mark]*
E.g.
```
trackName = input("Enter track name with no spaces.")
while noSpace(trackName) == false
  print("Error. Spaces found in track name.")
  trackName = input("Enter track name with no spaces.")
endwhile
```
Your answer must be given in OCR Exam Reference Language or a high-level programming language or award no marks.

Glossary and Index

A

abstraction Picking out the important bits of information. **64**

accumulator The part of the ALU that stores the intermediate results when doing a calculation. **3**

active attack (networks) A network attack where the hacker attempts to change data or introduce malware. **44**

algorithmic thinking Coming up with an algorithm to solve a problem. **64**

algorithm A step-by-step set of rules or instructions. **64-72**

alphanumeric The collective name for letters, digits and symbols. **27, 80**

analogue signal A continuous signal which can't be processed by a computer. **29**

AND One of the Boolean operators.
   logic gate 88
   operator 90

anti-malware software Software designed to stop malware from damaging a computer or network. **46**

application A piece of software written to help users do various tasks, often through a graphical user interface with menus and toolbars. **1, 6, 12, 13**

architecture Describes how the CPU works and interacts with the other parts of the computer system. **2, 3**

argument A value that a parameter of a sub program actually takes. **99**

arithmetic logic unit (ALU) The part of the CPU that carries out arithmetic and Boolean operations. **2, 3**

arithmetic operator An operator that programs use to carry out simple mathematical operations. **77**

array A data structure where all the data is stored and defined under one variable name. **94, 95**
   one-dimensional 94
   two-dimensional 95

ASCII A 7-bit character set consisting of 128 characters. **27**

assembly language A low-level language. **112**

assignment operator (=) Assigns the value on the right hand side to the name on the left hand side. **78**

authentication A process for checking the identity of the user. **106**

auto-documentation A programming tool commonly used to make a summary of a program. **113**

B

backdoor A vulnerability in a computer or network's security that a hacker could exploit. **44**

bandwidth The amount of data that can be transferred on a network in a given time. **30, 36**

binary A counting system using base-2 consisting of 0s and 1s. **20-22**
   addition 21
   converting to/from denary 20
   converting to/from hexadecimal 24
   overflow 21
   shifts 22

binary search algorithm 69

binary shift Moving the bits in a binary number left or right and filling the gaps with 0s. **22**

BIOS (Basic Input Output System) Software stored in ROM responsible for booting up a computer system. **6**

bit A binary digit, either 0 or 1. **19**
   least significant 20
   most significant 20

bit depth The number of bits available for each audio sample. **29**

bitmap image A graphic that is made up of pixels. **28**

Bluetooth® A common type of wireless technology. **36**

Boolean A logical system using the operators OR, AND and NOT. The Boolean data can take one of two values, either true or false.
   data type 76
   logic gates 88, 89
   operators 90

boundary data Test data on the boundary of what the program will accept. **108**

breakpoint A programming tool used to halt a program at a specific place. **113**

brute force attack A network attack which uses software to crack security passwords through trial and error. **44**

bubble sort algorithm 70

buffer Memory that's used for temporary storage. **13**

bus topology A network topology in which all devices are connected to a single backbone cable. **38**

byte 8 bits. **19**

C

cache (CPU) Quick access memory inside the CPU. **2, 7**

casting A way of changing from one data type to another. **77**

cat 5e / cat 6 cable Standards for copper Ethernet cables used on LANs. **35**

censorship The control (usually by a government or organisation) of what information other people can access. **52**

character A single alphanumeric symbol. **27**
   (as a data type) 76

character set A group of characters that a computer recognises from their binary representation. **27**

client A device which requests data from a server. **37**

client-server network A type of network managed by a server, which takes requests from client devices. **37**

clock speed The number of instructions a processor can carry out each second. **7**

cloud computing (the cloud) The use of the Internet to store files, access software and provide increased computing power. **43, 52**

code editor Part of an IDE where you write and edit your source code. **113**

colour depth The number of bits used for each pixel in an image file. **28**

command-line interface A text-based user interface where the user types in commands. **13**

comment A note added to source code to say what part of a program does. **105**

comparison operator Compares two values and outputs either true or false. **78**

compiled code An executable file created by a compiler. **112**

compiler A programming tool to translate source code into machine code. **112**

compression The process of making the size of a file smaller. **15, 30**

computational thinking Tackling a problem through decomposition, abstraction and algorithmic thinking. **64**

Computer Misuse Act 59

concatenation Joining strings together. **80**

condition-controlled loop An iteration statement that repeats a set of instructions until a condition is met. **85**

constant A named value which cannot be altered as the program is running. **79**

control unit (CU) The part of the CPU that controls the flow of data. **2, 3**

copyright A legal right that prevents others from copying or modifying your work without permission. **59**

Copyright, Designs and Patents Act 59

core (CPU) A processing unit found inside the CPU. **7**

count-controlled loop An iteration statement that repeats a set of instructions a given number of times. **84**

Glossary and Index

CPU (or processor) The part of the computer system that processes the data. It contains the control unit, ALU and cache. **1-3**
   performance 7

cultural issue An issue which affects a particular religious, ethnic, national or other group. **51-55**

cyberbullying Using social media to deliberately harm someone else. **53**

D

database A collection of data records (made up of fields) often represented as tables. **98**

Data Protection Act 59

data type Tells you what kind of data it is, e.g. integer, real, string, etc. **76**

debugging Identifying and fixing errors in a program. **113**

decomposition Breaking a problem down into smaller problems. **64**

dedicated system A computer system designed to carry out a specific task. **1**

defensive design A method of designing a program so that it functions properly and doesn't crash. **105, 106**

defragmentation Reorganising data on a hard drive to put broken up files back together and collect up the free space. **15**

denary A number system using base-10. Also known as decimal. **20**
   converting to/from binary 20
   converting to/from hexadecimal 23

denial-of-service attack A network attack which stops users from accessing a part of a network or website. **44**

Designs and Patents Act 59

device driver A piece of software that allows applications to communicate with a piece of hardware. **12**

digital divide The inequality created by the fact that some people have greater access to technology than others. **55**

digital signal The representation of an analogue signal using binary data. **29**

disk management Organisation and maintenance of the hard disk. **14, 15**

domain name server (DNS) A server which stores website domain names and their IP addresses. **43**

dongle A small piece of hardware which allow devices to connect to a network wirelessly. **36**

DO UNTIL loop Type of iteration statement. **85**

E

ELSEIF 83

embedded system A computer built into another device, e.g. a Smart TV. **1**

encryption Coding ('encrypting') data so that it can only be decoded ('decrypted') with the correct key. **15, 46**

environmental issue An issue relating to how we impact the natural world. **51, 58**

erroneous data Test data with an incorrect data type that a program should reject. **108**

error diagnostics Information about an error once it's been detected. **113**

errors (programming) 107

Ethernet Network protocol used on LANs. **35, 41**

ethical issue Something which raises questions of right and wrong. **51-55**

E-waste Discarded computer material. **58**

extreme data Test data on the boundary of what the program will accept. **108**

F

fetch-execute cycle The process that the CPU uses to retrieve and execute instructions. **3**

fibre optic cable A high performance cable that uses light to carry data. **35, 36**

field An element of a record used to store one piece of data. A column of a database table. **97, 98**

file handling (programming) Reading from and writing to external files. **96**

file management The organisation, movement and deletion of files. **14**

file sharing Copying files between devices on a network. **37, 59**

file size 27-29
   images 28
   sound 29
   text 27

final testing Testing the whole program at the end of the development process. **108**

firmware Permanent software stored on ROM, used to control hardware or embedded systems. **6**

flash memory Solid state non-volatile data storage. **8**

flowchart A graphical way of showing an algorithm. **66**

FOR loop

FOR loop A type of count-controlled iteration statement. **84**

FTP (File Transfer Protocol) A protocol used to access, edit and move files on another device, like a server. **42**

function A sub program that takes parameters and returns a value. **99, 100**

G

gigabyte 1000 megabytes. **19**

global divide The digital divide between different countries. **55**

global variable (programming) A variable available throughout the whole program. **100**

GPU (Graphics Processing Unit) A circuit for handling the processing of graphics and images. **7**

graphical user interface (GUI) Allows the user to interact with the computer in a visual and intuitive way. **13**

graphics card A piece of hardware containing a GPU. **7**

GUI builder An IDE tool for giving a program a graphical user interface. **113**

H

hacker A person who tries to illegally access or attack a computer network or device. **44, 59**

hard disk drive (HDD) Traditional internal storage for PCs and laptops that stores data magnetically. **1, 8, 9**

hardware The physical parts of a computer system. **1, 12, 35**

heat sink Pulls heat away from the CPU to help maintain its temperature. **1**

hexadecimal A counting system using base-16 consisting of the digits 0-9 and the letters A-F. **23, 24**
   converting to/from binary 24
   converting to/from denary 23

high-level language A programming language like C++ and Java™ that is easy for humans to understand. **112**

hosting (Internet) When a business uses its servers to store the files of another organisation. **43**

HTTP (Hyper Text Transfer Protocol) Used by web browsers to access websites and communicate with web servers. **42**

Glossary and Index

Glossary and Index

Glossary and Index

solid state drive (SSD) Alternative to a traditional magnetic hard disk drive that uses flash memory. **8, 9**

sorting algorithm A set of instructions that you can follow to order a list of items. **70-72**
    bubble sort 70
    insertion sort 72
    merge sort 71

sound 29

source code The actual written code of a program. **60, 112**

spoof website A fake website that tricks users into thinking it's another well-known website. **45**

spyware A type of malware which secretly monitors and records user actions. **44**

SQL (Structured Query Language) A programming language used to manage and search databases. **45, 98**

SQL injection A piece of SQL code which can be typed into an input box to try and attack the SQL database. **45**

stakeholder Somebody who has an interest in or is affected by the decisions of an organisation. **51**

standards A set of agreed requirements for hardware and software. **41**

star topology A type of network topology where all devices are connected to a central switch or server which controls the network. **38**

storage device A device used to read and write data to a storage medium. **8, 9**

storage medium A thing that holds data. It can be part of the storage device (e.g. magnetic disks inside a hard drive) or separate (like a CD). **8, 9**

string A data type for text.
    data type 76
    manipulation 80

structure diagram A graphical way of showing a program where tasks are broken down into smaller tasks (modules). **105**

sub program A set of code within a program that can be called at any time from the main program. **99, 100, 105**

surveillance The act of monitoring what people are accessing on the Internet. **52**

switch (network) Connects devices together on a LAN and directs frames of data to the correct device. **35**

SWITCH statement A type of selection statement. **84**

syntax error An error in the code where the rules or grammar of the programming language have been broken. **107**

systems software Software designed to run or maintain a computer system. **12-15**

T

TCP/IP A set of protocols which dictate how data is sent over the Internet. Made up of Transmission Control Protocol (TCP) and Internet Protocol (IP). **41, 42**

terabyte 1000 gigabytes. **19**

tertiary storage High-capacity external storage used mainly for back ups. **8**

terminal testing Testing the whole program at the end of the development process. **108**

test data Inputs that are chosen to see if a program is behaving as intended. **108**

testing A way of checking if a program functions correctly and meets certain requirements. **107, 108**

test plan A detailed plan of how a program is going to be tested including what test data will be used. **108**

topology (networks) How the devices in a network are connected together. **38**

trace table A table that keeps track of the value of certain variables as a program is run. **111**

translator A program that turns a programming language into machine code. **112**

trojans A type of malware which is disguised as legitimate software. **44**

trolling The act of trying to provoke public arguments online. **53**

truth table A table listing all possible binary inputs through a logic circuit, with the corresponding outputs. **88, 89**

U

Unicode® A large character set that attempts to include all possible characters. **27**

units (of data) 19

URL (Uniform Resource Locator) An address used to access web servers and resources on them. **43**

user access levels Controls what files or areas of the network different groups of users can access. **46**

user account 14

user interface Provides a way for the user to interact with the computer. **13**

utility software Software designed to help maintain a computer system. **15**

V

validation Checking that an input meets certain criteria. **45, 106**

variable A named value which can be changed as the program is running. **79**
    global 100
    local 100

viral Content on the Internet which has spread rapidly via social media. **54**

virtual memory Area of secondary storage used by the OS as extra RAM. **6**

virtual server A software-based server. **58**

virus A type of malware which spreads by attaching itself to files. **44**

volatile memory Memory that loses its contents when it has no power. **6**

Von Neumann A type of CPU architecture. **2, 3**

W

WAN (Wide Area Network) A network which connects networks in different geographical locations. **34, 43**

Waste Electric and Electronic Equipment (WEEE) directive 58

WHILE loop Type of iteration statement. **85**

Wi-Fi® A common type of wireless technology. **36**

WIMP A GUI based on windows, icons, menus and pointers. **13**

wired / wireless networks 34-36

wireless access point (WAP) A piece of hardware that allows devices to connect wirelessly. **36**

world wide web (www) The collection of websites hosted on the Internet. **43**

worms A type of malware which replicates itself. **44**